A Hundred British Spas

By the same author

History and Heroes of Old Merton
  (*Charles Skilton*)
Preserving London
  (*Robert Hale*)

A Hundred British SPAS

A PICTORIAL HISTORY

With 42 maps and 81 illustrations based on old prints and photographs, drawn by the author

Kathleen Denbigh

SPA
PUBLICATIONS

To Ken who helped to track down
many an elusive spring

Acknowledgements

I should like to thank Mr J. W. Nunn,
Hon. Secretary of the British Spas Federation
and also the spa town authorities for their
invaluable help and advice.

K.D

© Kathleen Denbigh 1981
ISBN 0 9507574 0 3

Designed and typeset by Oxprint Ltd, Oxford
Printed in Hong Kong by the South China Printing
Company

Contents

Preface	page xiii
Introduction	xv

1 **EARLY SPAS OF NOBLE PATRONAGE**   1
   Bath 3, Tunbridge Wells 17, Astrop 27, Epsom 31, Buxton 37, Bristol 47

2 **LONDON'S OLD SPAS**   53
   Islington 57, Sadler's Wells 61, Clerk's Well, London Spa and Powis Well 64, Bagnigge Wells and White Conduit House 67, St Chad's and Pancras Spa 71

3 **A RING OF SPAS**   75
   The Streatham Spas 79, Sydenham and Dulwich 83, Spas south of the river (Lambeth, St George's, Camberwell, Shooter's Hill, Bromley, Ladywell, Bermondsey) 83, Beulah Spa 87, Richmond and East Sheen 89, Spas north of the river (Hyde Park, St. Govor's, Billing's Well, Notting Hill, Acton, Kilburn, Hampstead, Muswell Hill, Tottenham, Totteridge, Welwyn) 90, Barnet 97, Northaw Spring and Wanstead 100

4 **SPAS PATRONISED BY GEORGE III**   101
   Cheltenham 105, Weymouth 121, Southampton 127

5 **REGENCY AND EARLY VICTORIAN SPAS**   131
   Brighton 133, Scarborough 139, Dorton 143, Melksham 149, Ashby-de-la Zouch 151, Admaston, Sutton and Saltwell 153, Gloucester and Tewkesbury 155, Leamington 161

6 **EARLY HYDROPATHIC SPAS**   171
   Malvern 175, Ilkley (White Wells and Ben Rhydding) 185, Matlock 191

7 RURAL AND PROVINCIAL SPAS   197
Strathpeffer and Moffat 201, Spas of northern England (Gilsland, Shap) 202, Croft-on-Tees 203, Ripon and Aldfield 209, Malton and Hovingham 211, Skipton 213, Boston Spa 217, Askern 221, Other Yorkshire spas 223, Woodhall Spa 225, Spas of eastern England (Thetford, Mistley, Hockley, West Tilbury, Canterbury), Bakewell 230, Droitwich 233, Tenbury Wells 239, Minor Welsh spas (Trefriw, Llanwrtyd Wells, Llangammarch Wells) 243, Builth Wells 247, Llandrindod Wells 249

8 SPA OF THE NORTH   257
Harrogate, Knaresborough and Harlow Car 259

Pharmaceutical Notes   279
Bibliography   281
Index   283

Illustrations

Bath
　The King's and Queen's Baths in 1675　page 5
　The Pump Room of 1706 with the King's and Queen's Baths　7
　The Assembly Rooms in 1769–71　10
　The Cross Bath in about 1830　12
　The Pump Room in 1806　13

Tunbridge Wells
　The Chalybeate Spring and Walks in 1718　20
　The Bath House in 1827　23
　The Parade in 1880　24

Astrop
　St Rumbold's Well in the 19th century　29

Epsom
　The Wells in the early 19th century　34
　The Old Well in 1901　35

Buxton
　The Drinking-Place in 1800　41
　The Crescent in the 19th century　42
　St Ann's Well and Pump Room in about 1894　44

Bristol
　Old Hotwell House in the 18th century　50
　New Hotwell House in the early 19th century　51

London
　Islington Spa in 1733　59
　Sadler's Wells in 1792　62
　London Spa, Finsbury, in 1720　65
　Bagnigge Wells in about 1774　68
　St Chad's Well in about 1830　70
　St Pancras Well in about 1730　72

Streatham
　Old Mineral Spring as seen today　80
　The New Wells House in 1831　81

Norwood
　Beulah Spa in 1851　88

Kensington
　St Govor's Well, Kensington Gardens, in 1910　91

Acton
　Acton Wells Assembly House in 1793　93

vii

Hampstead
  Assembly and Pump Rooms in the early 18th century   94
Barnet
  Well-house in about 1796   98
  Well-house of today   99
Cheltenham
  The Original Spa in about 1813   106
  The Original or Royal Well in 1788   109
  Montpellier Wells in about 1809   110
  The Montpellier Rotunda, interior, in the 1840s   113
  The Sherborne Pump Room in about 1818   114
  The Cambray Pump Room in the 19th century   117
  The Pittville Pump Room as seen today   118
Weymouth
  Nottington Spa House in 1833   123
  Radipole Pump Room in about 1833   124
Southampton
  The Long Rooms and Bath in the 18th century   129
Brighton
  St Ann's Well at Hove in the early 19th century   134
  The Royal German Spa in the early 19th century   135
Scarborough
  The New Spa in about 1840   141
Dorton
  The Pump Room in the early 19th century   145
  The chalybeate spring as seen today   146
Ashby-de-la-Zouch
  The Ivanhoe Baths in the early 19th century   152
Gloucester
  The Pump Room in the 19th century   156
Tewkesbury
  Spa building in the 19th century   157
Leamington Spa
  The Aylesford Well in the 19th century   164
  Smart's Marble Baths in about 1820   165
  The Upper Assembly Rooms in 1826   166
  The Royal Pump Room as seen today   168
Malvern
  The Holy Well in the early 1870s   177
  St Ann's Well as seen today   178
  Spa Villa and Pump Room in the 19th century   179

Ilkley
   White Wells as seen today   187
   Ben Rhydding Hydro in about 1884   188

Matlock Bath
   The Old Pavilion and Royal Hotel in about 1884   193
   The Grand Pavilion as seen today   194

Strathpeffer
   Pump Room interior in the early 20th century   200

Croft-on-Tees
   New Sulphur Spa in the early 20th century   206

Skipton
   Pump-house (converted) as seen today   215

Boston Spa
   Spa building in the 19th century   218

Askern
   Spa scene in the 19th century   222

Woodhall Spa
   Hotel with bath-house and pump-room in about 1868   228
   Bath House and Pump Room in the 19th century   231

Droitwich
   The Saline Baths and Hotel in about 1840   235
   St Andrew's Brine Baths in 1975   236

Tenbury Wells
   The Pump Room in about 1960   240

Llanwrtyd Wells
   Spa buildings in the mid-20th century   244

Builth Wells
   Park Wells in the early 20th century   248

Llandrindod Wells
   Old Pump Room and Hotel in 1850   253
   Rock Park Pump Room as seen today   254

Harrogate
   The Tewit Well as seen today   263
   Knaresborough Spaw in the 19th century   264
   St John's Well in 1831   267
   The Sulphur Well in about 1806   269
   The Royal Promenade and Cheltenham Pump Room in about 1835   270
   The Royal Pump Room in about 1842   272
   St John's Well as seen today   273
   Montpellier Sulphur Well and Baths in 1831   275

Maps

British Spas   xiv
Bath   *page* 2
Tunbridge Wells   16
Astrop and King's Sutton   26
Epsom   32
Buxton   38
Bristol Hotwells   48
Central London spas   56
The Streatham Spas   78
Dulwich and Sydenham   84
Beulah Spa   86
Barnet   96
Cheltenham   104
Weymouth   120
Southampton   126
Brighton   132
Scarborough   138
Dorton   144
Melksham   148
Ashby-de-la-Zouch   150
Gloucester   154

Tewkesbury   158
Leamington Spa   162
Malvern   174
Ilkley   184
Matlock Bath   190
Croft-on-Tees   204
Ripon   208
Aldfield   208
Skipton   214
Boston Spa   216
Askern   220
Woodhall Spa   226
Droitwich   234
Tenbury Wells   238
Llanwrtyd Wells   242
Llangammarch Wells   242
Builth Wells   246
Llandrindod Wells   250
Knaresborough   260
Harrogate   260
Harlow Car   276

Preface

NOT MANY people realise that more than a hundred spas have existed in Britain and that traces of even those long since forgotten can often still be found.

The spa was a unique institution and, as such, it deserves a special place in social history. During the centuries preceding the rise of medical science it offered countless 'cures' for countless ills and, understandably was often revered. Although changing fashion and the fickleness of human nature could reverse a spa's popularity almost overnight, several of them became important meeting-places for fashionable society, leaving behind them some enduring and notable architecture.

In this book my aim has been to present a pictorial and descriptive record of all the major and most of the minor spas whilst it is still possible to obtain and assemble the necessary material. The record includes an account of each spa's origins, the nature of the waters, the sometimes colourful personalities associated with it, and how it achieved or failed to achieve fame.

Although two world wars hastened the demise of most British spas still in existence in the 20th century, there were a few notable survivors and, today, there are signs that some of these are seeking, and may well find, a new lease of life.

K.D.

Introduction

TAKING ITS name from Spa in the Ardennes, the British spa dates from the late 16th century. Originally it was simply a place possessing a 'curative' mineral spring or springs which was commercialised in some way—usually by the owner of the land who made the most of his good fortune by enclosing the newly discovered well and by providing accommodation for visitors.

To the genuinely sick and afflicted, the early spas were often places of pilgrimage and the primitive accommodation offered was generally accepted without complaint. But, as the message of the waters' healing qualities spread, a new and more demanding clientèle began to appear. This was the British aristocracy—a rich, influential and fashionable section of the population who began to see in the spas a means of obtaining relief from the effects of dissipation or other excesses at court but who had no wish to put up with uncomfortable lodgings and an almost total lack of entertainment during prolonged periods of absence from home.

Predictably the opportunities presented by high society's increasing interest in 'taking the waters' did not escape the notice of the entrepreneurs of the day and, by the early 18th century, most of the more promising and favoured spas were in the hands of proprietors only too ready and willing to cater for its needs. The result was the gradual appearance of the elegant pump and assembly rooms, colonnades, promenades and pleasure gardens that were to become almost synonymous with the successful spa.

As one might expect, the more remote country spas developed along more modest lines but, whatever their status, the mineral spring remained the vital element and focal point of interest, distinguishing the genuine spa from social imitations such as the seaside resort of later years.

It is easy to understand the immense importance of these springs at a time when there was little else to which the sick and ailing could look for help. In medieval times, man had revered them as holy wells because, to him, they were the sources of magical cures and all attempts to put them down, including those made during the Reformation of the 1530s, failed.

Some of Britain's mineral springs, notably the thermal springs of Bath, Bristol and Buxton, dated back even further—as far as the Roman era, when the invaders' addiction to bathing assured such places of a special place of honour. Most of the springs however were not discovered until the 17th, 18th and 19th centuries, by which time members of the British medical profession had joined their Continental colleagues in extolling the virtues of the waters and were even writing treatises on the subject.

Under the impetus of the new popular demand, scores of mineral springs began to be discovered up and down the country, sometimes by diligent searching, sometimes by accident. Certain parts of the country appeared to be better endowed than others but by the end of the 19th century most places in Britain were within reach of at least one minor spa. (The minor spas enjoyed local rather than national acclaim but their waters fell into the same groups as those of the major spas and were no less 'therapeutic'.)

There were three main groups. The purely saline waters contained dissolved salts such as magnesium sulphate (Epsom Salt) and were used chiefly for their purgative effects. Then there were the chalybeate (pronounced kal-ib-ee-at) waters characterised by the rust coloured iron oxide formed when ferrous carbonate is exposed to air. These waters contained various iron salts, notably ferrous sulphate renowned for its tonic and restorative properties. Thirdly, there were the sulphur waters characterised by the smell of hydrogen sulphide (the gas given off by bad eggs) containing sulphur compounds and traditionally drunk or used for bathing, particularly as a treatment for skin complaints.

An intriguing feature of the springs and wells on which the spas depended was, in fact, the variety of their waters. Most could be categorised as belonging to one of the three groups but some contained substances from two or, occasionally, from all three. Even when the same essential ingredients were present, the proportions were likely to differ, in addition to which there was yet another variant—the temperature factor. In fact so numerous were the minor variations that opportunities for comparisons and preferences were virtually limitless and, needless to say, they exercised the minds of many a spa-goer and prescribing physician.

The reasons for all these variations in composition and temperature are not far to seek. The depth of origin, the nature of the subsoil or rock over which the waters passed and the geological conditions which enabled them to rise to or near to the surface all played a part. Waters which passed over rocks containing very soluble substances naturally tended to have high mineral contents, as did those rising from a great depth. The latter also showed smaller seasonal variations in temperature and, like the waters of Bath, were more likely to be 'hot' than those of shallower origin.

The chemical composition and temperature of the spring waters were not, however, the only factors which contributed to the success or failure of any particular spa. The location, the business abilities of the proprietor and the vagaries of fashion all played a part. In fact there appeared to be no golden rule: one spa might prosper and remain in vogue for a long time while, for no apparent reason, another might enjoy only a brief spell of glory or barely get off the ground at all.

Even as early as the 17th century, the number and choice was so wide that Celia Fiennes, a lady-in-waiting with a remarkable urge to visit and sample the waters of every spa within reach, spent months on the project. Much is owed to this intrepid traveller and water-drinker whose personal and often amusingly critical account of the virtues and shortcomings of the early spas are faithfully recorded and preserved in *The Journals of Celia Fiennes*.

Other recordists were the diarists Samuel Pepys and John Evelyn, both untiring water-drinkers who regularly visited many of the smaller spas around London. Without their accounts, some of these lesser spas might well have passed into oblivion unnoticed.

Yet another group of people who left written evidence of both the early and the later spas were the so-called water poets. It is curious how much verse the spas inspired. Much of it was written by the wits of the day but there are also some pathetic verses such as the couplet attributed to Mary Queen of Scots:

'Buxton, whose fame thy milk-warm waters tell,
Whom I, perhaps, no more shall see, farewell!'

Sometimes faith and pathos went hand in hand with humour, as in the verse on a tombstone:

'Here lies I and my three daughters,
Died from drinking the Cheltenham waters,
If we had stuck to Epsom salts,
We shouldn't be lying in these cold vaults.'

As for the wits, their contributions were usually brief and to the point:

'The Malvern water, says Dr John Wall,
Is famed for containing just nothing at all.'

There were, of course, many who made notable contributions to the spa story in non-written form and perhaps none more so than Beau Nash. Beau Nash's primary impact was on Bath and Tunbridge but news of the strict code of conduct which he imposed at these two resorts quickly spread and became unwritten law at virtually every fashionable spa in the country.

Born in Swansea in 1674, Richard or 'Beau' Nash has been described as a fastidious Welsh opportunist. His parents were not well off but they were middle class and Nash received an Oxford education before attempting a career in the army and then in law. Neither suited him and within a short time he succumbed to the attractions and dissipations of society life, making a shifty living at gambling. It was not until 1705, shortly after he arrived in Bath, that he suddenly found his metier.

Nash's opportunity came with the death of the existing master-of-ceremonies in a duel over a game of cards. The newcomer was offered the post and so began the remarkable career that was to make Bath famous not only for the splendour of its balls and other public functions but also for the manner in which they were conducted. It is said that, under Nash, everyone knew exactly what to wear and how to behave and that for the first time, the young ladies were protected against unscrupulous adventurers.

In 1735 Beau Nash became, additionally, the first master-of-ceremonies at Tunbridge and remained so for twenty-six years. The seasons of the two resorts were complementary so he was able to move from one to the other, insisting on the same code of manners and morals which, by this time, every spa-goer had come to expect. Yet, under all the autocratic authority, ostentation and finery, Beau Nash was quite a poor man who frequently found himself in debt.

Some say that Nash's problems stemmed from an over generous and sentimental nature, but there were other factors too. Most of his income was derived from the gaming tables and when successive governments tried to suppress public gambling by means of legislation, his fortunes were inevitably affected. At all events, by 1754 Nash had become so financially embarrassed that he narrowly escaped the hand of the law and, when he died at Bath in 1762, he was in very poor circumstances—a strange ending for the man who had 'reigned' for over fifty years and who had left an indelible mark on the 18th century spa.

Although the social side of spa life had increased enormously in importance during Beau Nash's time, much faith and hope was still attached to the curative aspect of 'taking the waters' and quite heroic quantities were often drunk. Two glassfuls was a fairly common dosage but it was not unknown for quantities of up to a gallon to be consumed at a single session. In fact, such was the state of medical science, or lack of it, that even the highly intelligent

18th century statesman Lord Chesterfield went to Tunbridge with the naïve hope that his deafness might be cured by the chalybeate water. It was not until well into the 19th century, as more was learnt about the treatment of disease and more drugs were developed that the efficacy of the spa waters began to arouse even mild scepticism.

Meanwhile another personal account of Britain's spas had appeared in the literature. Published in three volumes in 1841 under the title *The Spas of England and Principal Sea-Bathing Places*, it was compiled and written by Dr Augustus Bozzi Granville (1783–1872), a strong-minded ex-Italian patriot whose travels and political adventures had eventually landed him in London in 1813.

As an important contributor to spa history and one whose work is occasionally quoted in this book, the antecedents and personality of Dr Granville are of some interest. After qualifying as a physician in 1802 and acceding to his mother's request to adopt an English name—his maternal grandmother was English—this resourceful character embarked on a varied and colourful career. In 1818 he acquired a fashionable Saville Row practice and about the same time launched out as a prolific writer of pamphlets on political and medical matters.

According to recorded descriptions, Dr Granville was of medium height, somewhat square-faced with a high forehead, keen looking and firm. He was happily endowed with suave and prepossessing manners which enabled him to impart confidence to his patients and he was also a lively, witty and learned conversationist. These were valuable gifts indeed for any society practitioner, but, as his frequent and sometimes alarming travels abroad bore witness, Dr Granville was also an adventurous soul who was subject to all kinds of enthusiasms. Earnestly preoccupied with matters of health and impressed by what he saw on the Continent, it was not long before he became a devoted exponent of spa therapy.

After publishing *The Spas of Germany* in 1837, Dr Granville set out to see what Britain had to offer—a venture which necessarily depended on the horse and carriage of the day and was one which, by the end, taxed even the energies of this remarkable investigator. Although the somewhat lengthy travel saga which resulted contains much extraneous information, it throws some very valuable light on the early Victorian spas and on the attitudes of those who patronised them.

Despite its merits, Dr Granville's work ran to only one edition and it is doubtful whether it made much contribution to the impending Victorian spa boom. That particular phenomenon is generally attributed to the railways whose arrival suddenly placed virtually every spa in the country within reach of those who could afford the fare, notably the rising middle classes. Only too glad to escape from the dirt and grime of their industrial cities, this new and prosperous section of the community had little compunction about spending large sums of money on lengthy visits to spas obligingly prescribed or recommended by their doctors.

The result was the rebirth of established resorts such as Harrogate, Buxton, Leamington, Matlock and Cheltenham and the rapid development of relative newcomers such as Woodhall and Llandrindod. All these resorts were highly respectable, capable of bestowing social benefits on the visitor as well as the promise of improved health.

But for all their undoubted attractions, the Victorian spas were a far cry from the old spas of the 17th and 18th centuries. 'Taking the waters' was once again a serious business and there was no place for frivolities. Concerts and music still provided an acceptable form of relaxation but unedifying diversions such as gambling were definitely out. Even more noticeable was the replacement of many of the old elegant buildings by larger and more commodious ones—a true reflection of the wealth of the new clientèle and the solidity of the age.

One of the more obvious examples of the new approach to spa treatment was the growth in popularity of the hydropathic establishment with its Spartan regimes that bore little, if any, resemblance to what had gone on at Bath a couple of centuries earlier. In fact so different were the Victorian and Edwardian spas from their predecessors that they can almost be said to represent a new spa age rather than an extension of the old.

It is difficult to say exactly how long the final phase lasted. By 1914 when the First World War broke out, it had already reached its zenith and the subsequent story is one of continuous decline. It has been estimated that by 1919 there were between thirty and forty hydropathic establishments still in existence in the country, but the social order had changed and the number of people left who could afford to patronise them was fast diminishing. This was the period when many of these great Gothic-styled establishments fell victim to a series of disastrous fires—accidental or otherwise—while others anticipated events by converting themselves into ordinary hotels, municipal and private offices, or by allowing themselves to be pulled down for redevelopment.

Spa towns as a whole were also in trouble. With the appearance of more synthetic medicines, the mineral water 'cure' had lost much of its credibility and was rapidly going out of fashion. Although few of these towns were willing to relinquish their spa identities completely, many realised that other means would have to be found of ensuring their prosperity and they, too, began looking towards urban, or even industrial, development as a means of salvation.

Harrogate is a good example of a town which managed to remain a spa for another twenty years or so while following an active programme of urban development. Other towns did likewise, with varying degrees of success, but none were immune from the post-war slump and, increasingly, excuses were found, usually on economic grounds, for reducing the number of spa buildings. It was a trend hastened by the Second World War and by the introduction of the National Health Service—a trend which finally led to the closure of most of the remaining pump-rooms.

Although 'taking the waters' was now popularly regarded as an anachronism, the demise of the British spa did not pass unlamented. Some of the Continental spas were, and still are, flourishing so why, it has been asked, must Britain's be relegated to oblivion? Various theories have been put forward in explanation, including the plausible suggestion that Britain has such a plentiful and excellent supply of drinking water that it has no need of its mineral springs.

Be that as it may, there are still some people who hope for a British spa revival and indeed there is now a small body of medical opinion in favour of reinstating any spa premises with bathing facilities which could once again be made viable. It is pointed out that for certain disabilities such as the rheumatic complaints, heated mineral water bathing provides as effective a treatment as any other so far devised, that it is relatively cheap and that the patient actually enjoys it! At the moment, only Leamington offers a service of this kind but the names of Bath, Droitwich, Harrogate, Llandrindod and Woodhall have all been put forward as possibilities for establishing a nation-wide network of modern therapeutic spa centres.

Consideration of such schemes are, however, outside the scope of this book and the only plea that can usefully be made here is for the preservation, on conservation grounds, of as many surviving springs, wells or spa buildings as possible. The last stages of the spa age, or ages, will soon be outside the span of living memory and for this reason, if for none other, all such reminders are of historic interest and value.

1
Early Spas of Noble Patronage

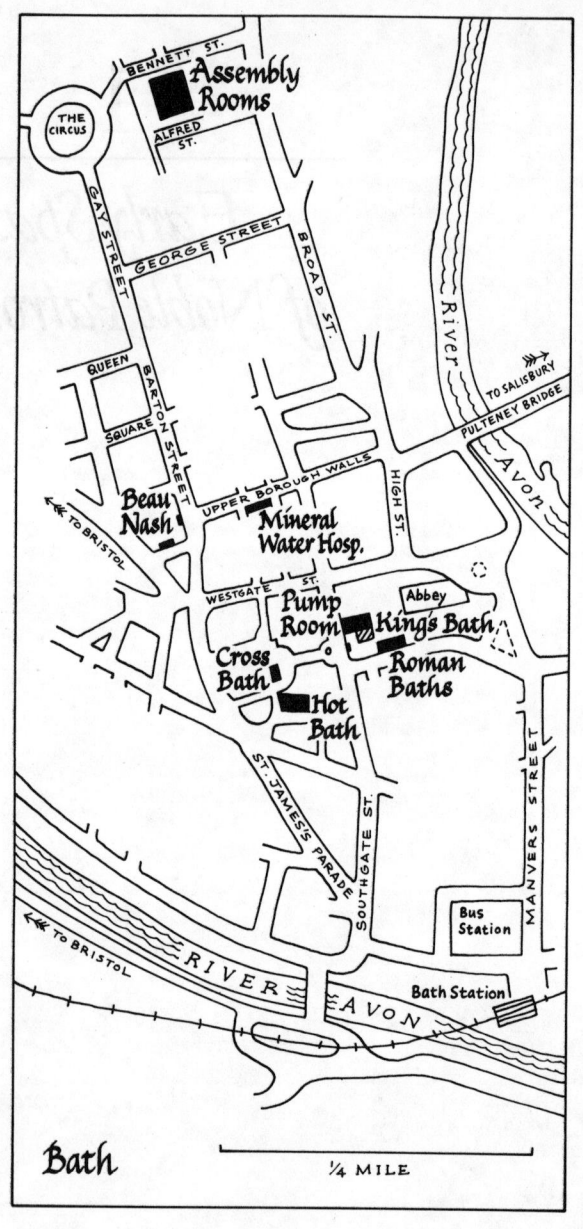

Bath

WHEN THE spa age dawned, Bath was ready and waiting. It had everything—legend, history and an abundant supply of hot mineral water from natural springs—all the ingredients in fact to place it in the forefront of British spas and to attract the most noble in the land.

The legend, believed by some historians to date back as far as 800 B.C., tells of the curative value of the waters through the adventures of a prince called Bladud who was banished from his father's kingdom after contracting leprosy. After years of wandering, the outcast found work as a swineherd on the banks of the Avon, only to discover that he had passed on the dreaded disease to the animals in his care. Fearful of dismissal, Bladud took the pigs away to the woods to forage where they scampered down the river bank and wallowed in the hot springs. Almost at once Bladud saw that the pigs were recovering and, drawing the correct conclusion, followed their example by plunging into the steaming swamp.

According to the legend the banished prince, who was destined to become the father of King Lear, was duly cured and returned to his father's kingdom where he identified himself by his mother's ring and eventually succeeded to the throne. During his reign he built a new capital city around the springs and called it Caer Baden—the city now known as Bath.

Almost a match for its legend, Bath's recorded history also reflects man's early interest in the hot saline springs—an interest which dates back at least to the time when the Roman invaders built their famous baths around the shrine of the goddess Sul-Minerva in about A.D. 76 and called the town Aquae Sulis—waters of Sul.

There are few records of what happened during the dark ages after the Romans left but the mere fact that Bath became known as Akemanceaster (meaning 'Sick Men's Town') suggests that, even during this time of decay and twilight desolation, people continued to use the water for curative purposes. Indeed, with the phenomenon of hyper-thermal water—the temperature was a constant 120°F—bubbling up before their eyes at the rate of 500,000 gallons a day, it would have been surprising if some use had not been found for it.

It is known that in Norman times new baths were built and that the original King's Bath, named after Henry I, appeared soon after 1100. It is also known that this bath was still in use in 1559 because in that year there were reports of scandalous behaviour among the bathers which led to intervention by the first Bishop of Bath and Wells and to the introduction of more decorous codes of conduct.

In those days, right up to the time of the dissolution of the monasteries, the springs and baths were administered by the bishop and prior of the Abbey. After that they passed to the city corporation, who appointed a keeper-of-the-baths—not a paid servant but one who paid for the privilege of receiving any income from the charges and tips.

The best known of the medieval baths were the King's Bath, the Cross Bath and the Hot Bath, all built directly over hot springs and standing within about a hundred yards of each other. The Cross Bath did not acquire its present name until five hundred years later but it was one of the earliest of the medieval baths, possibly dating back as far as 1180 when the adjacent St John's Hospital (now an almshouse) was founded. When Elizabeth I visited the city in 1574, all three of these baths were in existence as open-air structures and all were destined to be rebuilt in the latter part of the 18th century.

Towards the end of the 16th century, a small new rectangular bath was constructed for the exclusive use of women. Used in 1616 by James I's queen, Anne of Denmark, who came seeking relief from her dropsy, it became and remained known as the Queen's Bath until it was demolished in Victorian times to make way for the excavation of the Roman Baths discovered directly underneath.

By the 17th century, the message of the benefits and growing popularity of foreign spas had begun to reach England, and Bath should have been in a position to rival the best of them. As a town, however, it could still offer little more than a few tree-lined walks and facilities for bowls and, once again, its reputation was suspect. In 1630, Charles I's queen, Henrietta Maria, actually refused to visit because of renewed reports of violence and scandalous behaviour and went to Tunbridge instead.

Nor did the rest of the century produce much sign of improvement. According to the diarist John Evelyn, the streets in 1654 were still 'narrow, uneven and unpleasant' and fourteen years later, in 1688, Evelyn's fellow diarist Samuel Pepys expressed his own reservations. Following a visit with his wife to the Cross Bath at four o'clock in the morning, Pepys wrote that there was 'much company; very fine ladies; and the manner pretty enough, only methinks it cannot be clean to go so many bodies together in the same

Bath: *The King's and Queen's Baths, from an engraving of 1675 by Thomas Johnson.*
With the hot spring rising in the centre, the medieval King's Bath was built soon after 1100 and named after the reigning king, Henry I. The elaborate embellishments, as seen in this view from the abbey churchyard, were gradually acquired over the years and, by 1675, the bath had become a venue for fun and frolics rather than a centre of healing. The smaller rectangular Queen's Bath to the left of the picture dated from the end of the 16th century, when it was constructed for the exclusive use of women. It became known as the Queen's Bath after Anne of Denmark, wife of James I, used it in 1616 in the hope of curing her dropsy.

Both these ancient baths remained open to the skies and changed very little until 1705–6, when the first proper pump-room was built.

water'. The most dubious reputation of all, however, was attached to the King's Bath, where the associated sundry evils appear to have included not only uncleanliness, overcrowding and mixed bathing but also 'deplorable behaviour'.

In spite of these deterrents, Charles II's queen, Catherine of Braganza, paid a visit to Bath in 1663 in the hope that bathing in the warm and buoyant spring water would enable her to bear children. She was disappointed but, at the Cross Bath (so named in 1688 after being adorned with a cross to commemorate the birth of a royal son to James II's second wife, Mary of Modena, following her visit the previous year) bears witness, the waters sometimes appeared to live up to the powers attributed to them. (Whether or not Mary of Modena's production of the 'Old Pretender' speaks well for the Cross Bath is, of course, a matter of opinion!)

The last of the royal visitors before the transformation of Bath into a properly organised spa with fine buildings was Queen Anne who came in 1692, in 1702, and again in 1703 in search of a cure for her gout and dropsy. By this time, the bathing conditions at least had improved and even that indefatigable spa traveller and critical observer Celia Fiennes had noted with approval in her 'Journal' that the routine was conducted decorously and that the water was changed every night.

However, Bath still suffered from a chronic shortage of lodgings and, since it possessed little in the way of entertainments, boredom with its attendant quarrels, scandals and intrigues was rife.

The person responsible for changing all this was, of course, Richard or 'Beau' Nash, whose arrival and subsequent appointment as master-of-ceremonies in 1705 transformed the spa into the disciplined organisation that was to become a model for virtually every fashionable spa in the land. Nash's authority was all embracing. As well as keeping the beggars at bay and the sedan-chair carriers in order, he even supervised the paving, the lighting and the cleaning of the streets. Not surprisingly, his extravagantly dressed figure, with its fancy waistcoats and black wig topped by a jewelled cream beaver hat, became one of Bath's most famous and familiar sights.

At the height of his fame, Nash occupied a magnificent mansion in St John's Court (now the Garrick's Head), thereby encouraging, no doubt, the building aspirations of many a rich resident. Nash's 'reign' certainly opened the door to the great builders such as John Wood and Ralph Allen who soon moved in to meet the demand—a demand that included the provision of suitable lodging-houses for use during the season and which, as everyone

Bath: *The Pump Room of 1706, with the King's and Queen's Baths, from an old print.*

With its large arched windows reminiscent of an orangery, Bath's first proper pump-room, seen on the left, was commissioned in 1705 after the royal physician had recommended that the waters should be drunk as well as used for bathing. It was completed the following year by a local mason-builder, John Harvey. Although enlarged in 1745, this early pump-room was always regarded as too small and was destined to be replaced, in 1791, by the Great Pump Room.

The Queen's Bath, to the right, survived until the late 19th century, when it had to be demolished to allow excavation of the Roman bath, discovered almost directly underneath it. By that time the more important King's Bath was also disintegrating and the Victorians decided to rebuild it for show purposes. Only a few relics from the original structure were included in the reconstruction but the result provided (and still does after some dismantling in modern times for cleaning and excavation) a fascinating reminder of how the famous medieval bath once looked.

8   Bath

knows, resulted in the fine terraces, crescents and circuses that still characterise Bath today.

Following the recommendation of the royal physician that the waters of Bath should be drunk as well as used for bathing, a local mason-builder called John Harvey was commissioned in 1705 to build a proper pump-room and this was completed the following year. With its large arched windows, it looked like an orangery but, apart from the Corinthian columns on the side next to the Abbey churchyard away from the steaming corrosion of the King's Bath, it soon came under criticism as being too small and too low a building to be impressive—a criticism which persisted even after it was enlarged in 1745 and which ultimately led to its replacement in 1791 by the Great Pump Room.

Meanwhile, in 1708, Bath had acquired its first assembly rooms. Successively known as Harrison's, Simpson's and the Lower Rooms, this building stood south-east of the Abbey where toilets now stand in Parade Gardens facing Orange Grove. It provided one of the many new facilities which helped Nash to devise a clearly defined programme of activities for the increasing number of visitors.

For most visitors the day began with a bathe in the hot spring waters between 6 and 9 a.m. and was followed by a water-drinking session to the accompaniment of music. After that there was breakfast and, at noon, a service in the Abbey which all who could were expected to attend. Visitors were then free to do their shopping or to drive, ride, stroll or rest until it was time for dinner at 3 p.m. After dinner they normally paraded before making the second and last visit of the day to the pump-room. In the evening there was tea followed by a choice of entertainments, including balls, social visits, gambling and visits to the theatre. Seldom did a day go by without some kind of scandal but it was usually of a relatively innocuous nature and without the serious repercussions common in the days before Beau Nash.

In addition to his organisational and peace-keeping abilities, Beau Nash possessed enough psychological insight to understand the importance of royal visits and how to handle them. When the Prince of Orange came in 1734 he promptly added the prefix 'Orange' to the 'Grove' and had an obelisk erected in the centre. Whether or not he anticipated that this might lead to the need for another obelisk is not revealed but, following the Prince of Wales' visit in 1738, he again rose to the occasion and Queen Square was selected as the honoured site for an equally impressive monument.

Predictably, by the end of the century almost everyone who mattered in society was familiar with the spa at Bath. Most members of the aristocracy regarded a visit not just as socially advantageous but as a social necessity and, despite an increasing number of competitors and imitators, it remained supreme.

Any notion that nature had intended the waters of Bath to be solely for the benefit of the aristocracy was, however, obviously an untenable one and Beau Nash was among the first to recognise the needs and rights of the local poor. Indeed it is believed that, beneath all his flamboyance, Bath's leading citizen had a pronounced social conscience and that his organising of subscriptions for the building of the Mineral Water Hospital was no more than might have been expected of him.

Designed by John Wood's son and opened in 1742, the charity hospital (later known as the Royal National Hospital for Rheumatic Diseases) still stands in Upper Borough Walls, about 150 yards north of the central Pump Room area. In the early days, one of the senior physicians was Dr William Oliver, famous for his views on nutrition and, more particularly, for his Bath Oliver biscuits. However, it is worth remembering that for nearly a hundred years after it was built, the patients still had to walk or be carried to the hot springs for their treatment. There were no pipes to carry the water.

Towards the end of his long 'reign' as the 'uncrowned King of Bath', Beau Nash had to move out of his mansion into a smaller house in nearby Saw Close, a house which still stands today next to the Theatre Royal. There he died in virtual poverty in 1761 at the age of eighty-eight. In the last years of his life he was sadly neglected by his one-time friends and it was not until after his death that Bath recognised its loss and commissioned a statue of him by Prince Hoare. The statue was duly and ceremoniously erected in the original pump-room where it remained until, accompanied by a long case clock, it was transferred to the grander premises of the Great Pump Room later built on the site. Here both statue and clock remain today, adorning the apse on the east wall.

By the late 1760s a major programme of urban expansion was under way at Bath accompanied by the appearance of several new spa buildings. John Wood the younger had become the leading architect and between 1769 and 1771 his 'new' or Upper Assembly Rooms, built at a cost of £20,000, appeared on the north side of the town near the famous 'Circus'. In spite of its somewhat undistinguished exterior, the building possessed a magnificent ballroom, a tea-room and a card-room and was soon renowned for its public breakfasts and grand balls. Like the heroine in Jane Austen's *Northanger*

Bath: *The Upper Assembly Rooms, from a 20th century drawing.*

Built between 1769 and 1771 on the north side of the town, this spa building was designed by John Wood the younger. Externally it was never regarded as distinguished but the tall Corinthian columns, magnificent chandeliers and other impressive features of the interior earned it a reputation for being the finest of its kind in Europe.

By the 20th century the building had degenerated into a cinema and a saleroom and it was 1938 before it was re-opened to the public by the National Trust. In 1942 it was partly burnt out as the result of enemy action and again had to await restoration before finally being re-opened in 1963. As well as housing the Museum of Costume, it now serves as a conference centre and, appropriately, is once again the scene of balls and banquets.

Abbey (1789), most spa visitors now made a habit of patronising both the 'Upper' and the 'Lower' Rooms.

Having acquired its dramatic Royal Crescent (1767–75) and its famous Adam-built Pulteney Bridge (1769–74), the town also decided to embark on a programme of rebuilding its medieval baths. The first to be commissioned—in 1775—was the new Hot Bath which still survives today in altered form. As designed by Wood, the elaborate symmetrically planned building had no roof and the portico area with the four Tuscan columns that today serves as an entrance into the building was simply a shelter for a pump from which the public could obtain the water. Facing it was the smaller Hemming Bath, whose building also survives, though in very poor condition.

When the smaller neighbouring Cross Bath was rebuilt in 1784, the work fell to Thomas Baldwin. Thomas Baldwin was the principal architect of the day and he used the opportunity to provide a termination of his newly erected Bath Street—a street designed to link the various bathing establishments with the projected new Pump Room. Rebuilt in the baroque style, the Cross Bath was left, as it always had been, open to the skies.

Baldwin was responsible for the transformation of much of the central area but, due to a quarrel with the city fathers, he failed to complete the Great Pump Room which he had started in 1791 as a replacement for the old Pump Room erected nearly a century earlier by John Harvey. Because of the quarrel, John Palmer had to be appointed to finish the work and it was he who created the fine 60 ft-long Corinthian interior.

When, after innumerable delays, the great spa building was finally opened in 1795, it was acclaimed as one of the most elegant in the land. Embellished with a small gallery, three aspes (one containing the statue of Beau Nash) and with the all-important pump at one end—the pump was not moved to its present central alcove position overlooking the King's Bath until late Victorian times—it was seen as providing the perfect setting for the morning ceremony of water-drinking, and the spa-going public responded accordingly.

Fresh influxes of visitors were, of course, accompanied by the usual complement of wags and, as the caption verse beneath one of Rowlandson's drawings demonstrates, they made the most of their opportunities:

'It shocks me to see them look paler than ashes,
And as dead in the eye as the bust of Nash is,
Who the evening before were so blooming and plump,
I'm grieved to the heart when I go to the pump.'

Bath: *The Cross Bath, from a drawing of about 1830.*

Standing over a hot mineral spring in use since very early times, this roofless baroque-style building, with it round stone bath, was built in 1784 as a replacement for a medieval bath-house. The architect was Thomas Baldwin who designed it as a termination for his newly erected Bath Street—a street created to link the Pump Room with the various bathing establishments. The original bath had been used by Mary of Modena, second wife of James II and acquired its name the following year, in 1688, when a cross was erected over it to commemorate the birth of a prince. In 1954 the Cross Bath was renovated by the corporation and opened to the public at certain times of the week.

The building on the left of the picture is the Hot Bath. It was rebuilt in 1775 by John Wood and also survives today, though in altered form. Both the Cross Bath and the Hot Bath were closed in 1978 for the installation of modern purifying equipment.

Bath: *The Great Pump Room, from an old print of 1806.*
The classical style building was begun in 1791 to a design by the city architect, Thomas Baldwin, replacing the much smaller building of Beau Nash's time. After Baldwin lost his post in 1792, the Pump Room was finished by John Palmer and finally opened in 1796. Subsequent changes included a late 19th century enlargement by J. M. Brydon and, in modern times, the replacement of the old Pump Room Hotel, visible in the picture behind the colonnade, by neo-Georgian flats.

It is expected that the extensive cleaning and purifying operations, started in 1978 to the whole of the warm spring water system, will provide this famous pump-room with yet another long lease of life, bringing people from all over the world to drink the water and sit where the Regency beaux and belles once sat.

This was probably the heyday of the great spa and it is hard to believe that, within fifty years, Rowlandson and his contemporaries had all disappeared and that Bath was busy turning itself into a sedate Victorian watering-place complete with solid looking hotels and lodging-houses and fleets of big black bath-chairs. With the opening in 1867 of the city-owned Spa Centre (a fee-paying establishment which remained in operation until taken over by the NHS some eighty years later) such was to be the scene for many years to come.

In addition to providing the King's Bath with a new concrete floor, the Victorians constructed the Pump Room's central alcove with its pump, tap and basin. They also provided the tea, palms and music which were to become almost an institution at Bath and, according to present plans, are likely to remain so.

The end of the century saw a major east-side extension (1897) to the Pump Room and various internal alterations but, by this time, much of the town's attention was centred on the excavations arising out of the discovery in 1879 of the Roman Baths beneath the Queen's Bath. It was an attention which was to prove very rewarding in the years ahead when Bath began to shed its spa image in favour of its new role as a tourist centre.

Despite its changing image, the town continued to provide spa treatment even during the two world wars. In fact, throughout the Second World War, it kept the old octagonal Hot Bath (by this time protected by an iron and glass roof) open so that the warm buoyant waters could be enjoyed by the ordinary citizen for swimming purposes.

Nevertheless, a certain amount of decay was setting in and perhaps nowhere was it more apparent than in the condition of the small roofless Cross Bath, of Mary of Modena fame. It was not until 1954 that the corporation undertook and completed the restoration of this interesting old structure and opened it once again on certain days of the week to the public for bathing.

Unlike the Hot Bath and the Cross Bath, the King's Bath remains today as the Victorians intended it to remain when they rebuilt it—simply as a showpiece. As seen through the windows of the Pump Room, it still resembles the bath of the 17th and 18th century prints but the number of genuinely old features are few—notably the figure of the legendary Bladud, the bronze rings attached to the side for the support of bathers, and possibly part of the balustrade.

In 1976 Bath finally decided that the time had come for it to close its doors as a centre of spa therapy and that, in future, treatment at the Royal Mineral Hospital was to depend on heated tap water.

As it turned out, this may have been a temporary blessing in disguise for, in October 1978, came the alarming news that the warm spring water of Bath was polluted with a dangerous toxic organism and that the supply to the Pump Room, the street fountain, the Hot Bath, the Cross Bath and other outlets would have to be switched off whilst the whole system was opened up for cleaning and the installation of modern purifying equipment.

Shortly after work was started on the two-thousand-year-old reservoir beneath the King's Bath, it became clear that the operation was not going to be as simple as at first supposed. Not only were there many technical problems but it was realised that far more of the original structure of the King's Bath existed beneath the Victorian concrete than anyone had believed possible and that, however costly, the opportunity for further excavations was too important to miss.

Embedded in the sludge at the bottom of the reservoir were gifts, including numerous coins, once thrown to the goddess Sul Minerva, while another unexpected bonus was the discovery of wooden piles sunk by the Romans as part of a massive wall enclosing four springs. A collapsed roof added by the Saxons in about A.D. 300 made its own contribution to the story but caused further complications for the excavators.

The cost of the spa excavations at Bath has been high but the rewards are now plain to see and it is confidently believed that, with the water flowing again, this remarkable spa, for centuries the hope of the sick and at one time the fashionable stamping ground of England's high society, will soon once again be back in the limelight.

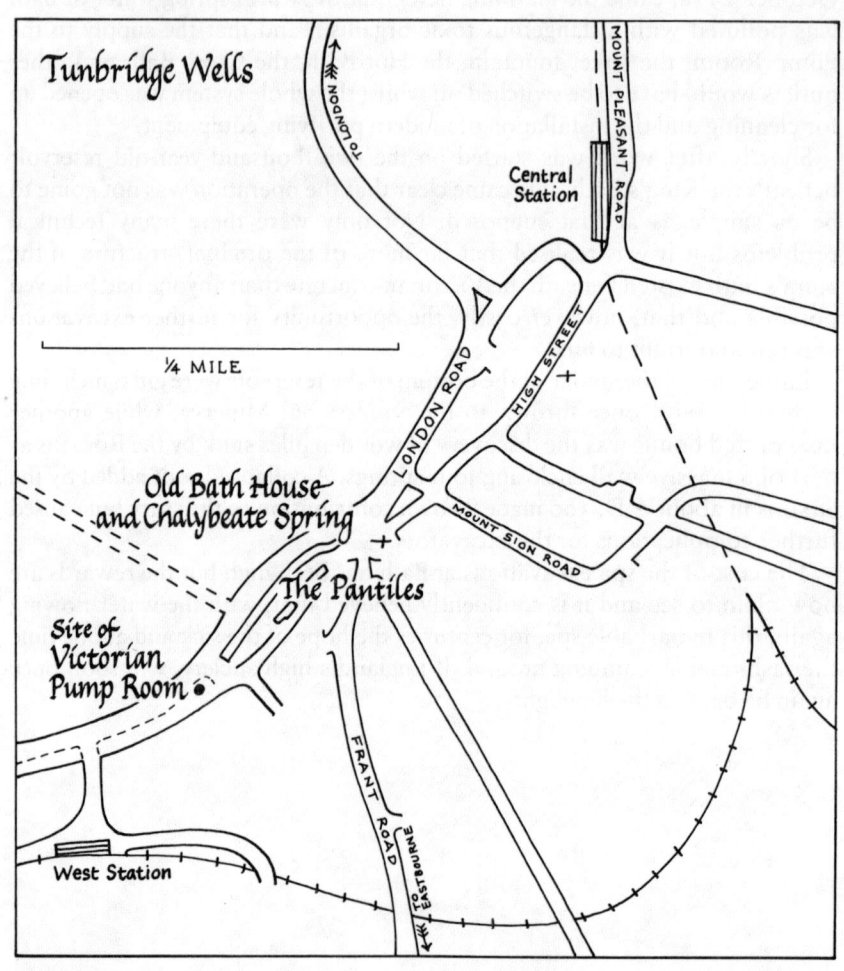

Tunbridge Wells

PROBABLY THE most important of Bath's contemporaries during the 17th century was Tunbridge Wells. Tunbridge was no more than a village but it had the advantage of being relatively close to London and, when a chalybeate (iron-bearing) spring was discovered there in 1606, it quickly became, like Bath, a spa of royal and noble patronage.

According to most accounts, the story of Tunbridge Wells began when the young and dissolute Dudley, Lord North, was riding back to London after staying at Lord Bergavenney's hunting lodge at Eridge two miles away. Although still unrecovered from his dissipations at James I's court, the young nobleman was sufficiently observant to notice a pool of strange rust-coloured water beside a stream in a densely wooded hollow. It reminded him of the water he had drunk at Spa during a recent health visit to the continent of Europe and he stopped to investigate. Having taken a drink from a cup lent him by the occupant of a nearby cottage, he collected some of the water in a bottle and took it back to London to show his physician.

After analysis, the physician declared that the water contained 'vitriol' (ferrous sulphate) which, according to the accepted opinion of the day, meant that it possessed some remarkable curative properties. Not only was it capable of curing the colic, the melancholy and the vapours and of making the lean fat and the fat lean but it could also kill flat worms in the belly, loosen the clammy humours of the body and dry the overmoist brain.

Encouraged by such promising news, Lord North returned to the site the following summer for a full course of treatment and was not disappointed. Within a short time he found himself fully recovered from his various ailments—he lived to be eighty-five!—and naturally lost little time in spreading the good news among his friends at court.

Since the newly discovered spring lay just within the Bergavenney (a name altered in the mid-18th century to Abergavenney) estate, Lord North's friend the baron immediately arranged for a clearing to be made, a well sunk over the principal spring—on investigation seven springs were found—and for a stone pavement to be laid round it. By 1608 the whole area had been enclosed within a triangular compound marked out with wooden rails.

Despite the primitive nature of these arrangements, by 1619 the well at Tunbridge was so well known that it was described as being 'much frequented by many great persons'. Yet a big problem remained: apart from what the neighbouring town of Tonbridge could provide some six miles away, there was virtually no accommodation and even Charles I's queen, Henrietta Maria, who arrived in 1630 for six weeks' convalescence after the birth of her son (the future Charles II) had to camp out like the rest of her entourage on nearby Bishop's Down Common.

Understandably, the royal visit aroused much interest and in 1632 a certain Dr Rowzee published a book about the waters of Tunbridge which, in its turn, highlighted the need not only for better accommodation but also for the provision of some form of amusement for visitors in between drinking sessions. The result was that in 1636 two cottage hostels were built. Designed to enable gentlemen to meet and smoke, one of them stood on the site of the Royal Sussex Assembly Rooms in Lower Walk and became known as the Pipe House. The other, which stood at the corner of Pink Alley, became a coffee and retiring house for ladies.

In addition to these welcome facilities, the green bank by the Well was levelled in 1683 and turned into a promenade. Planted out with a double row of elms and limes where tradesmen could set up booths and stalls with goods for sale to the visitors, this was the promenade that eventually became known as the Upper Walk.

Such activities had to cease during the Civil War, especially when Tunbridge became politically suspect, but, as soon as the monarchy was restored in 1660, life returned with a rush. With daily renderings from a trumpeter and a fiddler, the spa blossomed into stardom, attracting ever more important visitors, including Charles II and his queen, Catherine of Braganza. Catherine came in 1664 and stayed at the house of the royal physician in the hope that the waters would assist in the production of some royal children but, in the event, all these royal visits achieved was an endorsement of the spa's growing reputation for licentiousness—a reputation which introduced the phrase, 'the waters of scandal', and inspired the French ambassador to write: 'Well may they be called *les eaux de scandale*, for they have nearly ruined the good name of the maids and ladies (those who are not with their husbands). . . .'

By this time two terraces, an upper and a lower, had been laid out along the Walks. Taverns and lodging-houses had also sprung up and a large house on Mount Ephraim had become an assembly room—attractions which no doubt did much to keep the court occupied when it arrived in force in 1665 to escape the plague and again the following year.

By now the Tunbridge season was firmly established. It lasted from May to October and was obviously very gay, with a constant round of unfettered amusements in which the tradesmen and nobility mingled freely on the Walks and joined together in the evenings for country dancing.

One measure of the spa's growth and popularity was the appearance in 1684 of the church of King Charles the Martyr opposite the entrance to the Walks. Dedicated to the ill-fated Charles I, whose wife had been the spa's first royal patron, the church had begun as a chapel-of-ease, with Samuel Pepys among the subscribers, and it was soon reputed to have the best sermons outside London.

In 1687 a fire destroyed the booths and stalls on the Walks, but what appeared at the time to be a disaster led to the building of permanent shops and a handsome colonnade along the Upper Walk, much of which survives to this day. Since the butchers, fishmongers and market stall-holders showed no wish to move out of their own special preserve on the Lower Walk, the Colonnade soon became the seasonal domain of haberdashers, booksellers and jewellers, who arrived from London bringing with them high quality goods of the kind every spa visitor appeared to need. Added to these amenities was a band engaged to play every day and the introduction of new amusements, including gambling.

In the years before she came to the throne, the Princess Anne visited the spa at Tunbridge several times and made some generous donations before disenchantment set in. Following a fall by her young son, the Duke of Gloucester, in 1698, the future queen gave a hundred pounds for the Upper Walk to be paved and returned the following year to see how the work was getting on, only to find that nothing had been done. Understandably indignant, the Princess vowed never to return.

As a direct result of this unfortunate incident, the Walks were paved in 1700 at the inhabitants' own expense and in 1706 two taverns appeared. Although they failed to win back the royal personage, no doubt these additional amenities helped to attract other notable visitors, including the Duke of Marlborough's three handsome daughters who were the belles of the season in 1712.

With the entertainment of high society clearly taking precedence over the spa's therapeutic attractions, a new personality called Bell Causey emerged at Tunbridge. Bell installed herself in 1725 as unofficial organiser of the amusements and was often to be seen with apron outstretched at the top of the steps leading to the Upper Walk, demanding and obtaining subscriptions for any

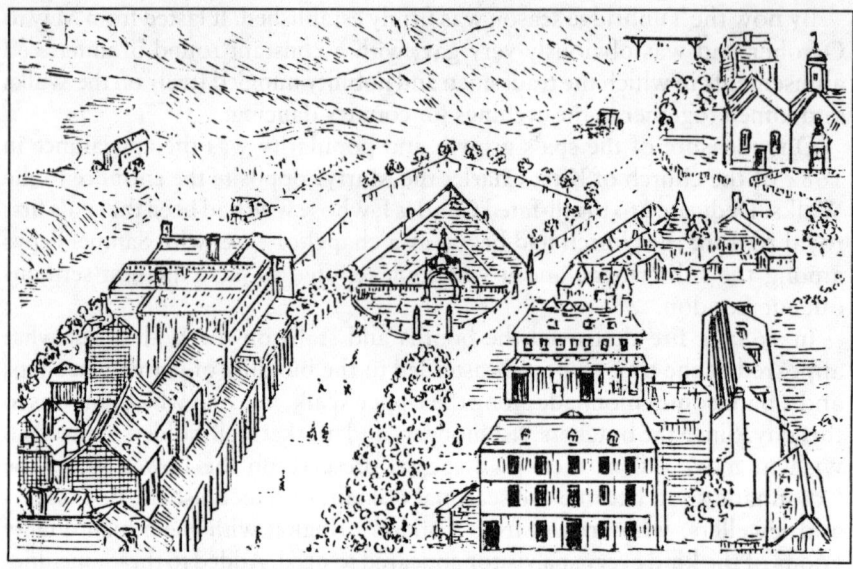

Tunbridge Wells: *The Chalybeate Spring and Walks, from a drawing of 1718.*

The paved triangular shaped enclosure was built by Lord Bergavenney around a spring discovered on the edge of his estate in about 1606 by his departing guest, Dudley, third Baron North, as he travelled home from Eridge through wooded country. Noting that the brownish spring water resembled the waters of Spa in Germany, the somewhat dissolute young nobleman collected a sample for confirmation in London, tried it on himself with beneficial results and began recommending it to his fashionable friends at court. Royal patronage dated back to 1630 when Charles I's queen, Henrietta Maria, came to recuperate after the birth of the future Charles II.

Although laid out in 1638, the Upper and Lower Walks, with their double row of trees, remained unpaved until 1700—two years after the Princess Anne's young son, the Duke of Gloucester, drew attention to their condition by slipping on them. Later on, the Walks became known as the Parade, the Royal Parade, Ye Olde Pantyles and, finally, as the Pantiles. The handsome colonnade on the left was lined with shops which had replaced booths and stalls destroyed by fire in 1687. Beau Nash was not to arrive from Bath until 1735, but there were already two inns (c. 1706) and various forms of entertainment. By 1718 a reputation for licentiousness acquired during the visits of Charles II and his court from 1663 onwards had died down and the 'waters of scandal' had become more respectable.

cause that took her fancy. So forceful a character was she that even Beau Nash deferred his arrival in Tunbridge until after her death in 1734.

Beau Nash finally appeared on the scene and became Tunbridge's first master-of-ceremonies in the late spring of 1735. Since the season and the waters of Tunbridge were different from those of Bath, there was no real rivalry between the two spas and Nash was simply accepted as 'king' of both.

After his arrival, the same rules of conduct were adopted as at Bath and the visitor's day followed much the same pattern, beginning with a water-drinking session between 7 and 9 a.m., followed by breakfast taken in lodgings or, weather permitting, on the shady terraces of the Upper Walk. The next engagement was attendance at chapel—a devotional exercise, though not always one devoid of other considerations such as fashion—after which the visitor was free to relax by engaging in one or more of the traditional leisure activities such as walking, riding, shopping, reading and, of course, the inevitable gossiping. Dinner was served in the visitors' lodgings at 3 p.m., after which the company would sally forth in full formal dress to parade up and down the Walks before taking their final glass of water.

The last venue of the day at Tunbridge was usually the new Assembly Rooms in the Lower Walk where balls, gambling and tea-drinking sessions were regularly held. An alternative entertainment was a visit to the theatre or, for the more serious minded, the occasional philosophical lecture. (In 1802, the theatre was transferred to the Lower Walk, where it remained in operation until 1842. It was later converted into the Corn Exchange and today only the portico remains unaltered.)

Of all the pastimes, the balls probably remained the most popular. They lasted from 6 to 11 p.m. and always consisted of two hours of minuets followed by supper and country dancing—a somewhat rigid programme but one which was accepted by dancers and chaperones alike until gradual changes in fashion and preferences decreed otherwise.

Change was not always easy to detect but, if the observations of one of the water poets in 1733 are any guide, even by the time of Beau Nash's arrival, the spa had passed its peak:

'Fair maid of Kent, regret no more
Thy dearth of beauty and thy triumphs o'er;
No longer to thy rocks proclaim
Thy faded honours and thy lessened fame.'

Lessened fame it no doubt was, but Tunbridge was still a fashionable spa and remained so until the younger set began following the Prince Regent to Brighton. Only then were the lodging-houses around the Walks finally forsaken by the older members of the nobility and left to await the arrival of a new breed of occupier—the permanent residents.

Inevitably these residents set a different tone and the transformation of Tunbridge from a seasonal spa into a residential town gathered pace and was to continue throughout the Victorian period. The image was now one of a rather elderly resort noted chiefly for its country air and mineral springs. People had probably come to expect less from the chalybeate waters but they still believed in them and it was not long before cold baths became an additional and popular form of treatment for certain ailments. Due partly to the presence of dissolved salts (mainly of iron, calcium, sodium and magnesium), the temperature of the water varied only between 50°F and 52°F, summer and winter alike.

A cold bath built in 1780 at the end of the Walks became a familiar feature of the old spa area and no doubt contributed to the decision in 1793 to replace the original pantiles by more modern paving. By this time, the Walks had become known as The Parade or The Royal Parade—names which were to be changed yet again to Ye Olde Pantyles and, finally, to The Pantiles.

In 1802-4, the bath-house of 1780 was replaced by the building which, in slightly altered form, still stands today. With a basin let into the front wall to receive the spring water, it was a conspicuous structure and must have contributed considerably to the revival which followed two Tunbridge visits, in 1825 and 1834, by the Duchess of Kent and the young Princess Victoria.

But neither the Bath House nor the Royal Wells Inn with its enormous coat of arms, built in 1834, could sustain the revival for long and, in 1840, when Dr A. B. Granville visited the spa, he reported that Tunbridge was at a low ebb and neglected. Not even a drink at the basin, it seems, could please the travelling physician and, after noting that the water produced neither a warming nor stimulating effect, he added cheerlessly that a single eructation of air incurs after ingestion!

Clearly it was not possible to do anything about some of these shortcomings but a few years later, in 1849, a subscription was raised so that alterations and 'improvements' could be made to the Bath House. They included the erection of the present portico and railing, together with an extended dippers' lodge and, after much difficulty due to water gushing out from below, the advancement of the basin itself by two feet to the present position. In 1865 the stone basin was replaced by two granite ones, the first of

Tunbridge Wells: *The Bath House, from a drawing of 1827.*

Seen in the centre background at this north-eastern end of the Parade, or Pantiles, in what was known as Bath Square, the bath-house, which is still recognisable today, was equipped with cold, warm and a variety of special baths. It was built in 1802–4, replacing an earlier structure of 1780 which only had a cold bath. People who came to drink the waters had to descend a few wet steps at the left-hand corner of the building to a basin set in the outside wall. This small marble basin, which had replaced an earlier stone one, had three round holes at the bottom out of which the iron-impregnated water appeared at a temperature of 50°–52°F, at the rate of a gallon a minute.

Adjacent to the spring and bath-house, on the colonnade side of the Upper Walk, were small shops such as haberdashers, jewellers and booksellers, while the Lower Walk remained the preserve of butchers, fishmongers and the like.

A visit in 1834 by the Princess Victoria and her mother, the Duchess of Kent, helped to revive Tunbridge Wells as a respectable spa but seven years later it was reported by Dr A. B. Granville as out of vogue and at a low ebb. No doubt this gloomy report helped to persuade the town to embark on the 'improvement' scheme of 1847. Under this scheme, railings were erected around the spring and bath-house, a new portico was built and the dipper's lodge was enlarged.

Today most of the bath-house building is occupied by Boots the Chemist (entrance at side), with only a large old bath surviving in the basement.

Tunbridge Wells: *The Parade from the Chalybeate Spring, from a drawing of 1880.*

This was the view from the north-eastern end of the Parade, or Pantiles. The railings in the foreground, which today still enclose the spring and bath-house building, were those erected in 1847 as part of the 'improvement' package. Two polished granite basins, installed in 1865 by the lord of the manor in place of the earlier marble one, received the water, the first direct from the source, the second as the overflow. A charge was made for water from the first but from the second it was free.

By 1880 the proportion of drinkers to the number of town residents and other visitors had greatly diminished but those who did come to take the waters were well catered for. Bath-chair men waited for hire outside nearby King Charles' church and women dippers used to brush out the basins every morning, hand out the water in glasses and finally provide the drinkers with sage leaves to rub their teeth! Although the main attractions were now the shops and leisurely atmosphere, implemented by the German band which continued to play throughout the summer, the old chalybeate spring still dominated the paved precinct.

Today most of the original square baked tiles have been replaced by ordinary paving but the spring water remains available, with a dipper in attendance from Easter to October.

which received the water direct and the second the overflow. A charge was made for water from the first but none for water from the second.

In 1877 the Victorians built a proper pump-room at the south end of The Pantiles on the site now known as Union Square. The building had a large room with a fountain and also reading and retiring rooms, but it came too late to be a success and soon fell into a state of decay. It was finally demolished in 1964 as part of a redevelopment scheme.

The redeveloped site, now sometimes called the new Pantiles, consists of a shopping precinct—there are car parks behind and underneath but these are out of sight—and, although a heavier version, it fits in quite well with the original Pantiles and is likewise blissfully free from traffic.

The Bath House still stands at the other end of the ever delightful tree-lined 'Walks', though most of it is now owned by Boots the Chemist, whose newly created entrance stands out of sight around the corner. With its Victorian railings and adjoining dippers' lodge, the frontage probably looks much as it did at the end of the last century and, once again, in the summer, a dipper is in attendance, drawing and serving glassfuls of the celebrated water from the ancient well. The charge, as in the old days, is only a few pence.

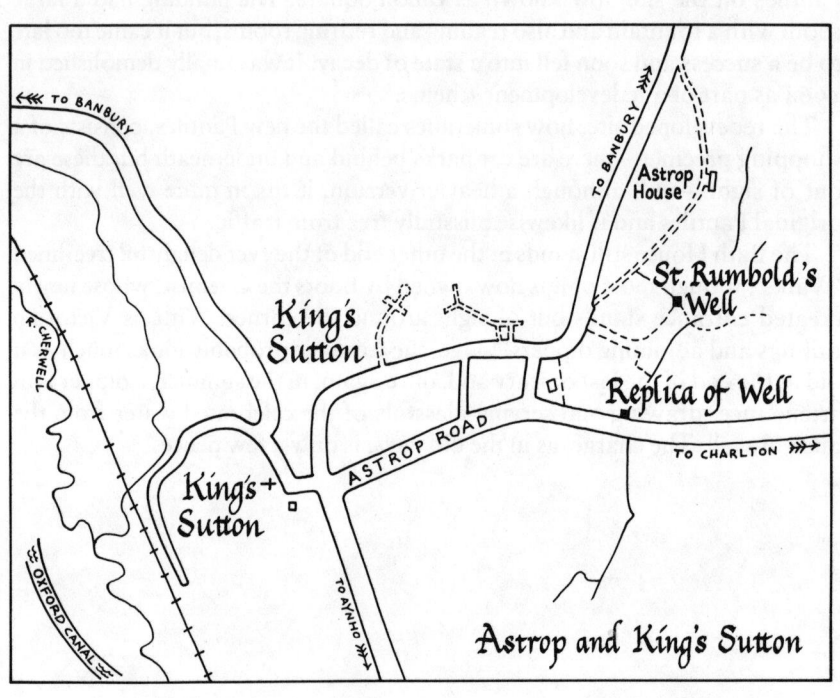

Astrop and King's Sutton

FAR LESS fortunate than Tunbridge Wells, both in terms of survival and of posthumous recognition, was the contemporary spa of Astrop and King's Sutton near Banbury. Today, very few people have heard of the chalybeate spring which now lies submerged in undergrowth within the farm grounds of an 18th century mansion called Astrop House but which, three centuries ago, succeeded in turning the adjacent village of King's Sutton into a prosperous, notable and fashionable spa. But then, apart from the size of the church and the age and quality of some of the surrounding houses, there are very few clues to the vanished glory that once placed this remote Northamptonshire village among Tunbridge's rivals.

The village of King's Sutton has a long history dating back to the time when King Alfred reputedly hunted in the area so it is possible that the Astrop spring was known long before it attracted the attention of a certain Dr Richard Lower. However, it was Dr Lower's 'discovery' in April 1664 that marks the beginning of the spa story.

Dr Lower was a local physician and the story is that whilst he and his partner Dr Willis were on their way to visit a patient, he noticed a pool of the characteristic rust-coloured spring water and decided to investigate. His companion, it seems, was, as usual, asleep on his horse but later joined in the investigation and in a number of experiments to determine the 'efficacy' of the water, which the two doctors subsequently declared to be medicinal.

The spring was named after St Rumbold and became known as Rumbold's Well. There are several St Rumbolds but the one associated with King's Sutton was the 7th century baby saint who is said to have been born near this spot. Despite his premature demise after only three days, legend has it that St Rumbold managed to declare himself a Christian and to ask that his body be allowed to remain at King's Sutton for a year, followed by two years at Brackley before being laid to rest at Buckingham.

Since it was not easy to portray such a saint as the guardian of a well, the statue of St Rumbold which eventually appeared in a stone niche above the spring wore the more familiar guise of a medieval knight in shining armour and, as such, provided the kind of protection considered suitable for a place of pilgrimage. People from considerable distances came seeking cures and spa buildings began to appear.

Astrop and King's Sutton

Among the early visitors was Celia Fiennes. Probably on her way from Oxford to Broughton Castle where some of her family lived, this intrepid traveller and untiring sampler of spa waters arrived in 1694 and wrote her account. The spa at Astrop, she declared in her Journal, was 'much frequented by the Gentry' and there was 'a fine Gravell Walke that is between 2 high cutt hedges where is a room for the Musick and Roome for the Company besides a Private Walkes'.

On the subject of the well itself, however, Celia was less enthusiastic, complaining that 'it runnes not very quick, they are not curious in keeping it, neither is there any bason for the spring to run off, only a dirty well full of moss's which is all changed yellow by the water'. In other words, the water sounds to have been almost as uninviting in 1694 as it looks today, though Celia did add that there were 'lodgings about for the Company'.

History does not relate whether or not the shortcomings noted by Celia Fiennes were rectified but in 1749 the water was piped to a new well constructed close by and Dr Radcliffe of Oxford was summoned to perform the opening ceremony. Complete with a basin, the well now stood at the bottom of a few steps in a small neat stone-flagged enclosure presided over by the statue of St Rumbold—an arrangement which must have met with general approval because high society soon came flocking. More lodging-houses were built in King's Sutton and balls were held every Monday, with the usual accompanying amusements such as cards to entertain the visitors during the rest of the week.

All went well until July 1785 when the village suffered a great fire in which forty houses were destroyed, leaving a trail of damage estimated at £30,000. It was a disaster from which recovery was virtually impossible and, by 1800, Tunbridge Wells had nothing more to fear from the spa near Banbury.

During the 19th century, an attempt was made to stage a revival at King's Sutton by exploiting the so-called Bog Well discovered in a marshy meadow near the railway station, but the project was doomed to failure. Far from bringing visitors into the area, it was soon realised that the new railway tended to take people away from it and any surviving local interest in spa water remained centred on the original spring at Astrop.

The final episode in the disappearance of this early Northamptonshire spa began in 1857. In that year the owner of Astrop Park Farm decided he was tired of seeing people crossing his land and made up his mind to close the footpath leading to the old well. To pacify the objecting villagers, the farmer laid a pipe to carry the water to a new site at the side of a public lane now

Astrop: *Statue and niche of St Rumbold's Well, from an old drawing.*
This stone statue presided over the ancient chalybeate spring of St Rumbold in the grounds of Astrop House, near King's Sutton, Northants—a spring discovered by a local physician in 1664. Celia Fiennes visited the well in 1694, when she found it dirty and without a basin, though she spoke well of the amenities.

Astrop Spa rose to fame in the 18th century and in 1749 the well was reconstructed on a nearby site and opened by Dr Radcliffe of Oxford. The now well stood in a small open stone-flagged enclosure at the bottom of a few steps, with a basin and the stone statue above. But after a disastrous fire in the adjacent village of King's Sutton, where most of the elegant and fashionable visitors lodged, the spa rapidly declined and in 1857 the owner of the land closed the footpath leading to it. He did, however, pipe the water to a new site in what is now Astrop Road and here he erected a replica well.

Today, that too is in derelict condition and the replica statue, like the original, is missing, though the niche remains. In recent years, there have been demands for a rescue operation.

known as Astrop Road, where he built a replica of St Rumbold's Well complete with stone statue and niche which he promised to maintain. But today, both this promise and the farmer's undertaking to keep the water flowing have long since been forgotten and the tap is dry. According to the villagers, the water began to disappear in about 1968 due, they think, to a fracture in the pipe from the original well. As for the statue, that too has disappeared from the scene, though the stone niche in which it once stood still stands, bramble-covered and forlorn, in a ditch beside the road.

During the past decade, there have been a number of demands for a rescue operation in the hope that one day St Rumbold will be restored to his rightful place and that the chalybeate water from the ancient spring will flow once again. So far, however, there are few signs of this becoming a reality and meanwhile much of the one-time hamlet of Astrop has been covered by a housing estate, leaving only the winding road by which the carriages once conveyed their noble occupants to drink at the well of St Rumbold as a reminder of this forgotten spa.

Epsom

ANOTHER EARLY contender for the position of rival to Tunbridge was Epsom. Although Daniel Defoe wrote in 1724 that 'as the nobility and gaiety go to Tunbridge, the merchants and rich citizens go to Epsom', a century earlier Epsom had its full share of noble patronage.

The famous well, from which the celebrated salt (magnesium sulphate) takes its name, stood on an open common some fifteen miles from London—a long enough journey in an age when travelling could be very hazardous, but nothing compared with the journey to Tunbridge. Predictably, the spa attracted the notice of the royal courts.

The date of discovery of the Epsom well is usually given at 1618, though one report (Brayley) suggests that the virtues of the water had been recognised earlier and that a physician who visited the well shortly after the accession of James I in 1603 found it impregnated with a bitter purging salt.

The other story is that a farmer called Henry Wicker recognised its peculiarities during the very dry summer of 1618 when his cows refused to drink from a water-filled hole on the common. Wicker's surprise led to local interest in the water and to the discovery, first that it was good for external scores such as ulcers, and then that it was an aperient and 'blood purifier'.

At all events, by 1621, strangers were on the scene testing its powers and the fortunate owner of the estate on which it stood lost no time in building an enclosing wall, together with a shed-like structure for the protection and convenience of visitors.

In 1645 the diarist John Aubrey arrived and gave himself the credit for making the waters of both Epsom and Tunbridge known to 'the citizens of London and to the king's people', though, in actual fact, the fame of both spas had already spread beyond London to several European countries.

By 1668 it was very common for doctors to prescribe a visit to Epsom and the country village was now poised for rapid expansion. The opportunity came two years later when Charles II presented neighbouring Nonsuch Palace to Barbara Villiers, who wasted no time in knocking it down and selling off its fine stone and other materials for the erection of sumptuous dwellings and taverns in and around Epsom. Some of the stone may have been used on the well when it was roofed over in 1675 but, whether it was or not, it made no difference to the unfavourable verdict recorded by Celia Fiennes

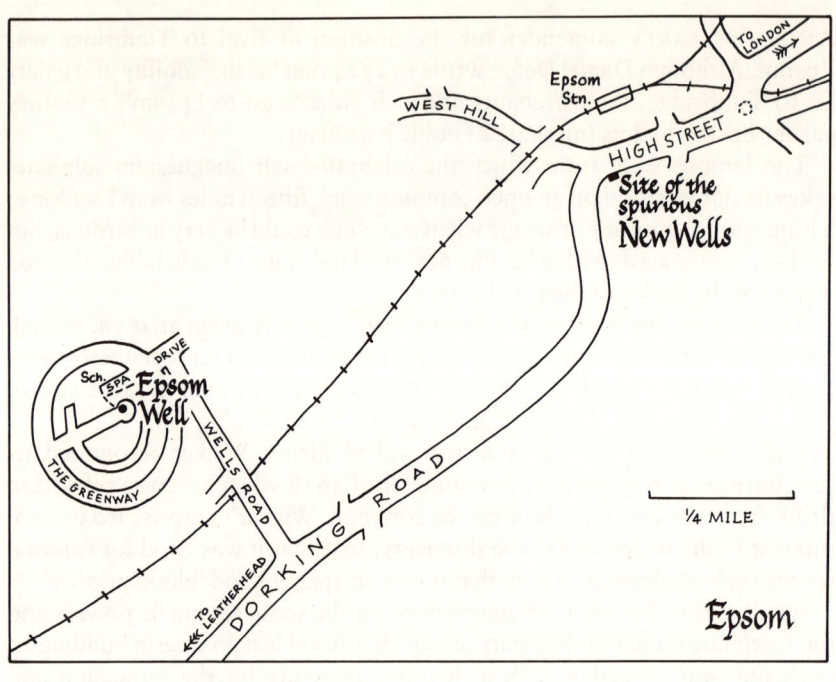

who wrote in her Journal that at the bottom of the steps it was dark and had no 'bason' and that, because the spring was slow and often ran dry, the local people filled it with water from 'common wells'.

Despite these criticisms, the Epsom spa prospered and, in about 1684, Charles II arrived with his court for the season. Nell Gwynne and other well-known figures such as Samuel Pepys were in attendance and there were the usual hordes of elegant men in white powdered wigs, elaborately dressed ladies in sedan chairs and all the attendant servants and post-boys—clear evidence that Epsom was now a centre of fashion.

The presence of such exalted company was obviously beyond dispute but at least one historian, quoting Thomas Shadwell's 'coarse' Restoration comedy as evidence, was of the opinion that the spa at Epsom had already been invaded by a lower class of society. Be this as it may, the prospects still looked good to the lord of the manor, John Parkhurst, who decided in 1690 to introduce 'prodigious and astonishing changes'.

Parkhurst's improvements included the laying out of a promenade lined with elms and lime trees all the way from the town to the well and the provision of a ballroom seventy feet long—improvements which, together with the effects of frequent visits by Queen Anne's consort, Prince George of Denmark, might well have ensured an extension of Epsom's career as a fashionable watering-place if a new situation had not arisen.

The chief culprit in the new situation was a local apothecary called Levingstone who had already made a fortune out of wealthy visitors but whose aspirations were not yet spent. In 1706 this ambitious man bought some land in the town and built the New Inn, described at the time as one of the finest and largest in England and approved of even by Celia Fiennes. (Standing at the west end of the High Street and later known as Waterloo House, a small section of the building still exists as part of new building society premises.) This alone might not have done much harm but, on the first floor, Levingstone created an assembly room equipped with a basin connected to the pump of a newly sunk well and then added a ballroom, gambling rooms, opulent shops and other allurements. Even facilities for horse-racing and cock-fighting were arranged, all of which drew people away from the Old Well.

The apothecary's final misdeed came in 1715 when he obtained a lease of the Old Well and, after a few years, had it locked up on the grounds that it did not pay—an act which forestalled any hope of the Well's recovery even when the word went round that the water of the New Wells was spurious, possessing few, if any, healing qualities.

Epsom

Epsom: *The Wells, from an old print.*

Standing on an open common about fifteen miles from London, Epsom's famous spring was reputedly discovered during the dry summer of 1618 after a farmer noticed his cows' refusal to drink at a water-filled hole. By 1621 the land-owner had built an enclosing wall and by 1668 the doctors were prescribing the water. In 1675 the well acquired a roof and steps leading down to it. Although one observer (Celia Fiennes) complained that it was dark and had no 'bason', its fame spread and the nearby village continued to expand into a fashionable spa. In 1684 Charles II came with his court for a whole season and in 1690 a tree-lined promenade was laid out by the lord of the manor.

Later royal visitors included Queen Anne's consort, Prince George of Denmark. Yet within twenty years decline had set in, due mainly to the opening of a spurious rival establishment in the town by a local apothecary. In 1715 the apothecary succeeded in closing down the Old Well and adjoining inn and it was not until after his death in 1727 that several abortive attempts were made to restore them to popularity.

Eventually a large private house called The Wells appeared on the site and what remained of the old buildings were incorporated into the back of a greenhouse. Only the well itself (probably inside the round structure seen in the distance) was preserved.

Epsom: *The Old Well, from a drawing of 1901.*

By 1901 the well from which Epsom Salts (magnesium sulphate) takes its name stood in the garden of a house called The Wells. At that time the water had the same qualities as it had when the well was first discovered high up on the common about half a mile from the village early in the 17th century.

The well brought fame to Epsom and by 1684 it was a fashionable centre full of sumptuous houses and large taverns to which Charles II brought his court for a season. Nell Gwynne and Samuel Pepys were among the patrons and all seemed set fair for a long and prosperous future. In 1690 major improvements, including the laying out of a tree-lined promenade between town and well, were carried out by the lord of the manor.

A later royal visitor was Queen Anne's consort, Prince George of Denmark. Yet by 1706 the seeds of decline had been sown. In that year an apothecary set up a lavish rival establishment in the town called the New Wells, based on a reputedly spurious water, and he had the Old Well locked up. After the apothecary died in 1727, several attempts were made to revive the Old Well but all failed and by the end of the century Epsom had ceased to be a spa. The house called The Wells was built on the site of the first inn to accommodate visitors and some of the original well structures were incorporated into its greenhouse.

Today the well alone survives, protected by a concrete lid and a double row of iron railings in the middle of a large housing estate. In 1950 the water was declared unfit for human consumption.

The Old Well remained locked up until the apothecary died in 1727. After that, several unsuccessful attempts were made to repair and re-open it and, even as late as 1754, a pathetic advertisement appeared declaring that 'the purging waters of this place are in excellent order'. By this time, however, visitors to Epsom were already more interested in horse-racing than in water-drinking and even the New Wells appears to have collapsed into oblivion. If ever there had been a chance of reviving this early spa, it was finally extinguished by the growing popularity of the sea-bathing 'cure'—a 'cure' which Epsom, like every other inland resort, was unable to provide.

The final abortive attempt came in 1760–70 when a Dr Dale Ingram advertised a preparation of magnesia obtained from the Old Well and opened the rooms there for public breakfasts. The response was poor, and, by the end of the 18th century, it was common knowledge that Epsom had lost its vogue as a health resort. Little now remained apart from the well itself and a few relics of Epsom's first real inn (an inn capable of accommodating visitors) which had stood close by. Eventually a large house called The Wells appeared on the site and the last of these original structures were built into the back wall of a greenhouse near a tennis lawn, leaving no further traces.

By this time, however, the well was pleasantly shielded by some fruit trees and the qualities of its waters were said to be unimpaired. In fact it was not until 1950 that the waters of Epsom were finally declared unfit for human consumption. Today the water is clearly undrinkable on many counts, but it is still there—several feet down in the old well, which now stands on a litter-strewn plot of grass at the centre of a large housing estate.

Since it is unlikely that anything can now be done to provide the remains of this ancient spring with a more worthy setting, perhaps it is best to remember it in terms of the verse found on a churchyard tombstone. A more impressive testimony to man's faith in its waters would certainly be hard to find:

'Here lies I and my three daughters,
Died from drinking the Cheltenham waters,
If we had stuck to Epsom salts,
We shouldn't be lying in these cold vaults.'

Buxton

WHATEVER POWERS were attributed to the waters of Tunbridge, Astrop and Epsom, they possessed no comforting warmth like those of Bath, Buxton and Bristol. Buxton's tepid waters were no match for those of Bath, either in temperature or quantity, but their taste was not unpleasant and the two towns had quite a lot in common. In fact, by the time John Carr of York was commissioned in 1781 to build the Crescent, the Square and the Great Stables, there were hopes that this delightful Derbyshire spa a thousand feet above sea level would actually rival it.

With a daily flow of about 200,000 gallons, the clear blue saline waters of Buxton come out of the ground at 82°F (28°C) and, as at Bath, the spa dates back to the time of the Roman occupation.

The Roman invaders called the place Aquae Arnemetiae—'the spa of the goddess of the grove'—and built two baths, neither of which survive. The saddest loss occurred in 1709 when a certain Sir Thomas Delves constructed a memorial arch above the spring which he believed had cured him and so unwittingly destroyed the unexcavated Roman bath beneath. The spring stood near the spot where the disused building of the Natural Mineral Water Baths stands today, a few yards from the south-west corner of the Crescent.

During Saxon times the springs of Buxton appear to have suffered from general neglect and, even by the end of the 12th century, the whole area amounted to little more than a hamlet. At this time, however, a chapel was erected and dedicated to St Ann, patron saint of cripples and of healing wells. During the centuries that followed, the chapel walls were adorned with the crutches of those who had been cured, though not even this, it seems, impressed Henry VIII who, in 1538, ordered that the chapel be destroyed and the adjacent medieval baths be sealed. Fortunately for Buxton, St Ann's remained a place of pilgrimage and, within a few years, the baths were re-opened.

Courtiers were sometimes sent by Elizabeth I to recuperate at 'the baynes of Buckstones' but the most noble of the early patrons was undoubtedly Mary Queen of Scots, who came several times between 1573 and 1584 at her own request in the hope that the waters would cure her rheumatism. During these visits, the ill-fated queen had to remain in the custody of the Earl of Shrewsbury at Buxton Hall (a house subsequently destroyed and rebuilt in 1670—

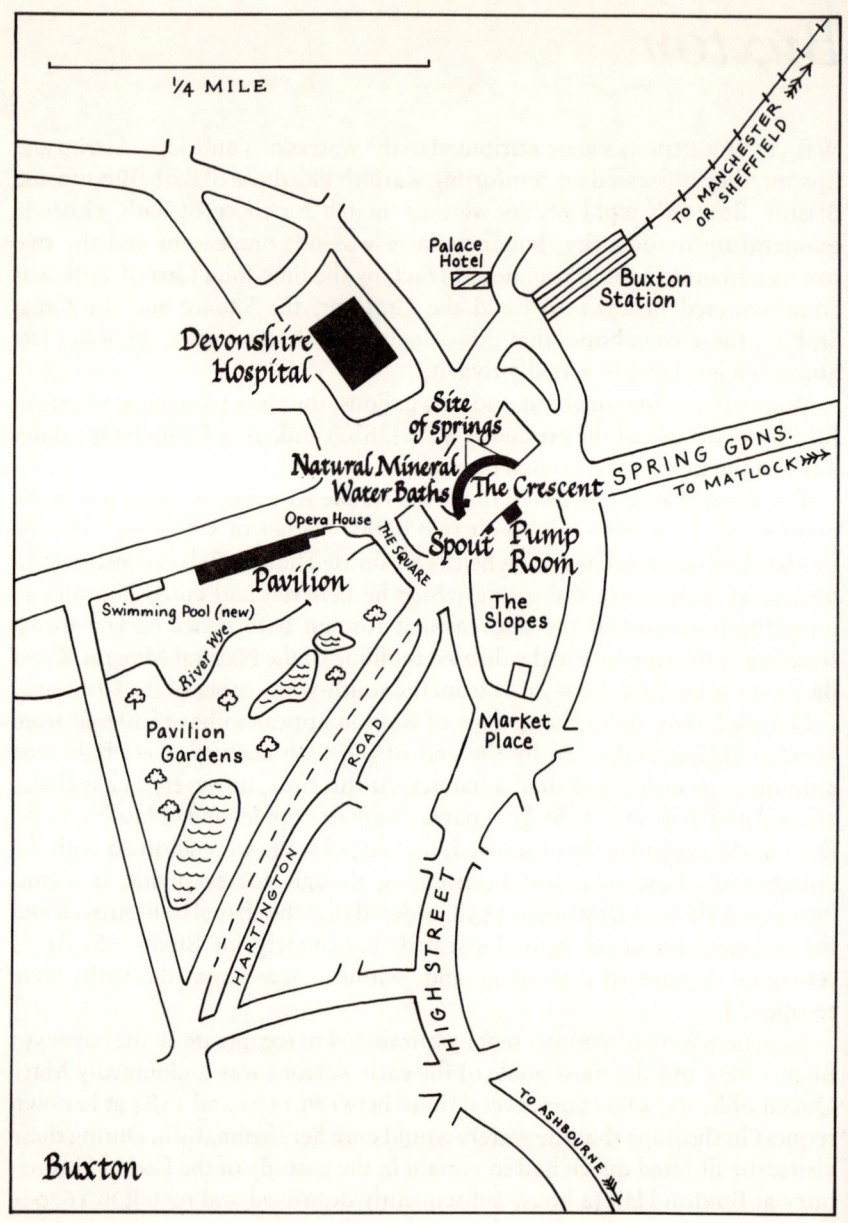

now the Old Hall Hotel) in whose grounds St Ann's Well stood. To Mary is attributed the celebrated couplet—found scratched on a pane of glass (now preserved in the Poole Caverns' Museum) which, translated from the Latin, reads:

'Buxton, whose fame they milk-warm waters tell,
Whom I, perhaps, no more shall see, farewell!'

During Elizabeth's reign, the Buxton waters also became very popular with poor people, many of whom were brought in from other places with the help of money raised by charging wealthier patrons according to their rank: from five pounds for an archbishop down to one shilling for a yeoman. This beneficence was not, however, always appreciated by the local population who soon began to object to large numbers of 'undesirable' strangers flocking to the pump placed against an outside wall of the Hall, and several attempts were made to have the arrangement discontinued.

Yet, for all its problems, St Ann's Well continued to be esteemed and a century later, in 1681, the translator and verse-writer Charles Cotton included some poetic descriptions of it in his *Wonders of the Peake*. There were, he wrote, 'Twin-sister springs only six feet apart, one of them hot, the other cold, like Love and cold Disdain.'

Buxton did, in fact, possess one chalybeate spring but the remainder, nine in all, were weakly saline due to small quantities of calcium and other salts. Most were discovered in the area now covered by the Crescent, the source being a subterranean reservoir about a mile below ground.

In spite of the abundance and popularity of its waters, Buxton suffered throughout the 17th and 18th centuries from a problem common to many spas—a shortage of accommodation. Spa visitors had to depend almost entirely on what the Earl of Shrewsbury could provide either at Buxton Hall or in nearby lodgings and, judging by Celia Fiennes' description of her experiences at Buxton Hall in 1697, the quality also left something to be desired: '. . . the beer they allowe at the meales is so bad that very little can be dranke . . . the Lodgings so bad, 2 beds in a room some 3 beds and some 4 in one roome . . . and sometymes they are so crowded that three must lye in a bed . . . We staid two nights by reason one of our company was ill but it was sore against our wills.'

This discouraging account of Buxton's shortcomings was borne out in 1705 by Sir Thomas Delves. In fact this distinguished patient's assessment of the place as 'a poor little Stony Town' may well have been a factor in his unfortunate decision to erect the thanksgiving fountain whose foundations destroyed the Roman bath. Erected in 1709 and described as 'an elegant structure', the Delves' Fountain was built almost directly over St Ann's Well in the form of an arched alcove.

In about 1709, the Delves' Foundation itself had to make way for the foundations of the famous Crescent which, for geographical reasons, could not be built elsewhere. However, a small pump-room subsequently designed by John Carr of York and erected at the foot of St Ann's Cliff (now known as The Slopes) opposite the south-western end of the newly built Crescent managed to survive until the early 1850s, and the decorative stone vase which surmounted it survives to this day at the apex of the southern gable of the Devonshire Hospital.

Equipped with a white marble basin and supplied with water from St Ann's Well by means of a channel, this original pump-room was looked after by a rota of four attendants. No charge was made for the water but gratuities were expected. The best known of the ministering matrons was a certain Martha Norton who was born in 1728 and died in 1820 at the ripe old age of 92. It seems that Martha held the record of fifty years continuous service in water-serving, first as the Delves' Memorial Fountain and then at the pump of its successor.

The story of the early spa at Buxton could well have been different if there had not been such a serious transport problem. Situated high up in the Derbyshire hills, Buxton was not only 'a poor little Stony Town' divided into two parts—then as now, the old village stood clustered around the market place at the top of the hill while the spa area occupied part of the valley below—but it was a very difficult place to reach. In fact, until the roads began to improve and journeys by stage coach began to be better organised, it was one of the most isolated spas in the country.

The person who decided that the time had come to provide the 'mountain spa' with more fitting facilities was the lord and land-owner, the fifth Duke of Devonshire. Like his grandfather Lord Burlington, the fifth duke was an admirer of the Palladian style of architecture and was particularly impressed with the work of the Woods at Bath. It was for this reason that the country's leading Palladian architect, John Carr of York, was engaged in 1780, the brief being that he should design buildings capable of placing Buxton on an equal footing with Bath and rapidly expanding Cheltenham. Clearly it was with this in mind that John Carr produced his famous Crescent.

This 'jewel of Buxton' had to be supported on piles because of the springs

Buxton: *The Drinking-Place, from a sketch published in 1800.*
Designed by John Carr of York, this simple building was erected in about 1790 as a replacement for the Delves fountain of 1709, which had to be demolished to make way for the foundations of the famous Crescent. With its classical façade and surmounting decorative stone vase, this original pump-room or 'drinking-place', as it was called, stood opposite the southwestern end of the newly built Crescent, several yards from the site of the Delves fountain and actual St Ann's Well. After being pumped along a channel, the tepid saline water was discharged into a white marble basin, where it was dispensed by a rota of four attendants. Payment for the dippers' services was on a voluntary basis.

By 1854, the building was regarded as too small and it was replaced by a double pump-room which, in its turn, gave way to the commodious late Victorian building which still survives. All that remains today of this original pump-room is the stone vase which adorns the southern gable of the Devonshire Royal Hospital.

42   Buxton

Buxton: *The Crescent and associated spa buildings, from a late 19th century engraving.*

With its forty rusticated pillars forming an arcade above street level, the Crescent was completed in 1786 for the fifth Duke of Devonshire to a design by John Carr of York. The Devonshire Hospital (left background), originally the Great Stables, was handed over by the sixth duke in 1858 for use as a hospital and the giant unsupported dome was added in 1879. The Palace Hotel (right background), in its dominating position above the railway station (right) was built in 1868 by John Currey, designer of the Pump Room.

and marshy land below. With its giant Tuscan pilasters rising from a rusticated base to form an arcade several feet above street level, it incorporated the Grand Assembly Room, some seventy feet long and thirty feet high, where elegant society could gather for balls and other social events. Lavishly decorated in the style of Robert Adam, this impressive room stood on the first floor of the E wing, leaving the remainder of the Crescent free for use as hotels, with shops at the front. Indeed, one of its three hotels still survives today.

Also included in the total cost of £120,000, was the Great Stables originally built to house one hundred and ten horses around an exercise court where visitors could ride in bad weather—a huge interior space destined to be covered over in about 1880 by the largest unsupported dome in Europe. (The building was converted into a hospital in 1858 and now, as the Devonshire Royal Hospital, is another of Buxton's landmarks).

Other developments, including the Square, the Quadrant and a row of fashionable shops, helped to turn Buxton into a popular and spacious Regency spa, specially noted for its fine mountain scenery and intimate atmosphere. One of the few remaining complaints was the condition of the public baths, which some people found offensive. However, even this problem was eventually solved by some hotels providing their own facilities, though it was 1818 before it was possible for visitors to bathe in the waters of Buxton at temperatures other than the natural 82°F.

In 1851-3 new thermal baths designed by Henry Currey and reputedly inspired by Joseph Paxton's lily-house at Chatsworth were built at the eastern end of the Crescent. Another development was the replacement, in 1854, of the pump-room which John Carr had designed some sixty years earlier with a simple but more commodious double building. Such innovations, however, were nothing compared with what was to come after the railway arrived from Derby in 1863 and from Manchester the following year.

As the trains pulled in to two identical stations built side by side and more and more visitors alighted, no one was left in any doubt about Buxton's destiny as an expanding and prosperous Victorian spa. The new visitors came from the large industrial centres and were members of the so-called middle classes but their enthusiasm was no less great and their needs no less exacting than those of their predecessors. Already they spoke affectionately of Buxton as 'the spa of the blue waters' and, in order to accommodate them, Henry Currey was hurriedly commissioned to build the Palace Hotel on the steep rise near the station—as enormous edifice which was soon to be followed by

Buxton: *St Ann's Well and Pump Room interior, from an early sketch.*

The neo-classical Pump Room, with its sunken oval basin supplied with water from St Ann's Well, was presented to the town by the seventh Duke of Devonshire. Designed by Henry Currey and opened in June 1894, it succeeded the two smaller pump-rooms of 1790 and 1854. Originally the whole of the floor space above the well was furnished with small tables and chairs for the use of drinkers, who used to come to the balustrade to receive their glassfuls of freshly drawn water handed up to them by the dippers. A small charge was made for the service.

Today the blue water continues to flow into the oval basin in the centre of a marble-tiled enclosure and is still available to the public during the summer months. But only a couple of tables and chairs remain as reminders of the past: the rest of the room is now in use as a tourist and information centre.

other large hotels (many with striking cast-iron verandahs) and improved facilities for leisure and entertainment.

Land through which the infant River Wye still flows before it passes into a culvert was donated by the seventh Duke of Devonshire and, in 1871, the 23-acre Pavilion Gardens were laid out by Edward Milner of Sydenham. They were followed by the glass and iron supported Pavilion (said to be reminiscent of Crystal Palace) which was designed by R. R. Duke. In 1876 the Pavilion was extended to include the octagonal concert hall, though the Opera House next door did not appear until 1903.

By the 1890s, even the double pump-room of 1854 was regarded as wholly inadequate and Henry Currey was once again consulted and commissioned. The building which the ageing architect designed as a gift from the Duke of Devonshire to the town was the Pump Room, partly used today as a tourist and information centre. Completed and opened in 1894, this well proportioned neo-classical building was provided with a large sunken oval basin built in marble from which the dippers used to (and still do) hand up freshly drawn mineral water to waiting clients at a modest charge. In the old days, of course, before the well was confined to a small enclosure, most of the floor space was furnished with small tables and chairs.

In order to comply with the Enclosure Act which declared that access to St Ann's Well must always be free, a pump was also placed outside the Pump Room on the west side and remained there until the 1940s, when it was replaced by the one which now stands several yards away, nearly opposite the Natural Mineral Water Baths.

This bewildering succession of pumps is a measure of the many phases through which Buxton passed. It reached the peak of its popularity during the late Victorian and Edwardian era and then, like so many other spas, declined. But even today there is still something of the old aura and, recently, following some important restoration work, even signs of a spirit of regeneration.

In 1970 the Grand Assembly Room, complete with original chandeliers and finely painted ceiling, was renovated by the county council at a cost of £120,000 and is now in use as a reference library. The Pavilion and its beautiful gardens also appear to have been given a new lease of life, though the old tea-room, whose decapitated onion dome now rests on the terrace, had to make way in 1972 for the modern swimming bath opened by Princess Anne. Finally, in 1979, the magnificently restored Edwardian baroque Opera House was re-opened.

As for the water itself, it now provides the swimming pool with all it is ever likely to need and continues to supply the 200-bed Devonshire Royal Hospital, which still specialises in physiotherapy and hydrotherapy for rheumatic patients. The water is also pumped through silver-lined lead pipes to the flourishing Buxton Bottling Company just behind the Crescent. With so much demand, it would be unwise to say that the blue waters of Buxton can yet be written off as a thing of the past.

Bristol

UNLIKE BUXTON, Bristol never had much hope of holding on to its spa identity. The position of its springs beside the River Avon made this impossible and today the 'healing' waters that once flowed out of the cliff face near the entrance to the Avon Gorge (a site on the east bank almost directly beneath the present-day suspension bridge) have completely disappeared. Nor, apart from a small section of the Colonnade, is there any sign of the old spa buildings.

But all this is a far cry from the 18th century when it was quite usual for fashionable visitors who had been to Bath in search of a cure to go on to Bristol's 'hot well' about a mile downstream from the town, where they could sample a warm weakly saline water not very different from that of Buxton.

At a temperature of 76°F, the Bristol water was not quite as warm as that of Buxton but it had been regarded as curative ever since the 16th century. Samuel Pepys recorded a visit to the spring in 1654 and Charles II's queen, Catherine of Braganza, visited it in 1677. Another early visitor was the inevitable Celia Fiennes who for once seems to have unreservedly approved of what she found, describing the water as 'exceeding clear and warm as new milk and much of that sweetness.'

With so much to recommend it, it is not surprising that attempts were made to protect the water from the high tides of the muddy river. A small brick reservoir built early in the 17th century had proved less than successful in avoiding pollution and a high enclosing wall erected in 1691 had merely diverted the spring. Obviously the time had come to build a proper spa building, and this was done in 1696.

Standing on a small rocky ledge that jutted out over the river, the resulting Hotwell House was given a special foundation to enable the pumps to raise the water thirty feet to the pump-room, while dual-purpose valves were fitted to the pipes to allow the waste to flow back into the river and to close off the river water at high tide.

Despite these ingenious devices, there were occasional suspicions that the spring was still polluted, but they were discreetly voiced and by the early 18th century the Hotwell spa had become a fashionable resort. Even Sarah, Duchess of Marlborough, and the Duchess of Kent were on the list of high-ranking visitors. Literary figures, including Addison, Pope, Cowper,

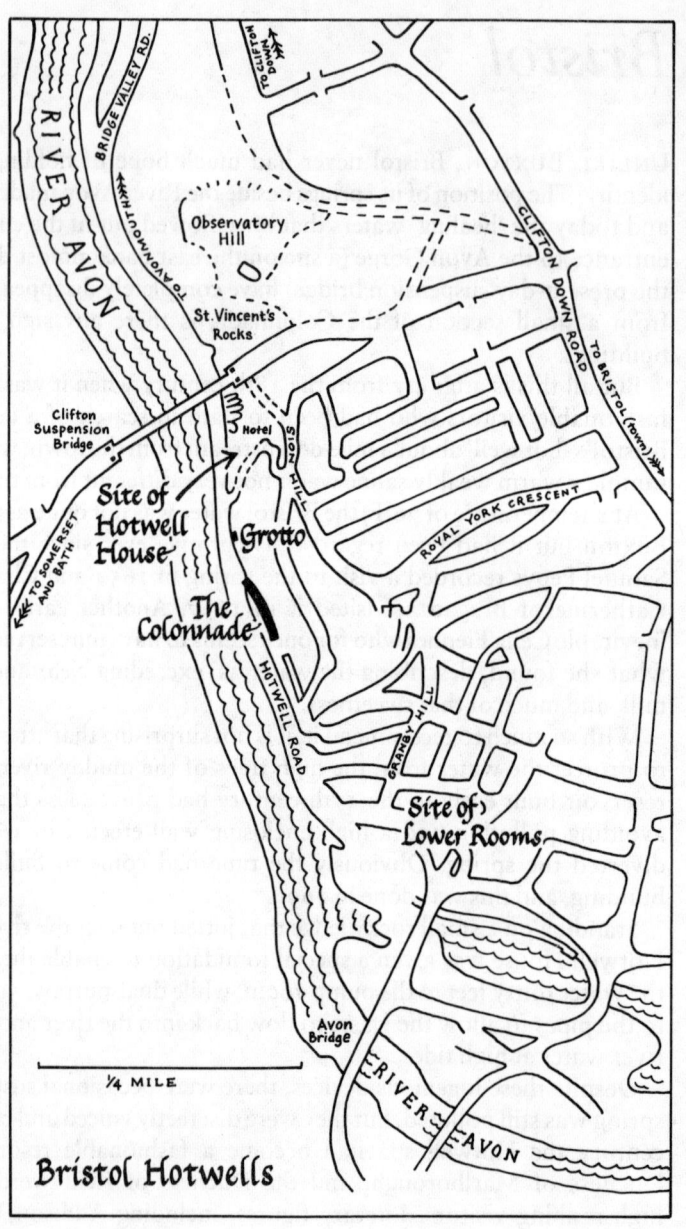

Gay and Sheridan also came and much was made of the reputedly 'safe' nature of the waters as a treatment for kidney complaints, 'hot livers', 'feeble brains', red pimply faces, diabetes and tuberculosis.

Between 1702 and 1793, several other mineral springs were discovered in the surrounding area and three of them acquired pump-rooms. None lasted very long, though one enjoyed a brief period of celebrity following reports in 1754 that its waters had cured John Wesley of suspected tuberculosis.

Meanwhile the Hotwell water was being bottled and shipped not only to other towns but also to distant parts of the world, where it appears to have commanded high prices. This flourishing industry continued for quite a long time despite the belief expressed by Pope and others that, to be effective and palatable, the Bristol water needed to be drunk fresh from the spring.

The Hotwell season began in late April and lasted until the end of September. There was limited accommodation on the upper floors of Hotwell House but most visitors had to stay in lodgings, arriving early each morning by carriage. The regime was much the same as at other contemporary spas: after drinking the prescribed number of glasses, it was customary to 'sit with the company', play cards, listen to the small orchestra or take a walk along the tree-lined promenade beside the river. After dinner, these activities were resumed and continued until five o'clock, when it was time to return to the pump-room for several more glassfuls of the water.

As elsewhere, Bristol had its full quota of scandal, public breakfasts and evening balls to break the monotony and in 1786 the replacement of the old piazza by a two-storeyed colonnade with a row of shops at ground level added new interest. An attractive piece of architecture, part of which still survives as a small group of private residences, the Colonnade provided cover for promenading in wet weather and was seen as a valuable amenity. Yet, in spite of it, decline was only a few years away.

Part of the trouble was that two years earlier, in 1784, the Society of Merchant Venturers had advertised for a new lessee for Hotwell House, with the stipulation that he be willing to build a quay wall, provide further protection from the tide and repair the pump-room. Not surprisingly perhaps, no such person presented himself and the Society had to appoint a salaried caretaker whilst they themselves undertook the repairs—an undertaking which proved so costly that they tried to recoup by putting up the rent. In 1790 the higher rent was accepted by a new tenant called Samuel Powell, who tried to defray it by drastically raising the spa charges—a course of action which quickly drove away the visitors.

Bristol: *Old Hotwell House, from a sketch by Turner.*

Situated about a mile from the centre of the town on the bank of the River Avon, the original or 'old' Hotwell House was built in 1696 over Bristol's famous spring which gushed out of an opening at the foot of the St Vincent rock. It stood on a small rocky ledge which jutted out a few feet over the river—a site previously occupied by an early 17th century reservoir which had failed to protect the mineral spring from high tides and by a high stone enclosure of 1691 which had diverted it. Although gaunt and somewhat austere in appearance, the spa building with its pump-room and fine river views proved a success. The nobility, many of whom came on from neighbouring Bath, looked favourably on the weakly saline semi-tepid water—'hot' was a misnomer—recommended as a 'safe' remedy for diabetes, kidney and other complaints and once drunk by Charles II's queen.

By the early 18th century Hotwells had become a fashionable spa patronised by many leading figures of the day including Sarah, Duchess of Marlborough, and there were the usual entertainments. In 1785 a master-of-ceremonies was appointed and about 1786 the colonnade replaced a small piazza for use in bad weather. By this time, however, change was in the air and from 1790, when a new tenant put up the charges, the spa dramatically declined.

Hotwell House was finally demolished in 1822 to enable a new road (later called Bridge Valley Road) to be built, leaving only a short stretch of colonnade to mark the spot.

Bristol: *The 'New' or 'Second' Hotwell House, from an old print.*
Standing close to the site of its demolished predecessor, the 'new' or 'second' Hotwell House was built in 1822 by the Society of Merchant Venturers, lords of the manor, in an attempt to revive the spa. Designed in the so-called Tuscan style, it was a somewhat complicated structure with a central pump-room and three projections shaped like the sides of a hexagon. There was a suite of mineral baths at the rear but not even these could win back the fashionable clientèle of the previous century. Many of the visitors were now incurable consumptives, which did nothing to restore confidence, and in 1867 the building was pulled down as part of a river-widening navigation-improvement scheme.

The spring was subsequently enclosed and its water piped to a small grotto hollowed out of the rock but in 1913, after river water had been found seeping in and causing pollution, the entrance to the pump was blocked up. Attempts were made in 1913 and again in 1925 to find the unpolluted original spring but without success.

Another factor which appears to have contributed to the sudden decline was the high mortality rate among the few patrons who remained. Since most of these were incurable consumptives, their presence merely added to the spa's depressing reputation and, by 1816, it was reported that the place was almost deserted. There was now no apparent hope of a revival and in 1822 Hotwell House was demolished to make way for a through road—the Bridge Valley Road and Hotwell Road of later years.

Once the building had gone, however, a cry went up to save Hotwell spa from oblivion and, at the instigation of a certain James Bolton, the Society of Merchant Venturers was prevailed upon to build the 'new' or 'second' Hotwell House beside the new road, a few yards further downstream.

The new building was in Tuscan style, with a pump-room in the centre and a suite of baths at the back. Once again, however, the charges were high and, in spite of James Bolton's commercial efforts—they included the sale of articles ranging from Indian soap to boomerangs!—the new spa failed to prosper. One trouble was that invalids found the journey up and down Granby Hill a harrowing experience and, by 1840, Dr Granville reported that 'few people, if any, drink of the semi-tepid sparkling water—fewer still bathe in it'. Finally, in 1867, it was decided to demolish the building as part of a river widening scheme for the benefit and safety of shipping.

With this news, however, the public was once again roused to protest and, following agitations and complaints to the local press about the need to preserve the spa, the spring was enclosed and the water pumped to a small grotto hollowed out of the road at the roadside, where a small pump was set up.

By 1913 the new pump was reported to be supplying as many as '350 persons a day' but, once again, river pollution was found to be a problem and, later that year, the wooden door of the grotto was locked and sealed. It can still be seen today in Hotwell Road standing next to another abandoned construction—the terminal of the hydraulic cliff railway built for the Spa Hotel (now the Avon Gorge Hotel) and its well-known assembly rooms. (The spa's first assembly rooms stood not far from the bottom of Granby Hill in a building now converted into a school.)

In 1913 and again in 1925 attempts were made by Bristolians to find the original unpolluted spring, but both projects failed. The loss of the spa now had to be accepted and, today, apart from the surviving stretch of the Colonnade and a few nearby houses overlooking the busy riverside road to Avonmouth, virtually nothing remains of Bristol's once famous 'hot wells'. Its waters have vanished more completely than those of any other early spa of noble patronage outside London.

2
London's Old Spas

AMONG THE pioneers of the spa age, but in a class of their own, were the old spas of London. Most have now disappeared without trace, though the names of a few linger on as street names or in association with the old music halls, of which they were the forerunners.

Many of these old spas stood in the valley of the Fleet—a river which, three hundred years ago, had already been described by the antiquary John Stow as 'the valley of the wells' and which bore little, if any, resemblance to the brook that now forms part of London's sewerage system.

After its journey from the ponds of Hampstead and Highgate, this open and still unpolluted river flowed on to join the Thames at Blackfriars and it was here, between St Pancras and Holborn—an area where many homeless people had camped out and set up home after the Great Fire of London in 1666—that a whole galaxy of mineral springs was discovered during the 17th and 18th centuries.

Such were the capital's medical and social needs that it was possible at that time for an enterprising entrepreneur to develop a spa around virtually any mineral spring with a plentiful supply of water. Whether or not the spa would succeed was a different matter.

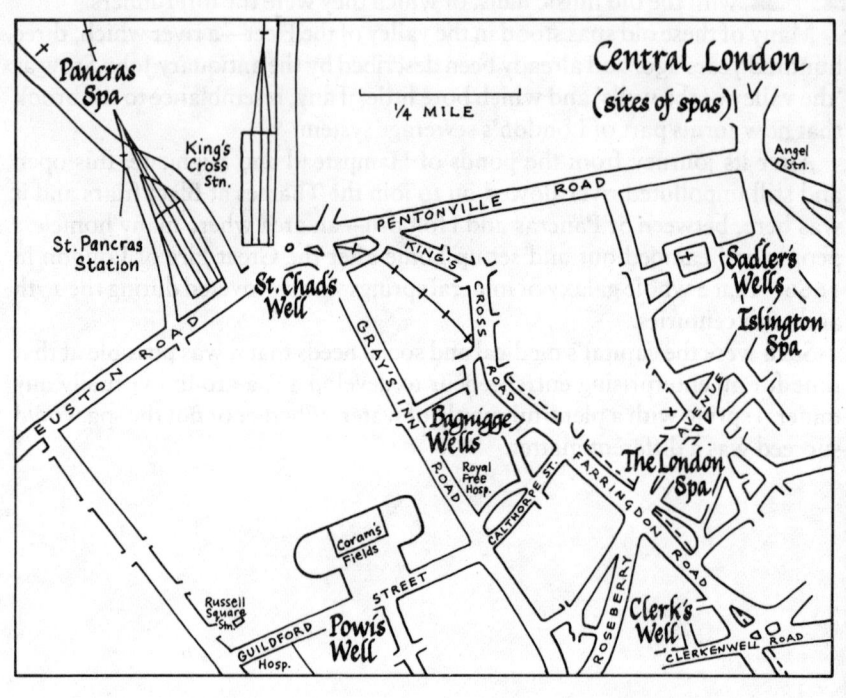

Islington

ISLINGTON SPA was among the first of the London spas to be developed. It grew up around a chalybeate spring discovered in 1683-4 and stood where a block of flats now stands beside the green known as Spa Fields opposite Sadler's Wells Theatre. The site had formerly been that of Gooseberry Fair— a fair noted for its stalls of gooseberry fool and threepenny tea-booths—and was quite extensive, covering a larger area than that of Sadler's Wells discovered shortly afterwards on the other side of the New River.

With development in the air, the discovery of the Islington spring soon led to the announcement (in 1685) in the *London Gazette* that a Mr John Langley, merchant, had bought Islington Wells. Few personal details are known about John Langley, but the site transformation that followed this announcement must have exceeded most expectations. The emerging spa even threatened to capture much of the aristocratic clientèle which normally bestowed its patronage on Tunbridge and it caused considerable consternation in that quarter, especially when, in 1690, the proprietor decided to change the name to New Tunbridge Wells.

By this time, the Islington spa had been laid out with gardens, tree-lined groves and secluded walks with plenty of shady arbours. There was also a coffee-house forty feet long, a dancing-room, a card-room and a raffling shop, and plans were already in hand for the holding of public breakfasts and regular dancing sessions. A French traveller later described the spa as 'a large village, half a league from London, where you drink waters that do you neither Good nor Harm, provided you don't take too much of them'.

However innocuous its offerings, the enthusiasm of those who followed the example of John Evelyn, who visited the well in 1686, and the recommendations of Lady Mary Wortley-Montagu a few years later soon died away and, by 1714, the Islington spa had fallen out of favour. *The Field Spy* reported on the situation:

'The ancient drooping trees unprun'd appear'd;
No ladies seen; no fiddles heard.'

However, this sad state of affairs was quickly changed in May and June of 1733 when George II's daughters, the Princesses Amelia and Caroline, began taking a regular course of the waters. Their arrival was usually greeted by a royal salute of twenty-one guns—a clarion call which quickly resulted in vastly increased takings for the proprietor. On one day alone, it was estimated that sixteen hundred people were present in the gardens and the proceeds amounted to thirty pounds. After than, the trees of Islington Spa no longer dropped and ladies were once again in evidence. In fact, according to a song of the day, there were now:

'Scrapes, curtsies, nods, winks, smiles and frowns,
Lords, milkmaids, duchesses and clowns,
In their all-various dishabille.'

Fashion, however, was fickle and the spa again lost its popularity before returning to favour for twenty years between 1750 and 1770.

When the water-drinkers came back, some of them actually stayed at the Wells which, according to one young lady's letter home to her family in 1753, was 'a very pretty Romantick place'. The writer added, however, that the water 'makes one vastly cold and Hungary'. Other drinkers also expressed occasional reservations, some complaining that, unless mixed with ordinary water, the water from the well made them giddy and sleepy. Nevertheless, the Islington water continued to be recommended for 'the gouty, the nervous, the weak-kneed and the stiff-jointed'.

In 1770, Islington Spa had a new proprietor called John Holland, who concentrated his efforts on popularising it as a 'genteel' tea-garden—the 'gentility' consisting, according to a farce called *The Spleen*, of publicans and tradespeople. But nothing, it seemed, could save John Holland from bankcruptcy and, seven years later, yet another proprietor called John Howard took over.

John Howard decided to introduce further innovations, including a bowling green and a series of 'astronomical lectures in Lent'. He also engaged a band, whose morning playing was followed by afternoon tea-drinking to the accompaniment of French horns. No doubt, to some people, the amusements became the chief attraction but health-seekers still came to drink the Islington waters, including Sir John Hawkins, author of *The History of Music*. Unfortunately, in May 1789, Sir John returned from his visit with a pain in his head and died the next morning of a fever of the brain.

Such reports cannot have helped the struggling spa and, by 1810, the proprietor seems to have realised that, despite its still beautiful ornamental gardens, it had lost its appeal. At all events, he decided to pull down most of the coffee-house and to reduce the size of the gardens to allow new streets to

London: *Islington Spa from an engraving of 1733.*
Advertised at this time as New Tunbridge Wells because its chalybeate spring (discovered about 1680) was similar to the springs of the Kent resort, Islington was one of London's earliest spas. The steps in the foreground lead down to the famous well. The original entrance to the gardens, with its 'pedestals and vases grouped with taste under some extremely picturesque trees' stood opposite the New River Head on a site now partly covered over by Lloyds Row and Rosebery Avenue.

By 1776 the spa had fallen on bad times but people still visited the gardens. The water continued to flow as late as 1860, though by this time the well had been enclosed in a private grotto and the spa gardens had disappeared beneath two rows of houses.

be formed. To do so, he had to take away the original garden entrance facing the New River Head, which he replaced by one in Lloyd's Row next to his own house, adjacent to the well.

In 1826, a later proprietor named Hardy opened the gardens of Islington Spa but enclosed the well in a private grotto, until finally, in 1840, the gardens themselves disappeared beneath two rows of houses called Spa Cottages. For a time, the well was preserved by a surgeon named Molloy, who took over and lived at the proprietor's house in Lloyd's Row. By 1894, however, all that remained was part of Hardy's grotto contained in a small cellar beneath a room of the house. The water had ceased to flow.

Today Rosebery Avenue (opened 1892) covers the site of the original entrance to Islington Spa and, apart from some small nearby gardens and an inscription on the wire fence of the Hugh Myddelton Infants School at the corner of Lloyds Row and St John Street, nothing is left to remind people of its one-time existence. The inscription reads: This was the site of New Tunbridge Wells (or Islington Spa) Pleasure Grounds and Medicinal Well which flourished here from about 1685 to 1840.

Sadler's Wells

THE CHALYBEATE spring belonging to Sadler's Wells on the opposite side of the New River originally belonged to St John's Priory, Clerkenwell. It was a medieval 'holy' well but, when Henry VIII dissolved the monasteries in 1539, it was lost or forgotten and was not re-discovered until 1683.

Meanwhile the New River had been constructed and the land on the north side of the reservoir into which the river flowed as an open stream now belonged to an inspector of highways called Thomas Sadler. It was here, in Sadler's garden, that a group of workmen accidentally unearthed the medieval well. It was arched over and curiously carved.

After submitting a sample of the water for analysis, the owner of the land found his hopeful expectations confirmed: despite the fact that it was neither offensive nor unpleasant to taste and that it made excellent beer, the water was declared 'ferruginous chalybeate'.

As Sadler saw it, there was no point in waiting and he immediately had a marble basin installed, while attractive gardens with poplars, willows and flowers were laid out along the sloping river bank. In addition, arrangements were made for some of the water to be bottled for sale and a reputation for excellent ale was also built up. Nor was that all: within a short time, Sadler's Wells had become famous for its entertainments held first in the open air and then in a single-storey wooden 'musick-house' attached to Sadler's own dwelling.

Understandably, all this added to the growing alarm of Tunbridge and Epsom and in 1684 they issued a tract protesting about 'this horrid plot'. 'Where at Clerkenwell', asked the aggrieved protestors, 'was the air, the diversions and the conveniences?'

But the older established spas need not have worried. Within three or four years the novelty of Sadler's Wells had worn off and, with it, much of its popularity. In fact in 1697 it was found necessary to launch a vigorous advertising campaign reminding people of the advantages of 'Sadler's excellent steel waters' which were claimed to be 'as full of vigour, strength and virtue as ever' and to be still 'very effectual for curing all hectic hypochondriacal heat, for beginning consumptions and for melancholy distempers'.

By this time, however, even allurements and assurances such as these fell on deaf ears and the early 18th century saw a virtual end to water-drinking at

London: *Sadler's Wells from a drawing of 1792.*
After an ancient chalybeate well was discovered by some workmen in his garden in 1683 Thomas Sadler promptly constructed a marble basin to receive the water and built a wooden theatre as an added attraction. The picture shows the replacement 'musick-house' built by Thomas Rosoman in 1765.

By this time water-drinking had virtually ceased but the new Sadler's Wells, still surrounded by fields and standing on the north side of the reservoir into which the New River flowed as an open stream, remained a successful resort almost to the end of the century.

Part of the building survives in the rebuilt (1931) theatre of today. The original medieval well is still there, under a trap-door at the back of the stalls.

Sadler's Wells, leaving only the gardens and Sadler's own house, including the adjacent 'musick-house', later known as Miles' Musick House, still in use.

It was, of course, the continuing popularity of the 'musick-house' which enabled the name of Sadler's Wells to live on. In 1765 Thomas Rosoman, the new proprietor, pulled down the old house in order to build a proper theatre, but he kept the well and called the theatre after it. According to reports sixty years later, in 1825, the well still stood, covered by a brick arch, in the centre of the coach yard, while the springs lay submerged beneath the orchestra and stage. When the theatre was rebuilt in 1931 to become the present-day opera house, the original medieval well was still there—as indeed it still is today. It lies under a trap door in a passage at the back of the stalls and is marked by a curious depression in the floor.

Clerk's Well, London Spa and Powis Well

ALTHOUGH DEVOID of any mineral content, Clerk's Well was another medieval well whose name lives on, in this case as the name of a whole district. Situated further south than Sadler's Wells, on a site now covered by Ray Street in the angle between Farringdon Road and Clerkenwell Road, it, too, belonged originally to St John's Priory and managed to survive for many centuries. In 1800 it was even provided with a new pump by the parishioners but finally it succumbed to the pressures of street development and ended up in the cellar of Nos 14–16 Farringdon Road.

Fresh water springs obviously provided less opportunity for spa development than did the mineral springs but there were a few people, inspired no doubt by the entrepreneurial activities going on around them, who were prepared to make the attempt. One such person was the proprietress of The Fountain, an inn which stood at the corner of what is now Exmouth Market, just off Rosebery Avenue. In 1685 this inn faced on to Spa Fields and in that year a spring of 'excellent town water' was discovered in its garden. The discovery was evidently considered too good to ignore and the innkeeper decided to try her luck by changing the name to the London Spaw, later adapted to the London Spa, alias Finsbury Spa.

The London Spa was provided with appropriate amusements, including May Day celebrations, but it remained better known for the strength of its ale than for the excellence of its waters and in 1754, it finally, and no doubt wisely, reverted to its original role. The last traces of the London Spa disappeared in 1835 when a new public house was built on the same site.

The waters of several of London's old wells were regarded as good for the eyes but even some of the better known ones such as Crowder's Well by Cripplegate, whose water was said to taste like new milk, never developed into what might properly be called a spa.

Perhaps the one that came nearest to attaining the distinction was the Powis Well, recommended both as an eye well and as one good for 'several distempers'. It stood on a site known as Lamb's Conduit Fields by the Foundling Hospital which, in terms of modern geography, means that it stood just south of Guildford Street. The Powis Well was provided with a

London: *The London Spa, Finsbury, from a May Day illustration of 1720.*
Standing near the angle of present-day Rosoman Street and Exmouth Market, the 'London Spaw' was the name given by the proprietor to the Fountain tavern after the discovery of a spring on the premises in 1685. Despite the declared change of status, the London Spa remained better known for the strength of its ale than for the excellence of its waters. The picture portrays the May Day celebrations when milk-maids and their swains danced in the gardens to the music of a fiddler.

After 1754 the premises reverted to their original role as a tavern and eventually, in 1835, a new public house was built on the site.

house of entertainment and also some pleasure walks, but it suffered from the memory of one grave misfortune. In the words of the *Weekly Journal* of 17 January, 1721, 'a man going to a little spring at the back of Lord Powis's house in Lamb's Conduit Fields stooped to wash his eyes and fell headlong in and was suffocated'.

Bagnigge Wells and White Conduit House

FORTUNATELY NO such misadventure was associated with Bagnigge Wells, which developed into quite an impressive spa. The rather strange name was that of the owner of a mansion which stood on a site now occupied by Cubitt Street, adjacent to the Royal Free Hospital. In the 18th century, the River Fleet flowed through the grounds of this mansion and there was an entrance from Bagnigge Wells Road, later to become King's Cross Road.

The story began in 1757 when the tenant of the house tried to encourage his plants to grow by watering them from two garden wells, one situated just behind the house, the other about forty yards to the north. Instead of benefiting from these ministrations, the plants promptly wilted. Investigations were initiated and, after a well-known physician had been consulted, the water from the first well was pronounces chalybeate, while that of the second was declared to have purgative properties.

Following these promising pronouncements, events moved quickly: the panelled banqueting hall was made into a long-room and gardens were laid out along the banks of the river. Soon there were formal walks with shady arbours for tea-drinking, a fountain, a fish pond, a grotto, a temple, three rustic bridges over the stream and some unusual statuary consisting of grotesque costumed figures. There was also a bust of Nell Gwynne in support of the tradition that the mansion had once been her country home.

With so many inducements, Bagnigge Wells started out with a fashionable and aristocratic clientèle. Those who wished to take the waters usually came in the mornings, encouraged no doubt by songs and verses such as the one that appeared in the June number, 1759, of the *London Magazine*:

'The headache shall vanish, the heartache shall cease,
And your lives be enjoyed in more pleasure and peace,
Obey then the summons, to Bagnigge repair,
And drink an oblivion to pain and to care.'

Whether or not the hoped-for oblivion was achieved, the aristocracy eventually grew tired of Bagnigge Wells. A familiar objection was its invasion by 'less refined' elements of society, meaning tradespeople or the so-called

London: *Bagnigge Wells from a pencil drawing of about 1774.*
Situated just west of King's Cross Road (formerly called Bagnigge Wells Road), the spa took its name from Bagnigge House, once the property of the Bagnigge family. It was opened about 1759 after the tenant's discovery of two springs, one saline and one chalybeate.

The domed room with the vane above it was the well-house while, typically, the fishpond in the garden shows a fountain in the form of a Cupid bestriding a swan. The grounds, with the River Fleet running through them, lay behind the Long Room (originally the banqueting hall).

Although very successful in its heyday, Bagnigge Wells gradually lost its fashionable clientèle and in 1813 the proprietor was adjudged bankrupt. However, the curtailed grounds remained open, under new ownership, until the arrival of the railways in 1841.

'cits' who had already invaded Islington Spa and who often turned up in hundreds on Sunday afternoons to drink tea in the Long Room or in the gardens.

However, by 1813, even the 'cits' had begun to tire of Bagnigge Wells and Thomas Salter, the lessee, was adjudged bankrupt. Practically all the fittings, including the chandeliers and two hundred tables for drinking went under the auctioneer's hammer and the tea-gardens, shorn of all their best shrubs and trees, were reduced in size, leaving behind only the ground east of the increasingly ditch-like and, on warm evenings, malodorous River Fleet.

The following year the curtailed premises were taken over by a Mr W. Stock, who tried in vain to revive them. Other lessees followed and Bagnigge Wells limped on until 1841, when the railway arrived. By 1843, the old well had been filled with rubbish, mosaics and oyster shells and in 1844 the final break-up occurred. Not long after this, an ordinary public house appeared on part of the site, at the corner of Pakenham Street and King's Cross Road, and what was left of the gardens was built over. All that remained to remind passers-by that a spa had once flourished here was the name given to the street opposite Mecklenburg Square—Wells Street.

A little further north, in the Pentonville Road, stood White Conduit House, so called because of a white stone conduit near the entrance. This was only a small spa but it was renowned for its feasts of hot rolls and butter and it was patronised by Oliver Goldsmith.

London: *St Chad's Well, from a pencil drawing of about 1830.*

Believed to be of great antiquity, the mineral spring stood at the north end of Gray's Inn Road (east side). According to tradition, the water resembled that which had cured St Chad (Anglo-Saxon Cedd or Ceadda) of some awful disease.

The site was developed as a spa about 1762 and, although the picture of the pump-room, house and garden reflects its declining fortunes, it never lost its respectability. In 1832 a new and larger pump-room with forecourt adjoining Gray's Inn Road was built and this, patronised mainly by local tradespeople, was still in existence in 1860. The well finally disappeared during building operations for the Metropolitan Railway.

St Chad's and Pancras Spa

A SPA WHICH had no time for gimmicks and which deliberately resisted the trend towards dissipation was St Chad's. Based on one of the most ancient wells in the area, St Chad's stood near Battle Bridge at the north end of present-day Gray's Inn Road, its name derived from the saint, originally Cedd or Ceadda, who had reputedly been cured of some awful disease by drinking water from a well of similar kind. (The water of St Chad's Well contained sodium and magnesium sulphates—Glauber's and Epsom Salts—and a small quantity of iron salts in solution.)

About the middle of the 18th century, spacious gardens reaching some way down Gray's Inn Lane were laid out around the wall and in 1762, after the usual laudatory notices had begun to appear in the newspapers, a good local reputation was built up. The waters were described as 'actively purgative, mildly tonic and powerfully diuretic' and one pint without any added salt was recommended for most persons. A special feature of the spa was the practice of heating the water in a large cauldron and then drawing it off by a cock into glasses. The pump-room normally opened at 5 a.m.

In 1832 the original pump-room at St Chad's was replaced by a larger one, but by this time the spa was already declining and, when the new Metropolitan Railway started operations in 1860, the building was demolished. It was a familiar story, but at least St Chad's, unlike some of its contemporaries, was able to claim that it retained its respectability to the end!

In 1760, about the time that St Chad's was turning itself into a spa, there were open fields with uninterrupted views leading to a spa some sixty years older which also prided itself on its reputation for appealing to the health-seeker rather than the pleasure lover. It stood on a site now occupied by railway sidings near old St Pancras church.

The Pancras spa was first opened in May 1697 and, as the handbill for that year shows, the emphasis from the start was on its therapeutic value. The waters were claimed to be a powerful antidote against 'the rising of the vapours and against stone and gravel' and were also recommended as 'a general body purifier and blood sweetener'. The only concession made to entertainment was dancing held on Tuesdays and Thursdays during the season.

Such a high moral tone was not, however, always easy to maintain and by

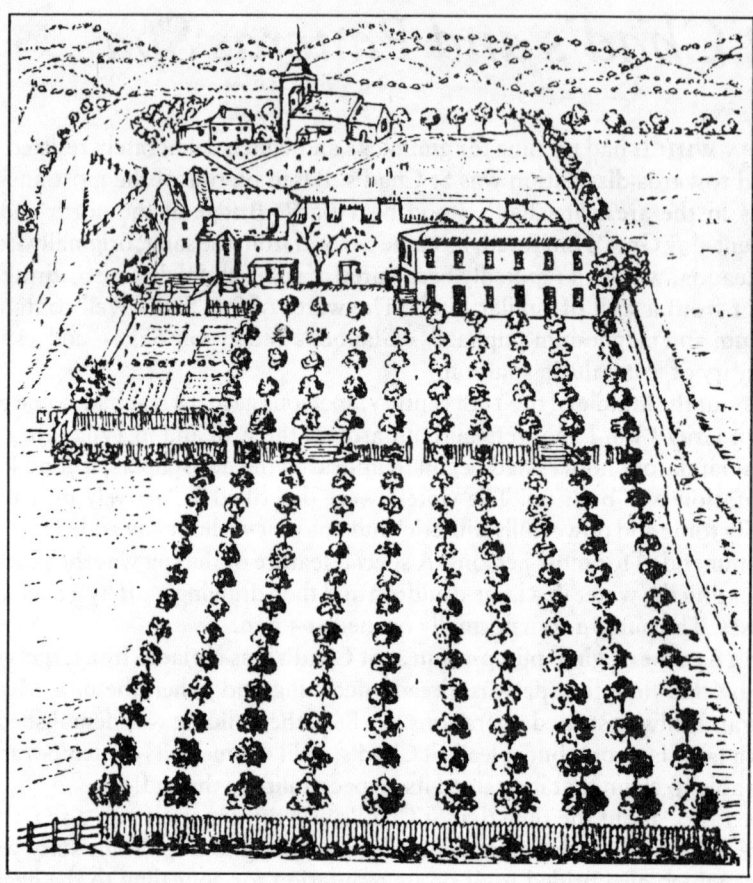

London: *Saint Pancras Wells, from a handbill of about 1730.*

Beyond the 'new' plantation stood the Long Room, adjoined by two small pump-houses. The castellated building was the House of Entertainment, joined on its west side by the Ladies' Hall. Further north, beyond the 'new' and 'old' churchyards, St Pancras church can be seen, with the Adam and Eve tavern close by.

The outer footpath on the right of the picture purports to lead to the City of London via Gray's Inn, the inner one to Southampton Row, while the coach road on the far left indicates the route to Hampstead and Highgate situated on the tree-lined brow of the distant hills. Railway sidings now cover the site.

1722 it was reported that the owner of the Pancras spa had to take steps to exclude undesirable characters who were 'encouraging scandalous company'. In 1729–30 the premises came up for sale, yet, despite this additional complication, the spa managed to recover its reputation. In fact Lysons later reported that the Pancras water continued to be esteemed until some years before 1795.

Inevitably, however, decline set in and, after being enclosed in the garden of a private house near the church, it was reported that the Pancras spa suffered a period of neglect before finally it 'passed out of mind'. Not even its honest reputation, it seemed, could save it from the big changes now taking place.

Such, in fact, were the changes that there was very little that could save any of the old spas of London. Most had begun with hope and perhaps a little glory and a few had achieved an honourable degree of fame, but the story had been rather like that of a Greek tragedy, with the end in sight almost from the beginning. Given inner London's unique situation, the early invasion of the middle classes and the aristocracy's flight back to their more exclusive haunts of Bath, Tunbridge and even Epsom was probably inevitable as no doubt was the gradual transition of the old spas into pleasure gardens, tea-rooms or music halls.

Another key figure in the changing scene was the early 18th century developer, anxious to make his fortune by transforming open vistas into streets and houses and prepared to make good offers to any spa proprietor willing to hand over some of his land. They were offers which few proprietors, already worried by declining takings, could afford to refuse, and the result was predictable: even the surviving gardens deteriorated and the old spa buildings began to undergo drastic alterations.

Finally, as if to aid and abet the whole inexorable process, the middle-class clientèle looked with disfavour on these changes and, just as the aristocracy had done before them, they, too, began looking further afield. Only short distances away, in the more rarified atmosphere of country districts surrounding the capital, new springs were being discovered and new spas opened up. There was no longer any need to confine the quest for health and pleasure to the 'valley of the wells'.

3
A Ring of Spas

THE IDEA of relaxing from their labours for a day and maybe improving their health at the same time by drinking natural mineral water in pleasant surroundings away from the stuffiness of the developing city was something that appealed very much to the middle classes. The roads and means of travel were beginning to improve and they saw no reason why they should not avail themselves of the opportunities on offer. After all, fashionable society had already been doing just that at spas such as Streatham, Richmond, Hampstead and Barnet.

As the demand grew, almost every 18th century land-owner within striking distance of London who found himself in possession of a mineral spring decided that opportunity was calling, and hastened to respond. The result was that, within a short space of time, the capital was ringed with small spas, some quite accessible, others less so.

In setting up a spa, the accepted yardstick, as in inner London, was Tunbridge. Make it as much like Tunbridge as possible, was the prescription, and people would come! Consequently, the new outlying spas had much in common, though in terms of success, there was enormous variation. Like those which had gone before, they depended for success on a host of factors, not least the expertise of the proprietor, the amount of capital available for development, and that ever essential ingredient—luck. A few enjoyed a fleeting fame, but the majority never attained more than a low-key existence, offering little more than the basic facilities—perhaps one or two rooms for refreshments and dancing. Understandably, Londoners looked first to the spas which were already well established, with spacious grounds and plenty of amenities.

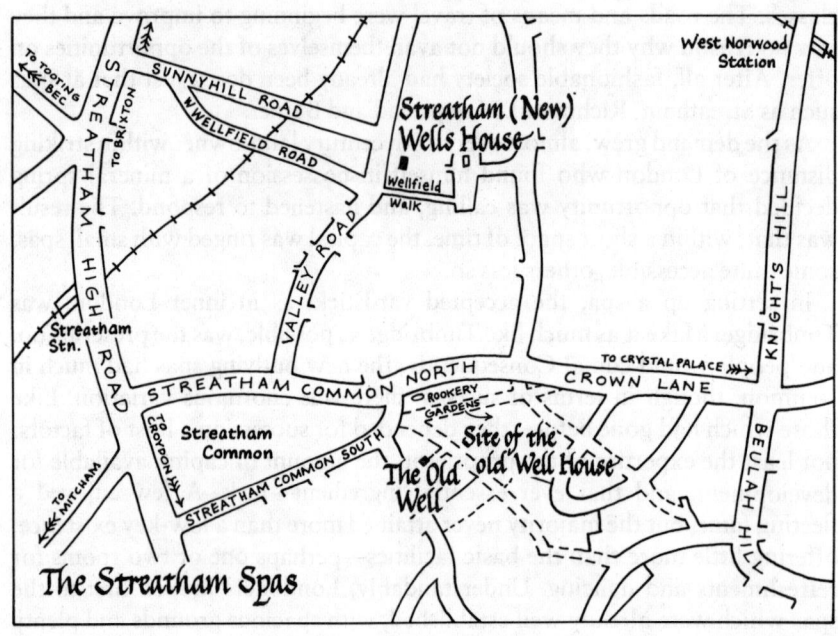

The Streatham Spas

STREATHAM WAS just such a spa and, for those who lived on the south side of the city, it was relatively easy to reach. As long ago as 1660 the first group of three underground springs had been discovered here by ploughmen working in a field. Fourteen years later the field, which stood just below a large house at the top of Streatham Common, had become the centre of a distinguished and beautiful resort, with John Aubrey among its early visitors. A spa 'much resorted to by distempered people' was how the antiquary had described it, declaring that the common dosage was three cupfuls of the water, the equivalent of nine at Epsom.

By the early decades of the 18th century, there was still no reason to doubt the efficacy of the Streatham water, described as saline with some sulphur. In fact the *Post Boy* of 28 May, 1707 went so far as to declare it 'the best for purging in England'—a recommendation which, exaggerated or not, brought the cumbrous family coaches rumbling down the hill each day towards the well, while other conveyances plied their way in the opposite direction, transporting large quantities of the water to the London hospitals!

This was the time when the original spa at Streatham was at the height of its reputation. By now the house had been enlarged or rebuilt to accommodate visitors and was known as the Well House. It provided regular concerts and assemblies and was able to offer its visitors plenty of beautiful tree-lined promenades along the high road and across the common.

By the middle of the 18th century, two of Streatham's three original wells were reported to be still in use, both arched over, though by this time subject to some local prejudice due to the sulphureous smell. This temporary loss of popularity, however, was remedied by a new proprietor and, according to a Dr Rutty in 1747, the Streatham waters, in company with those of Acton and Dulwich, were 'most in vogue'.

It was true that the old spa at Streatham had a longer run than many, but by the end of the 18th century it had reached the end of its career. The main source of the water was failing and most of its patrons showed little compunction about forsaking it for new pastures. A hundred years later, the old lead pump which had once raised the water thirty-five feet stood idle, its apparatus in decay, though a quaint little Elizabethan-style well-house which protected it was still there. As for the mansion on the terrace above, that had long since

The Streatham Spas

Streatham: *Streatham Old Mineral Spring as it stands today in Rookery Gardens at the top of Streatham Common.*

About 35 feet deep, this well and two others close by were discovered in 1659–60 after some labourers at the plough had noticed their horses floundering about in a quagmire. It was soon realised that the spring waters had medicinal (cathartic) properties, though it was 1674 before they came into vogue. With its fine promenade, Streatham Spa became very fashionable and remained so for about a hundred years, finally going out of use around 1792.

Until replaced by a Regency-styled house known as the Well House and later on as the Rookery, an old house stood near the top of the present steps and served as the spa building. After the council acquired the estate in 1912, the Rookery was demolished and so too was the quaint little round wellhouse in Elizabethan style which enclosed the actual well, with its old lead pump and adjoining lead bath.

Streatham: *The (New) Wells House at Streatham from an Indian-ink drawing of 1831.*

With its later extensions, this late 18th century white-washed stucco-faced house still stands on the east side of Valley Road. The room shown on the left contained the pump and well of a mineral spring discovered about the end of the 18th century after the original springs on Streatham Common had lost their popularity. The new saline spring was highly regarded by the local population and, up to 1810 at least, the water was supplied daily to several London hospitals.

About 1875 the premises were taken over by a family of dairy farmers who bottled the water and delivered it, along with the milk, right up to 1942, when the building was bomb-damaged.

In 1976 the Wells House was brought by Lambeth council from the United Dairies and there are plans to preserve it. The bust over the doorway is of Aesculapius, the god of healing.

been altered and converted into a Regency-style private residence with a new name—the Rookery. It was in the kitchen gardens of the Rookery that the main well now stood, with the secondary well lower down the hill, out of sight behind a high wall.

The end of the story came in 1912 when the council of the day took over the estate, demolished the old mansion and created the extensive present-day Rookery Gardens. The old well-house was also demolished and replaced by the modern structure which today stands in the rose garden, with the fish pond (probably once a lead bath adjoining the well) close at hand.

One factor in the decline of the original spa at Streatham was the discovery at the end of the 18th century of the 'new' Streatham spring and its development into a small spa. Situated about half a mile away, near the bottom of the hill in Valley Road, the new Wells House, which still survives, was a plain but substantial building with a bust of Aesculapius (god of healing) over the central doorway. The annexe at the side contained the well and pump and here people could come and drink the water (saline with a little iron and 'free' sulphur) or buy it in bottles.

Combined with a tea-garden, the new spa operated on a commercial basis and remained fairly popular until the 1860s. About 1875 the premises were taken over by a family of dairy farmers, who continued to bottle the water and to deliver it with the milk up to 1942, when the building was damaged by a bomb. By 1976 the premises were badly in need of restoration and were bought, as part of a parcel of development land, from the United Dairies by the Lambeth council. Although the building now has a preservation order on it, a decision regarding its future use is still awaited.

Sydenham and Dulwich

UNLIKE STREATHAM, where at least something still remains to remind people of the water-drinking era, the spas at nearby Sydenham and Dulwich have disappeared completely—despite the fact that Sydenham alone possessed as many as twelve wells, the first of which was discovered in 1640. 'A certain cure for every ill to which humanity is heir' was how one authority described the waters of Sydenham Wells (at one time erroneously referred to as Dulwich Wells), so perhaps it is not surprising that in its early days the spa was honoured by a visit from John Evelyn. According to tradition, it was also visited, some hundred years later, by George III, escorted by the Life Guards, who surrounded the cottage where he was drinking.

But in spite of this exalted early reputation, reports suggest that Sydenham Wells later acquired a rather rough clientèle and that, although the water continued to be drunk as late as 1859, the well-house eventually ended up as a place of entertainment. Today it is believed that the most important well lies beneath the font of St Philip's church, adjacent to Wells Park, under which most of the other springs lie.

The spring of the real Dulwich Wells was discovered in 1739 in the grounds of the Green Man tavern lower down the hill to the north. It stood where the Grove Hotel now stands at the corner of Lordship Lane and Dulwich Common. By the time the 'great breakfast room' was opened here in 1748, the new saline spring with the sulphureous taste and smell was already very popular with visitors from London and the waters were being regularly supplied to St Bartholomew's Hospital, as well as being sold in the city streets.

Dulwich Wells probably went into decline about 1780, partly due to a lawsuit involving the lessee and partly due to changing habits among London's water-drinking community. By 1814 it was no longer in use and today nothing of it remains.

Spas south of the river

Similar fates befell other small spas in this south-eastern corner of what is now Greater London, sometimes for the simple reason that there were too many of them. With the draining of the marshes, the number of 'discoveries' had increased rapidly and, since the 'opportunity' to exploit usually proved irresistible to somebody, supply soon outstripped demand.

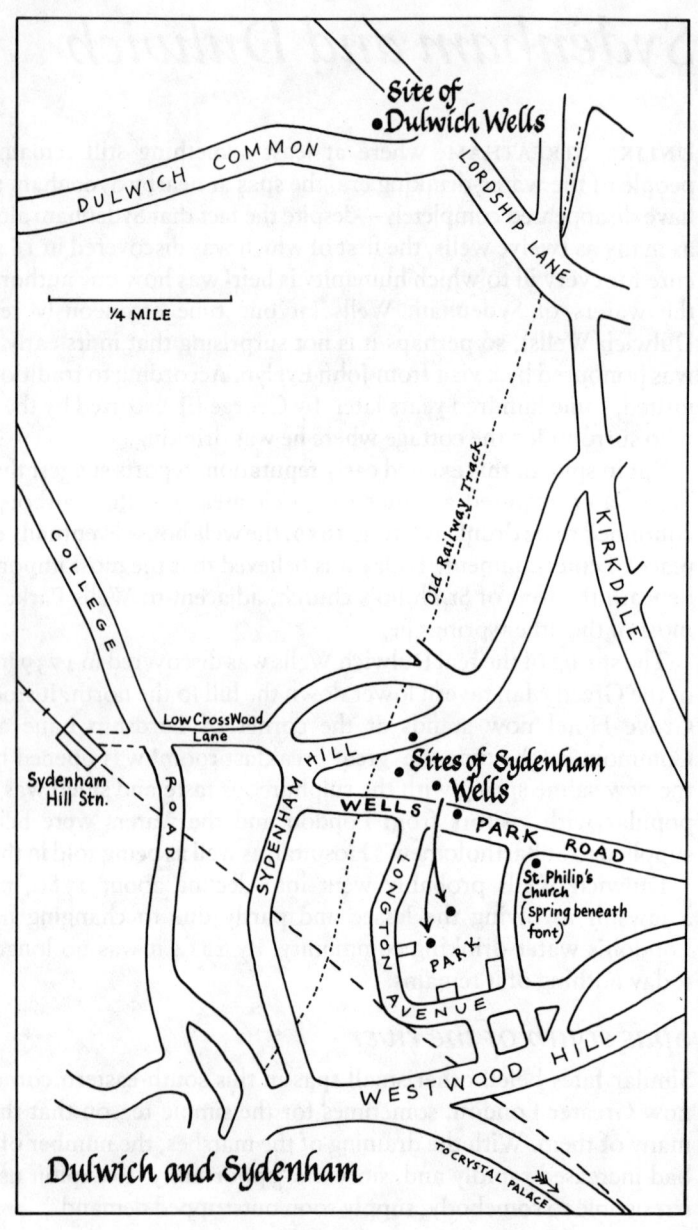

Spas south of the river 85

There was Lambeth Wells, with its two saline springs, first opened in 1697 on a site now occupied by Lambeth Walk. There was also its neighbour, St George's Spa, today covered by a huge traffic junction; and Camberwell, whose chalybeate spring was discovered in 1650. Further out, Shooter's Hill Wells, visited by John Evelyn in 1657, was still functioning in the 1880s and so, too, was a well at Bromley which had been rediscovered in 1756. At Ladywell near Lewisham there was a small spa whose well-house was still in existence in 1842 (its coping stones were subsequently unearthed during repairs to the Mid-Kent railway in 1880 and later used to form part of a fountain in the grounds of Ladywell Public Baths).

A chalybeate spa to enjoy a brief period of fame was that of Bermondsey, established in 1770 and noted for its fine music and firework displays. Alas, together with the fields and market gardens which once surrounded it, Bermondsey Spa was destined to vanish beneath some of south London's heaviest development and today the only reminder of its one-time existence is the name of Spa Road.

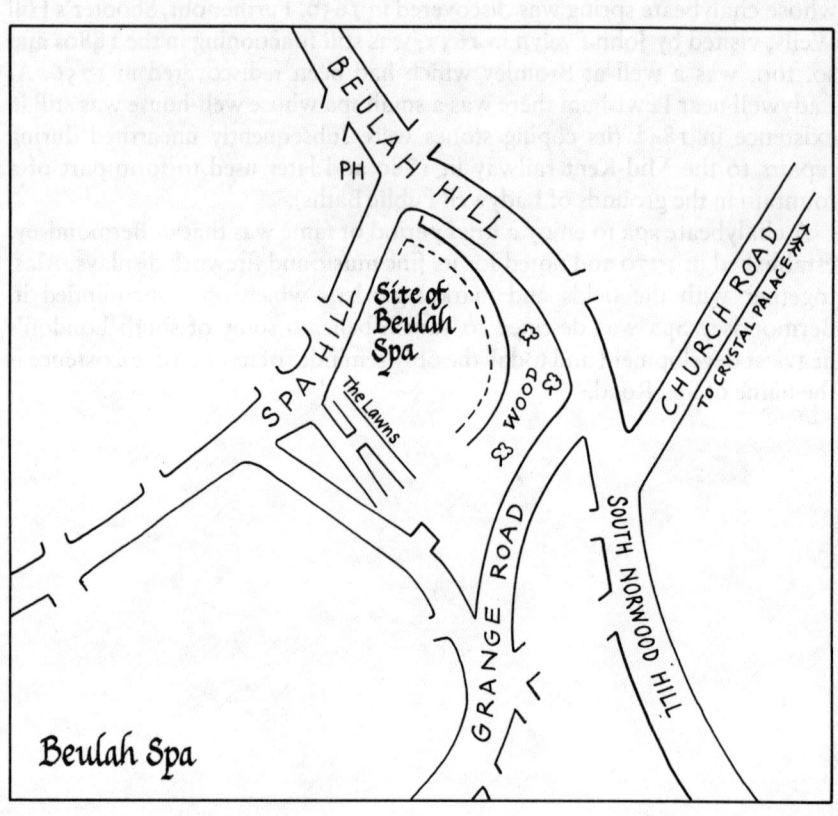

Beulah Spa

ALL THESE sad stories of decline pointed the same way—to the fact that Londoners were growing tired of water-drinking. Yet, curiously enough, a new spa on quite a grand scale was founded in 1831 on Beulah Hill at Upper Norwood. Situated on the slopes of the hill between what is now Grange Road and Spa Hill, it covered thirty acres and was handsomely laid out by no less an architect than Decimus Burton. There were undulating lawns, carriage drives and many winding footpaths with magnificent views over the Surrey hills.

Beulah Spa was built around a pure and strongly saline 12-foot-deep well whose water—the chief active constituent was magnesium sulphate (Epsom Salt)—was analysed by the famous Michael Faraday. The well was enclosed within a thatched cottage shaped like a wigwam and ropes were used to draw up the water. With its handsome ancillary buildings, the spa attracted 'several personages of rank', including Mrs Fitzherbert, the Duke of Gloucester, Lady Salisbury and, later on, Charles Dickens.

As time went on, various mid-Victorian gimmicks, including a maze, a camera obscura and an archery ground became part of the establishment. Such additions inevitably altered the character of the spa but they increased its popularity and might well have enabled Beulah to remain viable for many more decades if it had not been for the opening, in 1854, of the re-erected Crystal Palace near by.

Faced with this formidable competition, decline set in suddenly and Beulah Spa had to close in 1855. The spa buildings were finally demolished in 1876 and inevitably led to some encroachments by developing suburbia, though most of the abandoned site remained open land. There has been more development in recent years, but at least part of this grassy hillside with its fine views and adjoining wood still stands as a reminder of one of the last and most scenic of London's outer spas.

Beulah Spa

Norwood: *Beulah Spa (Upper Norwood) from an illustration of 1851.*
Set in beautiful undulating grounds of nearly thirty acres on the southern slopes of Beulah Hill (now The Lawns Estate), the spa buildings were designed in 1831 by a local architect called Decimus Burton. The hut, built in the form of an Indian wigwam, housed the Magnesia Well whose water was regarded as among the purest and most strongly saline in the country.

There were some building additions between 1831 and 1851 but the spa was short-lived due partly to the arrival near by of Crystal Palace with its counter attractions.

Richmond and East Sheen

LONG BEFORE Beulah Spa was dreamed of, another hillside spa was attracting water-drinkers from London. This was the early 18th century spa out at Richmond, which grew up around a saline chalybeate spring discovered in about 1689 on land later occupied by Cardigan House (home of the fifth Earl).

Some idea of what this Thames-side spa offered can be gleaned from the notification of its opening in the *London Gazette* in April 1696: 'The New Wells on Richmond Hill will be compleated for the reception of Company this following May.. There is a large and lofty Dining Room, broad walks, open and shady, near 300 feet long, cut into the descent of the Hill, with the prospect of country about.' (If 'the prospect of country about' meant the fine view from Richmond Hill over the Thames valley and beyond, which presumably it did, the advertisers could hardly have been accused of making exaggerated claims.) There were two entrances to the spa, one in the lower road leading to Petersham and one where the entrance gates to Cardigan House (demolished in 1971 to make way for British Legion flats) later stood.

Richmond Spa became a fashionable resort renowned for its concerts, dances and other entertainments as well as for its chalybeate waters, but it was of short duration, probably reaching its peak in the 1720s. Assemblies were still being advertised in 1750 but reports suggest that the atmosphere was rapidly changing, that there was much card-playing but little water-drinking, and that wealthier patrons were withdrawing their support. At all events, prices of admission had to be lowered and, shortly after this, there were complaints of 'noise and tumult' which eventually caused the two lady founders of the Houblon charity who lived opposite to buy the place for four hundred pounds in order to close it down.

After being leased out, it was reported that the spa's heavily corniced ornamental structures were allowed to fall into a dilapidated state and were finally demolished. As for the old chalybeate well itself, many searches were made in later years in the grounds and cellars of Cardigan House but nothing was found.

The nearest mineral spring to Richmond was, in fact, about two miles away, near Palewell Common, East Sheen, and that had never amounted to anything more than a local well used for bathing the eyes or the legs of children with skin complaints. Today even that has disappeared—unless it lies beneath a rusty well-cover in the small wood adjoining the common.

Spas north of the river

For Londoners who preferred to remain on the north bank of the river, there was natural mineral water available much closer at hand—as close in fact as Hyde Park and Kensington. Of the two springs in Hyde Park, only one ranked as medicinal, but in Kensington Gardens there was St Govor's Well. Situated just off the Broad Walk, a little to the south of the Round Pond and now commemorated by a round stone memorial in the centre of a paved area, this well had been known since ancient times, though the name of St Govor was not adopted until 1856.

Also close to the centre of developing London was Billing's Well at Earl's Court and a chalybeate well at Notting Hill House (later called Aubrey House) near Holland Park, but both appear to have disappeared about 1720 without having been developed into proper spas.

Further out at Acton, a few miles to the west, it was different. Here real efforts were made in about 1750 to exploit the potential of three strongly saline wells, and a well-house with assembly room was erected. Small though it was, the Acton spa stood in a large garden at the corner of Old Oak Common—Acton means 'farm by the oak trees'—close to what was to become Wormwood Scrubs prison, and it was soon attracting the fashionable and the gay as well as the sick.

Acton Wells remained popular until shortly after 1790, when the visitors began to be divided into two classes—those who were reportedly 'allured by the hope of recovery' and those 'tempted by the love of dissipation'. From then on, the spa began to decay and it was not long before the assembly room had to be converted to other uses. First it became a private dwelling, then a school, and finally it was reduced to the status of a farm building wedged between the Great Western and the Midland railway lines. Today, nothing of it remains.

Rather more accessible for the inhabitants of London was a secularised holy well at Kilburn which had once belonged to an Augustinian nunnery. In the early 18th century a spa grew up here behind the original Bell tavern, predecessor of the present-day public house in Belsize Road, and became known as Kilburn Wells. Its milky looking saline water was claimed to be more strongly impregnated with carbonic acid than any other spring in

Spas north of the river 91

Kensington: *St Govor's Well in Kensington Gardens, from a photograph of 1910.*

This ancient spring, situated just south of the Round Pond, was named in 1856 after the 6th-century patron saint of a church near Abergavenny in Wales. (The name was chosen by Lord Llanover, owner of the Welsh parish and London's first Commissioner of Works.) By this time, the two neighbouring springs in Hyde Park were out of use but it is quite possible that the St Govor's water was still available, being handed out in glassfuls by a woman attendant for a small charge. By 1880, however, the water was reported to be 'loaded with organic matter' and it seems unlikely that many people were prepared to drink it.

Today the spring is covered over with lids and the only clear reminder is the inscribed circular fountain, built in stone, which stands in the centre of a small paved area.

England and in 1773 the proprietor described the spa as 'a happy spot, only a morning's walk from the metropolis'.

The morning's walk was across the fields from Marylebone but there was also a road to Kilburn Wells and, after the great room had been specially adapted for 'the use of the politest companies', the little spa flourished. Even after people stopped drinking the water, the tea-gardens, at one time favoured by Oliver Goldsmith, remained in use until 1829. After that, however, the entire premises were overwhelmed by the expanding metropolis and today it requires some imagination to believe that Kilburn Wells ever existed at all.

More fortunate in this respect was Hampstead, though, here too, the springs have long since vanished. Situated less than two miles further north, they had a shorter history than the well at Kilburn but a much more spectacular one.

Chalybeate springs had been discovered in Hampstead during the reign of Charles II but little had been done about them and it was not until the early 18th century, when a local physician called Gibbons suddenly decided to publish a list of various 'cures' effected by the water, that the story really began.

Almost overnight a spa developed and Hampstead became 'a resort of the wealthy, the idle and the sickly'. The elm-lined approach promenade, still known as Well Walk, was laid out and the water, bottled daily in flasks at the Flask tavern and elsewhere, was despatched to the capital for sale in the streets. Lodging-houses sprang up and, as more and more people decided to actually come and live in Hampstead, it soon became a hive of activity, colour and fashion.

But none of this, it seemed, could ensure the continued success of the spa. Soon 'riotous assemblies' began to develop, giving the place such a bad name that the proprietor of the first Long Room went bankrupt and had to sell out. The premises were converted first into a chapel and then into a drill-hall, before finally being demolished in 1882.

Even Hampstead's second Long Room, built on the site of the present-day Wells House flats, failed to survive for long and nothing now remains of it apart from its name. Today, the only reminder of the early 18th century spa is the fountain later erected on the north side of Well Walk to mark the site of the original outflow. But even here, modern drain work and other innovations have had their effect and little, if any, water flows.

Modern drainage and road-making also accounted for the disappearance of the water from a one-time holy well at Muswell Hill. Situated about six

Acton: *Acton Wells Assembly House from an illustration of 1793.*
This simple spa building stood in a garden containing three saline wells at the south-west corner of Old Oak Common—on a site later engulfed by two converging railway lines near Wormwood Scrubbs.

With its powerfully cathartic waters, Acton Spa became quite celebrated around 1750, attracting both the sick and the gay from London. By 1790, however, its popularity had waned and shortly afterwards the Assembly House was converted into a private dwelling, later used as a boarding-school and finally reduced to a farm outhouse. Nevertheless in 1870 the gardens were re-made, becoming first a 'people's garden', then a thriving Biergarten owned by the German Club of London. But the enterprise could not survive the First World War and Acton Spa was finally buried in a labyrinth of factory land and railway sidings.

Hampstead: *Hampstead Assembly and Pump Rooms, from an early 18th century drawing.*

This building stood on the south side of the elm-lined promenade, Well Walk—a product of Hampstead's sudden rise to fame as a spa. However, in 1719, after complaints of riotous assemblies and bad debts, the proprietor of this first Long Room—a second one stood on the north side of the road on the site of the present Wells House flats—found himself in the Chancery Court. Soon afterwards the premises were sold and converted into a chapel, which remained in use for about a hundred and thirty years.

In the 1860s, the building became a drill hall and was finally demolished in 1882, leaving only the adjoining house (now 46 Well Walk) seen on the right of the picture. With the digging of deep drains and a railway tunnel, water from the chalybeate spring was reduced to a trickle but a fountain erected last century on the north side of the road to mark the original outflow remains. Apart from street names, there are few other reminders of Hampstead's once popular spa.

miles north of Hampstead, this 'spring of faire water', once a place of pilgrimage, was still in good condition and resorted to during the early 18th century. It stood enclosed by wooden railings in a field. Today field, well and water lie somewhere beneath the grounds of Alexandra Palace.

A similar fate befell the nearby springs of Tottenham, one of which was known as Bishop's Well and is believed to have issued out of the side of the hill opposite the vicarage near the River Moselle. Another stood a little to the south of what is now Bruce Grove.

In those days, the still more distant villages of Totteridge and Welwyn also possessed mineral springs and no doubt tried to make the most of them. All these spas, however, were small and unimportant compared with the one at Chipping Barnet, south of the road to Elstree.

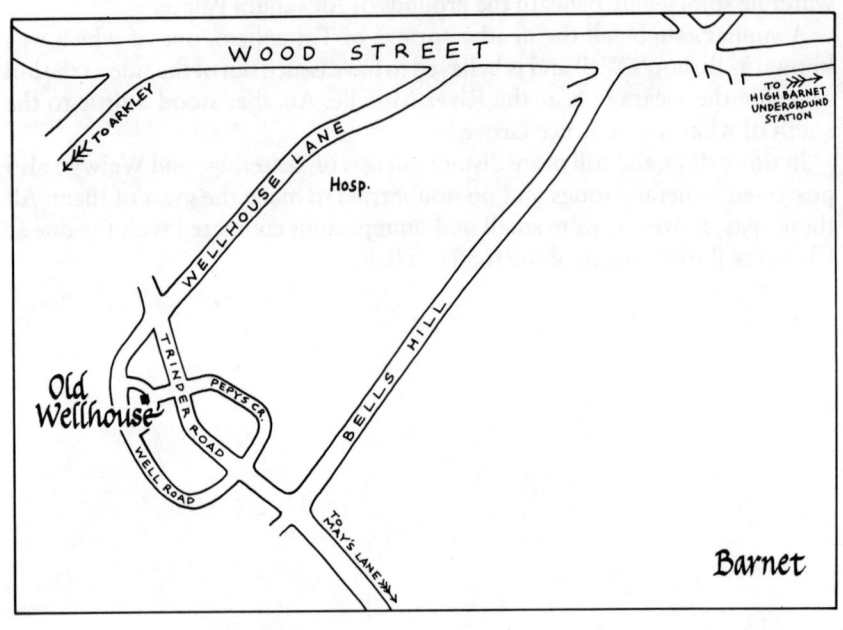

Barnet

EVEN THOMAS FULLER in his *Worthies of England*, published in 1662, referred to the Barnet spring, expressing the hope that the water would 'repair the blood shed hard by and save as many lives as were lost in the fatal battle of Barnet'. (The battle of Barnet took place in 1471 and ended with a Yorkist victory for Edward IV.)

The well also had the more doutbful advantage of a few comments from Samuel Pepys, who visited it in 1664 accompanied by his wife and his man Will. According to Pepys' account, he was persuaded to drink five glasses of the water and then felt so unwell that by the time he reached home he went straight to bed. During the night he got worse until, in his own words, he 'almost melted to water'. Very wisely, on his next visit in 1667, the famous diarist took the precaution of drinking only three glassfuls of Barnet's saline water!

In the early days, Celia Fiennes was also among Barnet's distinguished visitors and issued a warning, though of a different nature from that of Pepys. Her complaint concerned the conditions at the well rather than the effect of the water. She recorded that within the enclosing building of latticed wood, visitors who wished to drink had to descend some steps and that the water was so deep that she could not see the bottom. A connoisseur with a marked preference for stone basins, Celia seems to have thought badly of this arrangement and did not like the look of the water when it was drawn up. She said it was dirty and full of leaves and that she had to wait for the sediment to settle.

Yet, despite these criticisms, by the early 18th century, Barnet's so-called Physic Well had become quite fashionable and it remained in reasonably good condition until about 1790. It was still resorted to as late as 1812, but in about 1840 the old well-house was pulled down and a small farmhouse was erected on the foundations, leaving only the well itself. The well was protected and provided with a small iron pump so that any invalid who wished could still come and drink and, even by 1867, it was still being kept in repair with funds from a neighbouring boys' school. In fact it was 1907 before the water was finally declared unfit to drink.

The Barnet well came to light again in 1922 when the land was being excavated for a housing estate and the council decided to open it up. To everyone's surprise, the underground well-chamber, approached by a short

Barnet: *The original well-house (right), from an old illustration of about 1796.*

This and the adjacent building were pulled down and a small farm erected on the foundations in 1840 but the 'Physic Well' itself, first discovered about 1618, was left intact and covered over. A small iron pump, erected so that people could continue to draw the mineral water, could still be seen in the farmer's field in the early part of the 20th century, though by this time it was in bad condition and unusable. When the land was being excavated in 1922 for a housing estate, a large brick-built underground chamber containing the well, both in perfect condition, came to light again and a new pseudo-Tudor well-house was erected in order to preserve them.

Barnet: *The well-house, as seen in recent years.*
Designed to resemble the original Tudor well-house, this building was erected in 1922 over the newly discovered foundations of Barnet's ancient Physic Well. It stands on a plot of land in the middle of a housing estate and in 1960 was threatened with demolition because of damage by vandals. Fortunately, following protests by conservationists, it was saved and given a face-lift, though it still remains a target for graffiti.

flight of steps, was found to be in perfect and undisturbed condition due to the covering earth. As they emerged, it was seen that the walls, floor and barrel-like roof were all built of brick and that there was room for about twenty people.

In order to protect the well and the memory of it, a Tudor-style well-house designed to look as much as possible like the one described by Celia Fiennes was erected over it. However, by 1960, this new well-house had been so badly vandalised that it narrowly escaped demolition and it was only after representations by conservationists that the decision was taken to provide it with a new roof and a general face-lift. Today it remains vulnerable, but at least it still stands, marking the spot of a once fashionable and important spa.

Northaw Spring and Wanstead

The neighbouring Northaw Spring or King's Well (so named by Charles II because the courtiers of James I used to visit it while staying at the nearby palace of Theobalds) between Northaw and Cheshunt, had already disappeared by the 18th century, but the small spas of Woodford and Chigwell over in the north-east, both noted for their beautiful scenery around Epping Forest, were still functioning.

So, too, completing the circle, was Wanstead, established in 1619. Although unsuccessful in its original aspirations to rival Tunbridge, this pioneer spa managed to survive longer than most, and today it is commemorated by a memorial fountain in Blake Hall Road. Finally, however, like so many before and after it, Wanstead Spa could find no answer either to the caprices and fickleness of the public or to the commercial pressures of the suburban developer.

Although some of the spa gardens around the capital were saved for posterity, either by the action of local councils or by the generosity of private individuals, by the end of the 19th century most of the natural mineral water from London's outer ring of spas had joined that of the inner spas and was draining away into a massive sewerage system.

There were some, of course, further out in the surrounding countryside, that escaped this fate—as at the Surrey villages of Cobham (where a mineral spring still exists in the triangle between Plough Lane and Downside Road) and at Godstone (once renowned for its mineral spring at the southern tip of Tilburstow Hill). But few of these country spas amounted to much more than the spring itself and today, they, too, are almost forgotten.

4
Spas patronised by George III

B Y 1760, when George III came to the throne, new spas were appearing far beyond the confines of London. For those who could afford the journey and the luxury of a residential stay, they offered not only the excitement of fresh pastures but also the possibility of new cures.

To these rising establishments, royal patronage was of immense importance. As every aspiring spa proprietor already knew, wherever the monarch went others were sure to follow and, now that there was a king on the throne whose interest in 'taking the waters' was clearly no passing fancy, a royal visit was not beyond the bounds of possibility.

Today, when it is realised that George III cannot have been wholly unaware of the mysterious illness that was creeping up on him and would one day overwhelm him, it is not difficult to understand and sympathise with the royal interest in spas. Reasonably enough, the king favoured those spas which could offer some additional benefit such as sea and country air, or, as in the case of a relatively new spa such as Cheltenham, the possibility of an effective new remedy.

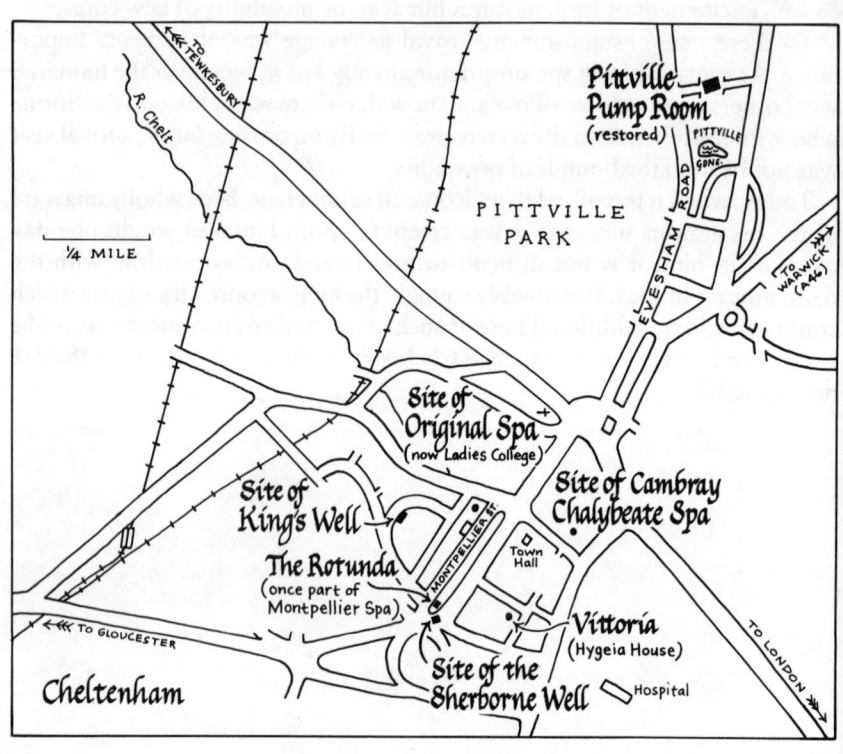

Cheltenham

THE STORY of Cheltenham Spa had begun with the Old Well, or Original Well, which now lies buried beneath the Ladies' College, just south of the River Chelt and the High Street. Officially the spring which fed the well was discovered about 1716, though it was said that old men knew of its existence long before that.

The 1716 discovery is attributed to the antics of a flock of pigeons which were observed pecking at salt crystals in a field where water had gushed up through the clay. Faced with so strange a phenomenon, people soon realised that this was no ordinary water and news that it possessed medicinal properties soon spread.

Understandably, the owner of the field, a Quaker named William Mason, did not share the enthusiasm of the numerous visitors who descended uninvited upon his property and it was only a matter of time before he decided to have the mineral spring 'railed in, locked up and a little shed thrown over it'.

These precautions by an uncommercially minded man forced Cheltenham's first spring back into a state of obscurity—but not for long. Mason eventually retired to Bristol and here his daughter Elizabeth met and married a widowed Manx sea captain called Henry Skillicorne. Skillicorne already knew something about the 'hot wells' at Bristol and, when Elizabeth inherited her father's property in 1738, he immediately decided to move to Cheltenham. Soon he had embarked on the systematic development of a spa.

The aspiring developer began by deepening and lining Mason's well, installing a pumping system and replacing the broken-down shed with a small brick structure similar to the one over the spring at Hotwells. With four supporting arches, this solid but simple pump-house was originally decorated with four stone pigeons, one at each corner—presumably as a reminder of the part played by the birds in the discovery of the well.

Skillicorne's next move was to lay out the famous Well Walk (now obliterated), with its numerous elms and limes leading from the river and town. Then, in 1742, he built the first public spa rooms. These facilities were later augmented by Grove House, or Mrs Field's Boarding House as it came to be called, where visitors could play cards or indulge in other forms of entertainment such as public breakfasts and dancing. This well-known

Cheltenham: *Entrance to the Original (Royal) Spa, from a print of about 1813.*

The picture shows Henry Skillicorne's first public rooms of 1742 on the right, and his son's Long Room of 1776 on the left. The actual well was through the archway.

After fifty years as the well's pumper, Hannah Forty died in 1816 at the age of seventy-two—an event which is said to have hastened the Original Spa's decline. Although the centenary celebrations of Henry Skillicorne's establishment of the spa were staged in Old Well Walk in 1838, not even this could reverse the trend which was now taking most of the fashionable clientèle to rival establishments such as Montpellier and Pittville. For the Original Spa, the end was already in sight in 1873 when the Ladies' College took over the site for development. Already the spring had been covered over, probably by Oxley's Music Hall, and it was only a matter of time before any remaining buildings and the once beautiful tree-lined avenue were swallowed up by the school.

It is believed that the spring now lies buried underneath the school's Princess Hall which replaced the Music Hall.

lodging-house stood on the west side of Well Walk on the site now occupied by St Matthew's church.

As for the water itself—later analysis showed that it contained small quantities of dissolved magnesium and sodium chlorides; magnesium, sodium and calcium sulphates; ferrous oxide; and traces of iodine and bromine—it was soon acclaimed as a cure for virtually everything, and the spa's reputation grew.

But all was not well. Within a short time visitors were complaining of a shortage of good accommodation, exorbitant prices and an inhospitable population. In particular, the unpaved High Street with its muddy stepping-stones aroused much unfavourable comment from the ladies who, with their long gowns, found it extremely hazardous.

Then there was the problem of the journey which, even from places as near as Gloucester, was far from easy. So, when an outbreak of smallpox was added to the list of deterrents, most people decided to stay away—a trend which not even a few brief appearances by celebrities such as Dr Johnson could reverse. In fact, by 1757, the prospects for the spa looked so bleak that Thomas Hughes, a 'foreigner' from Wales, who had leased the well from the ageing Skillicorne, was excused payment of his rates.

This state of affairs continued until Skillicorne died in 1763—as can be seen from an immensely long epitaph in the parish church of St Mary, he reached the age of eighty-four—after which his son William took over and set about making improvements.

William took as his partner a certain William Miller from London and in 1776 the two men opened a new and more elegant long room large enough for balls and card-playing. This, together with improving communications and more willingness on the part of the inhabitants to provide suitable lodgings, helped to re-establish some of the spa's lost popularity.

One of those who decided to participate in the revival was Thomas Hughes. Having married a local heiress in 1780, Hughes was soon busy building and opening the first assembly rooms on a prime site in the main street—a building which, with its Corinthian pilasters, chandeliers, lustres and music gallery, was soon recognised as a serious rival to the ballrooms built by Skillicorne and Miller.

The year 1780 also saw the arrival of Simon Moreau, who was to establish himself as the first master-of-ceremonies. In the words of a locally published doggerel verse said to have been inspired by Mrs Field of Grove House,

Moreau was an upstart from Bath who had come 'at the balls to preside, to preserve etiquette and pay homage to Pride'.

Whatever the newcomer's credentials and motives, it was not long before he and young Skillicorne's partner, William Miller, were at loggerheads. There was a struggle for supremacy and, as can be judged from the notes of one observer, the Honourable John Byng, a good deal of pettiness. Byng wrote: 'Mr Miller of the Long Room continued his impertinence and tyranny to Mr and Mrs Moreau by refusing them waters—tho' Mrs C's mangy dog drank of it constantly.' Such were the goings-on in Cheltenham in 1781!

But, whatever the private vendettas, the actual spa regime had now fallen into line with that of the other major spas such as Bath and Tunbridge. In other words, water-drinking began early in the day, the fiddles played from eight o'clock until ten, and there was a public breakfast every Monday at a shilling a head.

Although these were advances as far as the spa itself was concerned, the town was still badly in need of improvement and in 1786 the first Act was passed to this end. Perhaps its most important effect was the transformation of the High Street into a good thoroughfare with foot pavements and lamps— a change which no doubt played an important part in the choice of Cheltenham for the royal visit.

The appearance of George III, Queen Charlotte, three princesses and a small entourage in July 1788 was greeted with great enthusiasm, and news of it, echoing throughout the country, ensured Cheltenham of an honoured place on the spa map for many years to come. Nobody knows who exactly recommended the Cheltenham waters for the mysterious royal complaint or whether it really did any good but the family stayed for five weeks and appeared to enjoy it.

As usual, however, there were a few dissentient voices, one being that of Fanny Burney, the queen's lady-in-waiting, who wrote in her diary that she found it all very fatiguing. Some problems arose from the fact that Bayshill House, lent by Lord Fauconberg for the visit, proved too small to accommodate the gentlemen of the entourage and they all had to be lodged in the town. Nevertheless the house had the advantage of being only two fields and an orchard distant from the Well, to which the royal party ceremoniously made its way every morning, arriving by half past five.

Following the first glass of water, the royal drinkers would walk for half an hour, no doubt taking in the discreetly placed temple to the goddess Cloacina a little way down the hill from the spring before returning for a second glass.

Cheltenham: *George III in 1788 at the Original (or Royal) Well, from an old print.*

This well with its saline chalybeate water had been sunk in about 1716, soon after pigeons pecking at salt near by had drawn attention to the presence of water bubbling up through the clay soil. The land belonged to a Quaker called William Mason, but it was left to his son-in-law, a retired Manx sea-captain called Henry Skillicorne, to recognise the full potentialities for a spa. After his wife inherited, Skillicorne settled in Cheltenham and in 1738 he lined the well, provided a pumping system and erected the simple brick canopy supported on four brick arches. During the next five years, this 'father of Cheltenham Spa' laid out gardens and tree-lined 'Well Walk' leading from the river. He also built the spa's first public rooms.

After Henry Skillicorne's death in 1763, his son William continued to run the spa, adding a larger and more elegant Long Room in 1776. Nevertheless, by 1788, the spa was badly in need of the boost provided by the five-week visit of George III, Queen Charlotte and three princesses. To redress a shortage of spa water, George III caused the King's Well to be sunk in the grounds of nearby Bayshill Lodge, home of Lord Fauconberg, where the royal party stayed. But royal interest and the boom it created also encouraged other land-owners to begin searching for mineral water and their success soon brought serious competition for the Old Wells.

Cheltenham: *The first Montpellier Wells, from an old print.*
This relatively modest long room of the *cottage ornée* type preceded the colonnaded building which survives today in Montpellier as Lloyds Bank. It was built in 1809 by the London merchant Henry Thompson on pasture land he had acquired south and east of Skillicorne's original well. Here, on the slopes of the hill south of the River Chelt and the High Street, the developer had made some eighty borings and had finally succeeded in his search for mineral water. The spa he created was approached by a charming tree-lined walk built in imitation of the avenue leading to Skillicorne's well, and, east of that, were suitably laid out grounds flanked by the so-called Rides and Walks. The enterprise was so successful that, after only eight years, Thompson decided to replace the wooden building by something more ambitious and embarked 'at almost incalculable cost' on the building to which his son was later to add the famous Rotunda.

Finally, the king would walk back to Bayshill House for breakfast, leaving the ladies to ride back in a carriage.

One problem that seems to have exercised George III's mind during the visit was the dwindling supply of mineral water from the Old Well and, before he left, he suggested that a new well be bored in Lord Fauconberg's grounds. The suggestion was acted on and the new well was duly named the King's Well. Although it never became very important, it did mark the beginning of a new and frantic search for more springs—a search which not even a combination of adverse circumstances, including the bad state of the roads and the Napoleonic Wars, held back for long.

In the forefront of the new developers was a certain Dr Jameson who made at least forty borings on the slopes of Bayshill above the original well and was finally rewarded by the discovery of a spring in the vicinity of present-day Suffolk Square. Jameson chose the name Sherborne, after the Earl of Suffolk's nearby mansion but, alas, this tiny spa with its rustic pump-room ran dry and the name languished until resurrected years later, in 1818, by two other promoters who adopted it for their own use when they created an attractive little spa lower down the hill.

The drying up of Dr Jameson's well was due to the rival borings of a developer called Henry Thompson who, in 1809, laid the foundations of the famous Montepellier Wells just below it. A shrewd merchant from London, Henry Thompson had bought a tract of pasture land south and east of Skillicorne's original well and was soon outstripping Dr Jameson's efforts by notching up more than eighty borings. His first Montepellier spa building consisted of little more than a simple long room of the *cottage ornée* type complemented by wooden pillars, verandah and a tree-lined approach, but it was so successful that only eighty years later, in 1817, Thompson was in a position to replace it by a much more elaborate establishment.

The new spa building erected by Henry Thompson was an oblong structure surrounded by a stone pillared verandah designed by G. A. Underwood. It was the building which was later to acquire the famous domed Rotunda and which today belongs to Lloyds Bank.

Another measure of Henry Thompson's success was the fine new house which he erected for himself—it, too, still stands today—close to the Bath road. He called it Hygeia after the goddess of health, but the name was later changed to Vittoria House.

Yet not even Henry Thompson could avoid competition and in 1816 new assembly rooms with a magnificent ballroom appeared in the High Street.

These rival premises replaced Thomas Hughes' earlier assembly rooms of 1784 and were opened by no less a person than the Duke of Wellington.

No doubt it was the threat posed by such competition that persuaded Henry Thompson's son, Pearson Thompson, to take action almost as soon as his father died in 1825 by engaging the London architect John Buonarotti Papworth to design the famous circular Rotunda and to improve the Promenade Room at Montpellier. In the event, the project ran into difficulties due to the financial crisis that occurred later that same year but, eventually, the major extension was completed and was soon attracting most of what remained of the fashionable clientèle from Skillicorne's Original Spa.

A minor rival of the Montepellier Spa was the new Sherborne Pump Room designed by G. A. Underwood for the two promoters, Samuel Harward and Thomas Henney, who adopted the name of Dr Jameson's abandoned spa higher up the hill. Built in the style of the Temple of Illyssus in Athens, this charming little spa first appeared in 1818 but was soon undergoing transformations. Its name was changed to the Imperial Spa, and then, in 1837, in order to make way for the Queen's Hotel, the building was pulled down and re-erected in the newly laid out Promenade. The hotel still stands on the earlier site.

Another small spa to make its appearance about this time was in the Cambray district of Cheltenham, at the junction of Rodney Road and Oriel Road. Consisting of an octagon-shaped pump-room erected in 1834 by Baynham-Jones of Cambray House over a chalybeate spring, most of its patrons were local people. Eventually, when they drifted away, the building was adapted as a Turkish Bath and was finally demolished in 1938. Also built in the Victorian style was a small spa out at Alstone, north of the town, but this was doomed to early failure.

The real competitor to Montpellier was the Pittville Pump Room. Although this, too, was situated well out of town—about half way between the High Street and the present-day racecourse—Pittville was the most spectacular of all Cheltenham's creations and was in a class of its own. Even the site was enormous, consisting of common land enclosed under an Act of Parliament of 1801 and acquired by Joseph Pitt M.P.

Joseph Pitt was an ambitious man who, before rising to become a successful lawyer and speculator, had begun his working life by holding horses at a penny a time. By 1824, this new land-owner had devised a scheme for developing a brand new town in Grecian style with an extensive park and major spa as its focal point. It was the grand project and, in May 1825, the

Cheltenham: *Interior of the Montpellier Rotunda, from a drawing of the 1840s.*

This interior of the domed circular drinking hall, reminiscent of the Pantheon in Rome, is fifty-one feet high and fifty feet in diameter. It was added to the rear of Henry Thompson's colonnaded Montpellier Spa in 1825 by his son Pearson Thompson. The architect was John Buonarotti Papworth of London, celebrated for his work in the Crimea and Egypt but not until now an exponent of the classical revival style.

The Rotunda soon became a well-known centre of activity where 'from the seventh hour of the morning until nearly the tenth, the animation and gaiety continue unabated . . . whilst the soothing sound of music heightens the charm . . . revives the invalid's hope—and softens his afflictions'. But inevitably these gentle diversions ended with the boom and were replaced by 'balls, billiards and bingo' until finally, in order to save it from ruin, the building was bought by the council.

In 1962 Lloyds Bank, which had occupied part of the Long Room since 1890, offered to restore the entire building for its own use, with the result that today the famous Rotunda is a central banking hall lined with modern counters. Despite these changes, however, something of the old elegance remains.

Cheltenham: *The Sherborne Pump Room, later known as the Imperial Spa, from an old print.*

This delightful little pump-room stood on the site now occupied by the Queen's Hotel. Designed in 1818 by G. A. Underwood for Samuel Harward and Thomas Henney, it took its name from Dr Jameson's rustic pump-room (on a site near the present Suffolk Square) which had run dry because of Henry Thompson's rival borings lower down the hill. With its portico supported by six Doric pillars, the new Sherborne Pump Room was the first of Cheltenham's buildings to be modelled on the Athenian Temple of Illyssus. It was further embellished by the 'colossal' statue of the goddess Hygeia on its roof dome and by the 'cocks of pure crystal' from which the mineral water was dispensed to the strains of the usual 'band of musick'.

This little spa was so highly regarded that the now famous Promenade was constructed to link it with the High Street, though ironically this major contribution to the town's future development led to its displacement in 1837 by the big hotel. In that year, the spa building was demolished and rebuilt in the Promenade, where it managed to survive until the 1930s before being replaced by the Regal cinema.

foundation stone of the Pittville Pump Room was laid with full religious and Masonic ritual.

But despite Pitt's exertions and the interest of the Duke of Wellington, who frequently visited the site, progress was slow. Like his rival Pearson Thompson, Pitt was seriously affected by the late 1825 banking crisis and had to abandon most of his new town plans, though the £90,000 Pump Room project went ahead and was finally completed after five years.

Although, like another portent of things to come, the opening ceremony had to be postponed due to the death of George III, the big day dawned on 22 July 1830, and the magnificent Pittville Pump Room, set on a gentle slope overlooking an artificial lake, made its début. There was a grand public breakfast, followed in the evening by an even grander ball.

With its Ionic colonnade based on the Erechtheion originals at Athens and its massive roof dome surmounting a great hall and gallery, it is hardly surprising that the Cotswold stone temple was regarded as the finest specifically designed spa structure in England. Indeed it still is. During the restoration of recent years, the statues made by Gahagan of Bath were replaced by replicas made by Cheltenham carvers, but the effect remains much the same. Hippocrates and Aesculapius still stand sentinel over the parapet wings while the goddess Hygeia dominates the centre.

Back in the 19th century, however, it soon became clear that the fortunes of Pittville Spa were no more assured that were those of its more centrally situated rivals, as highlighted by what was happening to Skillicorne's old establishment. In 1828 the Original Spa staged its famous and successful centenary celebrations, when the Old Well Walk was illuminated with a thousand lamps in arches of green and gold. Yet, within ten years, the old pump-room was being pulled down and Oxley's Music Hall erected in its place. The plain fact was that, despite Cheltenham's reputation as 'the merriest sick-resort on earth', it depended on a fashion that was already past its peak.

The decline in water-drinking was something which not even Montpellier Spa could combat for long and, magnificent though it still was, by 1890 the Long Room had to be let out for banking purposes. Thereafter the rest of the spa buildings deteriorated, gradually succumbing to 'balls, billiards and bingo', in that order. By the middle of the present century, even the fate of the building itself was in doubt and it was not until 1962 that a final solution was found. In that year, Lloyds Bank, whose predecessors had taken over the Long Room, reached agreement with the council whereby the entire building was handed over to the bank for restoration, and conversion to its own use. Today it may be difficult to imagine the invalids and fashionable people who once gathered to drink Cheltenham's saline water to the strains of soft music in the huge circular Pump Room, with its sixteen Corinthian pilasters and massive central dome—now the main banking hall—but at least some of the orginal features are still there to assist the imagination.

Meanwhile the 19th century had seen the gradual reduction of Pittville to the role of a white elephant and by 1891 that, too, had passed into the hands of the council. The price paid was a pitiful £5,400. The council of that time hoped to reinstate both Pittville and Montpellier as spas, but even an extensive advertising campaign failed to bring back the crowds.

Another sign of the times was the demolition in 1900 of the Regency building known as the Assembly Rooms which the Duke of Wellington had opened in 1816. The site was redeveloped with the High Street branch of Lloyds Bank.

Yet, in spite of all the discouragements, Cheltenham still clung to its spa image and, in order to compensate for its losses, it began dispensing four different waters, including the alkaline Pittville water, from an octagonal pump-room set up in the Town Hall. It even made another attempt during the post-war depression period of the 1930s to popularise the Pittville Pump Room, though again without success.

By this time the rebuilt Sherborne Spa at the corner of St George's Road on the Promenade was also in trouble. Known for a long time as the Imperial Rooms, it had been reduced to the role of a cabinet and carpet warehouse and in 1937 was finally demolished to make way for a cinema. So, even before the Second World War broke out, Cheltenham's prospects for a spa revival looked bleak.

At the beginning of the war, the Pittville Pump Room and its adjoining grounds were requisitioned for military purposes, first for occupation by British forces and then by the Americans. During this period dry rot set in and, since nothing was done to check it, the fungus gradually penetrated most of the woodwork, including the curved rafters of the dome. The result was that by the time the building was de-requisitioned, the cost of saving it was regarded as prohibitive and the only hope lay in a major public appeal.

To everyone's surprise, the appeal proved so successful that restoration was able to begin at a cost of £53,000, and in 1960 the partially restored Pittville Pump Room was re-opened by the seventh Duke of Wellington who recalled the part played by his celebrated forebear in 1830. As restoration

Cheltenham: *The Cambray Spa, from an old photograph.*

After the discovery of a chalybeate spring on the site, this small octagonal Gothic-style pump-room was opened in 1834 by a local worthy named Baynham Jones of nearby Cambray House. It stood on the northern side of Oriel Terrace at the junction of Rodney Road and Oriel Road and, although one of Cheltenham's lesser spas, it had the advantage of being able to offer the iron-impregnated water as well as the more familiar saline.

In later years, the building was adapted to become a Turkish bath until, in 1938, it was finally demolished.

Cheltenham: *Pittville Pump Room, as it is today.*
This surviving and most spectacular of Cheltenham's pump-rooms was begun in 1825 to a design by John Forbes for Joseph Pitt M.P., a successful lawyer and speculator of humble origin. It stands on land which Pitt had enclosed from common fields on the northern outskirts of the town. Pitt's idea was to build a new town in Grecian style with the Pump Room as a focal point, but the scheme collapsed due to the late 1825 financial crisis.

The Pump Room itself, facing an artificial lake, took five years to complete, the total cost being almost £90,000. The Ionic columns are based on the Erechtheion originals at Athens, while the figures on the parapet above—the present ones are replicas—represent Hippocrates, Hygeia and Aesculapius. The huge roof dome lights the centre of a fine galleried hall in which a marble drinking fountain originally stood at the northern end.

Magnificent though it all was, Pittville remained somewhat inaccessible and, with spa mania declining, soon ran into debt. In 1890 the heavily mortgaged property was sold to the council for a mere £5,400.

During the Second World War, when British and American forces were stationed here, dry rot spread unchecked and post-war rescue only became possible as a result of public and private subscriptions. The partially restored building was re-opened to the public in 1960. By 1978, restoration was complete and, despite a history of setbacks, Cheltenham water is once again available from May to September. It is pumped up from a well 80 feet deep and dispensed from the restored fountain set in a new curved recess.

continued, the sculptures of Hygeia, Hippocrates and Aesculapius were copied from the originals in the Bolton Workshop and by 1978 were back in position above the Ionic pillared colonnade.

Today the huge repainted hall, with its fine rosetted dome, is the scene of concerts and other regular functions. Also restored is the original fountain, though a new niche had to be found for it. After various misadventures, water from one of Pittville's alkaline mineral springs is again being drawn to the surface from eighty feet below ground and is available to the public during the summer months. The pump is electrically operated but no doubt the water tastes much as it did when the first Duke of Wellington opened this famous Cheltenham pump-room a hundred and fifty years ago. Indeed it is probably not very different from the water of the Old Well drunk by George III when he came to Cheltenham in 1788.

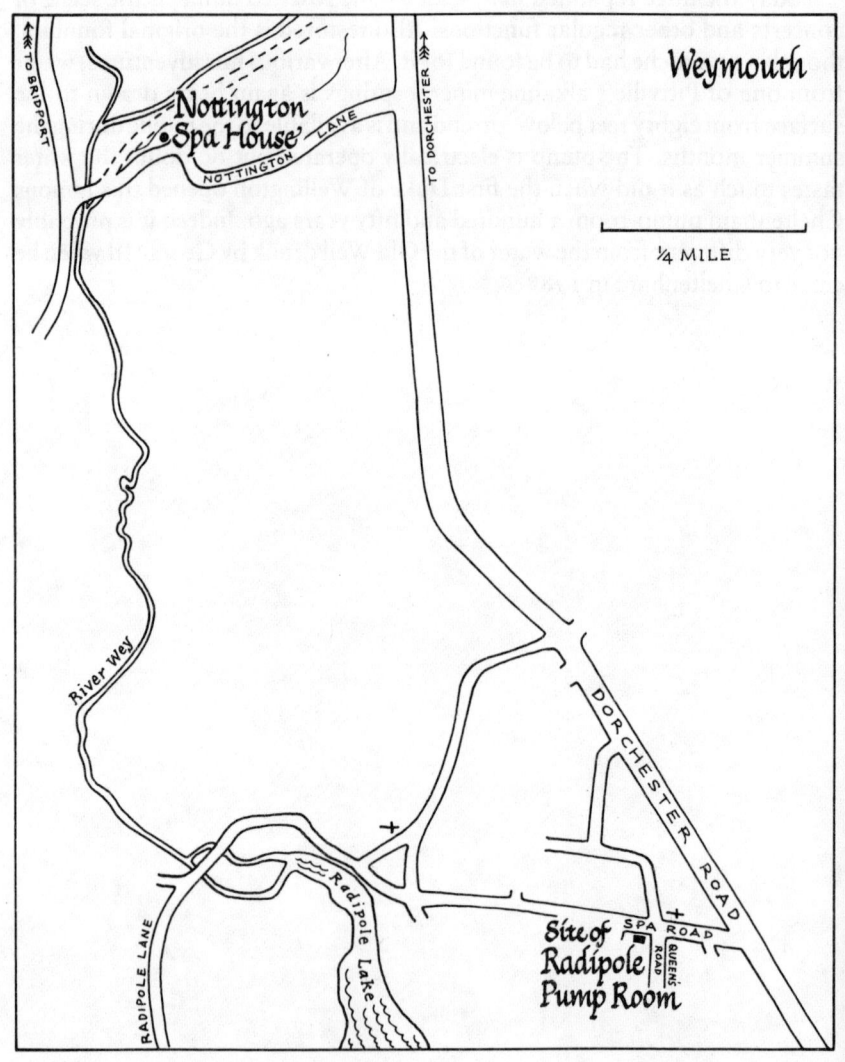

Weymouth

ANOTHER SPA resort greatly favoured by George III was Weymouth. Here, he and the royal party could visit two small spas, one chalybeate, the other sulphur, at the neighbouring villages of Radipole and Nottington, while also enjoying the benefits of sea-bathing.

The monarch regarded sea-bathing as a complementary therapy to water-drinking and, unlike some of his more faint hearted subjects, appears to have entered into the spirit of it with gusto! (With a band of musicians concealed in a nearby bathing machine ready to strike up 'God Save the King' as he entered the water, perhaps he could hardly have done otherwise!) At all events, George III became so attached to Weymouth that on several occasions he actually held his court here.

The weakly saline chalybeate spring at Radipole, some two miles north of the town, was the nearer of the two spas, but, during his 1789 visit at least, the king appears to have favoured Nottington a mile further out.

In those days, Nottington's saline sulphur spring, which lies between rising ground to the south and the meandering River Wey to the north, was surrounded by nothing more than a simple stone edifice. Tradition had it that its healing qualities were first recognised by a shepherd whose scab-ridden sheep had strayed off the road into a pool of water that had formed immediately above it. Apparently the animals drank and wallowed in the water, with noticeable and unexpected results, namely the gradual disappearance of their unpleasant symptoms.

As Nottington's fame spread, human beings sampled the water themselves and found it so beneficial that it became known as a preserver of health and beauty. Most people did, however, object to its taste and smell. The taste was said to resemble that of very hard boiled eggs, while the smell was compared with that given off during the scouring of guns!

Another problem was the formation of a white sediment which gave the water a 'light pearl colour' once the water had been exposed to the atmosphere, though it was pointed out that, when freshly drawn from the well, it was 'clear and transparent, as pure as fountain water'.

Presumably George III decided that he must take the bad with the good for he and the royal party, together with leading personalities from the surrounding countryside, regularly formed social gatherings around the well and dutifully drank their potions. Perhaps they drew encouragement from the reported similarity of the water to certain waters at Naples and Paris, where cures for almost everything from worms and gunshot wounds to nervous afflictions had been recorded.

Such was the reputation built up by the royal visits that the popularity of the Nottington water continued long after George III's departure. In fact, by 1830, a local worthy called Thomas Shore had already had it properly analysed and its efficacy confirmed by a professor at Guy's Hospital and was preparing to lay the foundation stone of the small octagonal pump-room which still survives.

The ceremony took place on Good Friday and was preceded by a service at Broadway church, from where a procession, led by a band, made its way to the site. The prospective proprietor was accompanied by his family, friends, artist, builder, workmen and 'a long train of respectable persons', including his most dutiful and appreciative son, George Shore.

It was George Shore who delivered the main speech, prefacing his remarks with the announcement that his honoured father was 'too overpowered by his feelings to say anything upon the present occasion' but that he himself had sufficient knowledge of his father's motives to be able to aver that Nottington Spa House had 'for its object the benefit of the community far more than any pecuniary consideration'. These sentiments were later echoed by other speakers from among the hundred people who subsequently sat down to a sumptuous dinner at Thomas Shore's house.

The octagonal spa building that arose during the following months contained both pump-room and baths. The well itself, complete with non-priming pump (a pump to which water has to be added to start it) stood in the cellar—and still does. Among the building's more conspicuous features were its gate-piers adorned by sculptured stone pelicans (later transferred to the adjacent property 'Greystones')—an additional landmark for the daily coaches from Weymouth and Dorchester which, by 1833, had begun to stop outside.

The premises were now being kept open from six in the morning to eight at night and appear to have been doing well, so it is not clear why Nottington Spa House changed hands. By 1836, however, it was owned by the new mayor of Weymouth, Charles Jesty, who continued to maintain it. No doubt the realisation that the water could not be satisfactorily bottled due to decomposition (hydrogen sulphide begins to oxidise as soon as it comes into contact with air to form 'free' sulphur) was a matter of some regret, but it

Weymouth: *Nottington Spa House, from a drawing of 1833.*

Situated close to the River Wey about a mile north of Radipole, this octagonal spa house was erected in 1830 by an architect called Robert Vining for its proprietor, Thomas Shore. It stands at a sharp bend in Nottington Lane, some third of a mile from the Dorchester road.

The discovery of the spring was attributed to a shepherd who noticed that his flock of sheep, suffering from scab, began to recover after they had wallowed in a pool of water on the ground above. After analysis, the mildly saline sulphur water was claimed to be equivalent to Harrogate water and good for a host of complaints, including cramps, rickets and gun-shot wounds! The spring was patronised by George III during his visits to Weymouth and soon became a meeting-place for leading personalities.

The eventual appearance of the spa house, equipped with vapour, warm, cold and marble shower baths in addition to the pump-room, was heralded with much pomp and ceremony. Because the sulphur content of the water decomposed quickly, people were advised to drink it on the spot and the attractive group of houses, which still stand adjacent to it, provided accommodation for invalids. The stone pelicans which adorn the gate-piers of one of them (Greystones) belonged originally to the spa house—still privately owned and now with a preservation order on it.

The spring still exists beneath the cellar and the old pump also survives.

Weymouth: *Radipole Pump Room, from a drawing of 1833.*

This early 19th century Gothic-style pump-room and its gardens overlooked the northern end of Radipole Lake, earlier known as the tidal backwater of Weymouth Bay.

After the spa, situated about two miles north of the town centre, had succumbed to urban development pressures, a laundry was built on the site, but in 1978 this too was sold for redevelopment, leaving the spot unmarked. In terms of present-day geography, the building stood at the north-west corner of Queen's Road with Spa Road, a short distance from the Spa Hotel in the Dorchester road. Originally the chalybeate spring, mentioned by Thomas Hardy in *The Trumpet Major*, was approached by a simple track from near the church of St Ann at the centre of the village.

Like the sulphur spring at nearby Nottington, it was patronised by George III and members of his family during their frequent visits to Weymouth. But, unlike Nottington which stands further out, its chances of survival were probably never good.

added weight to the strong recommendation that the water be drunk on the spot and therefore encouraged patients from a distance to take up residence in one of the lodging-houses (today a small group of private residences) established within a few yards of the spa building.

Nottington Spa House eventually came under the aegis of the lord of the manor and today, with a Grade I preservation order on it, it survives in excellent condition as a privately occupied house.

Less fortunate was the spa at Radipole, whose chalybeate waters earned a mention in Thomas Hardy's novel *The Trumpet Major*. When George III visited the Radipole well (the time of which Hardy was writing), it was surrounded by woods and probably possessed no more than a rudimentary cover. Later on, however, a pump-room was built over it in the Gothic-style of the day.

Set in gardens overlooking the northern end of the tidal backwater now known as Radipole Lake, the little spa managed to hold its own for a number of years before declining trade forced it to yield up its territory to Weymouth's expanding suburbia. Until quite recently, a laundry stood on the site, but now only the names of Spa Road and the nearby Spa Hotel are left to commemorate the spot where the Radipole spring once enjoyed its own small share of royal patronage.

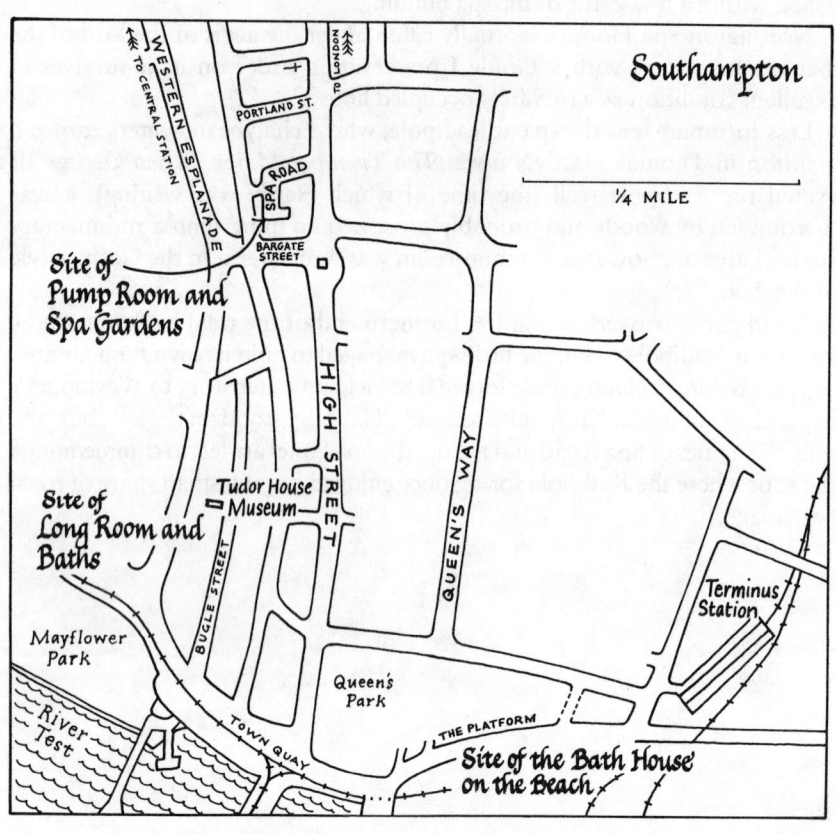

Southampton

FOR ALL its appeal, Weymouth was not the only resort where a king could enjoy sea air and drink spa waters at the same time. The old sea port of Southampton also had a spa and, since it was relatively easy to reach, it, too, found royal favour.

Southampton's spa story probably began in 1750—not with the discovery of the mineral spring but with a sea-bathing visit by Frederick, Prince of Wales, eldest son of George II. At that time, the Prince was staying in the New Forest and his brief excursion to the port, with its dark history of misfortune, turned out to be more successful than probably he or anyone else had anticipated. In fact Frederick enjoyed his bathe on the open foreshore so much that he recommended the experience to his brothers and, when they followed suit, so of course did the nobility and the gentry.

Having thus become a popular resort almost overnight, the little walled town quickly acquired three separate sea baths—Martin's, Seaward's and Simcox's, each named after their respective proprietors. By retaining the water at high tide, all these establishments were able to offer bathing facilities at any time of the day and, since the baths were fitted with false bottoms which could be raised or lowered by winches, they also offered a choice of water depth. Yet another popular feature of the sea baths was the 'observation chamber' available to spectators.

All that was needed now was the discovery of a mineral spring and for this there was not long to wait. About 1755, a year when Horace Walpole visited the town and described how 'we walked long by moonlight on the terrace above the beach', a spring containing compounds of both iron and sulphur was discovered at the bottom of what is now Bargate Street, where the land slopes down to the west.

When the word went round that the water was of nearly the same quality as that of Tunbridge Wells, the town authorities took immediate action by pumping it up into a fountain and allowing it to fall into a specially constructed basin on a fluted pedestal. (The basin is now preserved in the Tudor House Museum.) Steps were then taken to provide spa accommodation, including a reading-room, and this was followed by the laying out of extensive gardens that stretched right down to the River Test where they commanded fine views in all directions, including one of the New Forest shore.

(Apart from a few balconied houses around Portland Street, the whole of this area is now covered with down-town streets and the massive concrete building of Southern Newspapers Ltd.)

Once it had become apparent that Southampton possessed the ingredients of a real spa town, the proprietor of Martin's bathing establishment also acted promptly. The only existing assembly rooms were at the Royal George Inn in Lower High Street and they were already too small for the entertainment needs of the visitors. By 1761, the year after George III came to the throne, Martin had built the first section of some long rooms alongside his sea baths near the West Quay opposite the arcaded portion of the old town walls and, within a short time, had successfully appealed to the corporation for permission to alter part of the walls in order to provide easier access for vehicles.

Martin's assembly rooms, described by the owner as 'fitted out at vast expense', were noted for their magnificent pier-glasses and they quickly became the centre of fashionable life. As time went on, a series of extensions were built, producing a building of somewhat irregular shape but one which could offer a wide range of amusements. Balls were held twice a week during the season and card-playing and promenading became part of the daily routine. Neither the Dolphin Assembly Rooms (now incorporated into the Dolphin Hotel) in the High Street nor the Regency built Polygon which later appeared near the site of the present Polygon Hotel ever achieved the same degree of spa fame.

One of the town's later developments did, however, remain in use throughout the Regency period. This was the so-called Bath House on the Platform—a luxurious bathing establishment with fine views across the harbour which stood a little further to the east where the causeway road known as The Beach began.

To spa visitors, the shores of Southampton had always been an important attraction but, as they were to discover, this popular amenity could not be reserved for them alone. Ten years after Martin began building his assembly rooms, the rumour gained ground that sea water was an effective antidote for the bite of mad dogs and soon coach loads of victims and of precautionary minded people bringing with them their cats and dogs and other animals began arriving for a dip in the sea. Between January and September of 1773, it was estimated that one hundred and twenty people arrived for this purpose alone.

Just how much this curious influx affected the spa's popularity is not

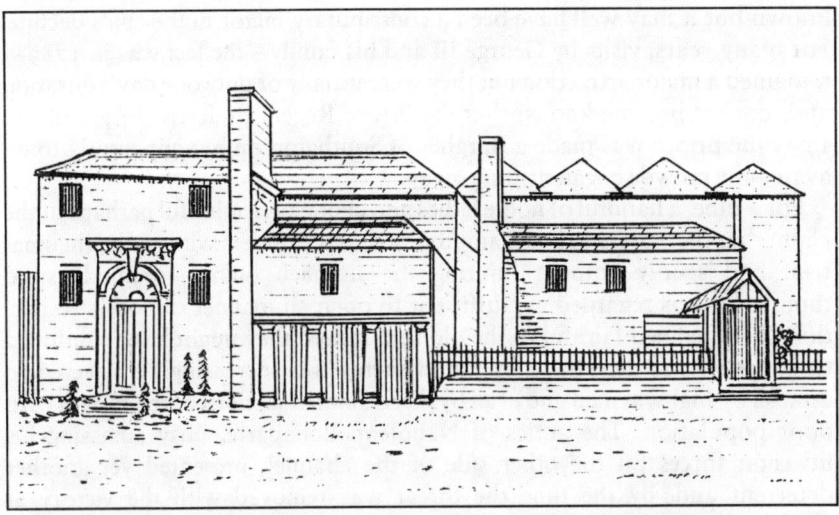

Southampton: *The Long Rooms and Baths, from an old drawing.*

This irregularly shaped building, the first part of which appeared in 1761, stood on the open foreshore of West Quay close to the West Gate, opposite the arcaded portion of the town walls. It was built by a Mr Martin alongside some sea-baths which he had already erected following a sea-bathing visit in 1750 by George II's eldest son. Having anticipated Southampton's potentialities, Mr Martin's hopes were fully justified by the discovery of an iron and sulphur spring near by and the subsequent establishment of a pump-room with fountain and fine gardens reaching right down to the shores of the River Test from the area now so dismally occupied by Spa Road and Southern Newspapers' concrete block.

The 18th century scene was one of increasing numbers of fashionable visitors in need of entertainment which the Long Rooms were ready to provide. With their 'magnificent pier glasses' and 'music judiciously disposed in the centre', they catered for balls, card-playing and promenading sessions, the only real competitor being the Dolphin Inn (now the Dolphin Hotel) in the High Street.

But royal patronage was still important and, although George III visited Southampton in 1789 on his way to Weymouth, by 1795 the Prince Regent had made it plain that he preferred Brighton. By 1818, nobody would take a lease of the spring and the Long Rooms followed the Spa Gardens into decline. The coming of the railway and development of the docks in the 1840s ruled out any prospect of recovery and, at the end of the century, these old spa buildings were pulled down.

known but it may well have been a contributary factor in the spa's decline. For many years, visits by George III and his family—the last was in 1789—remained a major attraction but they were usually of only one day's duration and, once it became known that the Prince Regent preferred Brighton—in 1795 the prince was made a Burgher of Southampton but apparently to no avail—the crowds began drifting away.

For a time, a handful of noble ladies and gentlemen, mindful perhaps of the claim that the waters of Southampton, worked wonders with palsy, rheumatism and scurvy without injuring the stomach lining,—a middle-sized tumblerful was regarded as 'sufficient to open all manner of bodily restrictions'!—remained faithful to the old spa. Indeed they might have continued to support it if they had not found themselves increasingly subjected to attacks by highwaymen and even by disenchanted factions of the town's own poor population. The antics of Napoleon Bonaparte, busy amassing his invasion forces on the other side of the channel, presented yet another deterrent and, by the time the threat was removed with the victory at Trafalgar, even this faithful band had gone elsewhere.

So few were the visitors by 1818 that nobody was prepared to risk taking a lease of the spa buildings and they quickly became derelict. Since nobody showed any interest in the water either, it was piped away and the pipes were covered over.

Finally, in the 1840s, as the railway and the docks arrived and established themselves, both the gardens and the last surviving relics of Southampton's spa days disappeared beneath the paving stones of the new expanding port—an obliteration probably more complete than that of any other spa on which Britain's water-drinking monarch had so hopefully bestowed his patronage.

5
Regency and Early Victorian Spas

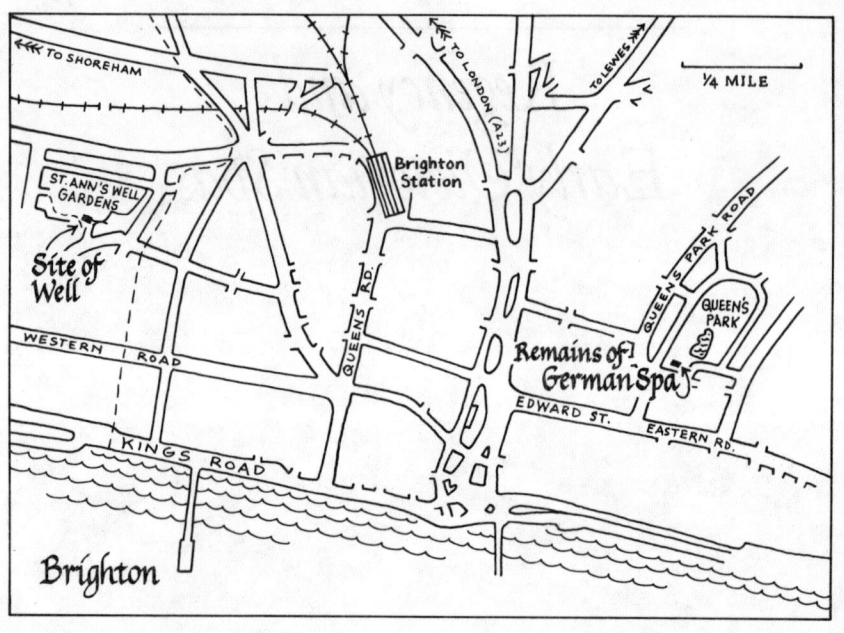

Brighton

THE PRINCE REGENT's liking for Brighton set a new trend. As the benefits of sea air, fine scenery, elevated locations and other external influences began to be generally recognised, several small towns and villages got the message and building sprees dominated by the new Regency style of architecture were soon under way, transforming them into resorts of distinction.

Among these new resorts was, of course, Brighton itself, already a town of some repute due to the activities of a local physician called Richard Russell. Dr Russell, who may well have heard of the sea-bathing-for-pleasure going on in the north at Scarborough, had introduced the idea of a combined sea-water-bathing and sea-water-drinking therapy and had even enrolled the dukes of Cumberland and Marlborough among his many devotees.

Sea-water-bathing and drinking were not, however, the only treatments prescribed by Dr Russell at Brighton. For some of his patients he also recommended the waters of a chalybeate spring known as St Ann's which had been found at Wick just outside the parish in what is now Hove. On Dr Russell's instructions, St Ann's Well was enclosed within a simple wooden building and a basin was installed for the convenience of his patients.

About 1800, these rather primitive arrangements at St Ann's were replaced by a small but properly furnished pump-room built in the classical style of the day with Ionic pillars. During the 1830s it was patronised by Queen Adelaide, wife of William IV, whenever she visited Brighton and it continued to flourish until about the middle of the century. After that, apart from a small number of consumptive patients, the clientèle began to disappear and the building became progressively more neglected.

For St Ann's, the end finally came in 1935 when the local council decided to demolish (many people said quite needlessly) and, today, all that remains of this once attractive little spa is the plateau on which the building once stood—there is a plaque to mark the spot—and a stream of rust-coloured water which still flows through the park.

By the end of his life, Dr Russell had made a great impression on the country's medical fraternity and, after his death in 1759, other doctors, notably a Dr Relhan, followed in his footsteps. A portrait of Brighton's pioneer of the sea-water 'cure', believed to have been commissioned by the proprietor of the Old Ship in recognition of the prosperity he had brought,

Brighton: *St Ann's Well, Hove, from an engraving.*

This low classical building, with its Ionic portico, set in a garden just outside the parish of Brighton, was erected about 1800. It replaced a simple wooden pump-room with basin, provided by Dr Richard Russell some fifty years earlier. Already a celebrated exponent of the so-called sea-water cure, Dr Russell added to his reputation by recommending the chalybeate waters and was soon followed by other 18th century physicians, including a Dr Relhan who proclaimed that 'bodies labouring under the consequences of irregular living and illicit pleasures are by the water greatly relieved'.

Even as late as 1869, the waters were being prescribed for consumptive patients, but by this time the spring had ceased to be fashionable and only the gardens, with the added attraction of a conservatory, available for concerts, built on to the pump-room, remained popular.

Regrettably, in 1935, Hove corporation destroyed the buildings of this once delightful little spa and the only visible reminder today is the rust-coloured water of a stream emerging from the paved area where the well once stood.

Brighton: *The Royal German Spa, from an engraving.*
The front portion of this small classical building with Ionic portico still survives at the south-west corner of Queen's Park. It was erected in 1825 for Dr Struve of Dresden after the German doctor had decided to give Brighton what nature had failed to provide. The result was an *artificial* spa where waters such as those found at Carlsbad, Marienbad, Spa and Seltzer were actually manufactured. Water for dissolving the various mineral salts was drawn from an artesian well and the products dispensed from a number of appropriately labelled and suitably embellished round-arched apertures in the wall behind the pump-room counter. Despite the comparatively spartan appointments, this unusual enterprise won the approval of George IV, and Brighton's fame as a fashionable health resort was further strengthened by the patronage of William IV and his family.

By 1886, the spa had ceased to function as such but it continued to operate as a manufactory of table waters. The business finally closed in 1960 and the premises lay derelict for some years before passing into the hands of Brighton corporation. In 1975, following efforts by conservationists to preserve the building, it was agreed to keep the fascia, which has now been restored.

hung in the assembly room at the inn until 1887, when it was presented to the town. At one time the portrait was attributed to Zoffany but it is now believed to have been painted by Benjamin Wilson. Today it hangs in the Brighton Art Gallery.

The next person to leave an indelible mark on the spa history of Brighton was Dr Struve of Dresden. About 1820, Struve had conceived the ingenious idea of introducing *artificial* spas and had translated the idea into reality by supplying first Dresden and then Leipzig with the mineral waters they lacked. On the grounds that 'no difference could be perceived between the natural and artificial productions' these imitative waters were chemically prepared to resemble those of the well-known Continental spas at Carlsbad, Seltzer and Spa itself. Spurred on by the success of his venture, Dr Struve decided to turn his attention to England.

With its existing fashionable clientèle and only one minor source of mineral water out at Wick, Brighton looked the ideal place for the establishment of a spa of manufactured waters, so in June 1825 Dr Struve opened the German Spa at the southern end of Brighton Park (now known as Queen's Park).

The building was in the classical style, with a low portico of six fluted Ionic columns and round-headed windows to the main room behind. It was small but attractive and it soon won royal patronage. George IV allowed the royal arms to be erected over the portico and, following visits by William IV and Queen Adelaide, it became known as the Royal German Spa.

Now at the height of its fashionable popularity, this unusual spa was visited in about 1840 by the redoubtable Dr Granville, who declared that it was his only reason for sending 'real patients' to Brighton, meaning presumably that he did not think much of the sea-water 'cure'.

Dr Granville's acceptance of the German Spa did not mean, however, that he wholly approved of it. On the contrary, he criticised the lack of space for walking and bemoaned the fact that, instead of bubbling up out of the ground, the various waters simply 'flowed from silver or glass spouts at the bidding of the smart lass in attendance'. Since it was common knowledge that the waters were made up behind the scenes by adding correct quantities of the appropriate mineral salts to ordinary water drawn up from an artesian well and by piping the product to suitably labelled taps in a row of round-arched apertures, no one could argue the point any more than they could argue with Dr Granville's final conclusions that 'the water-bibber drank in faith'!

In 1860, the German Spa was still being advertised but by 1886 it had ceased to function except as a manufactory of bottled table waters—a business which continued to operate in modern times under the name of Hoover Struve Ltd., with some of the founder's descendants among the directors. In 1960, however, the factory had to close and the premises quickly deteriorated.

Some years after the closure, the building was taken over by the council and became the subject of much controversy. In 1969 it was in danger of demolition, but eventually, following protests by various preservation societies, the decision was taken to retain and restore the colonnaded façade. So, today, this part of the old spa building still stands and, although now open to the elements, forms a striking and interesting memorial to the days when fashionable Brighton welcomed into its midst that strange contradiction—the artificial spa.

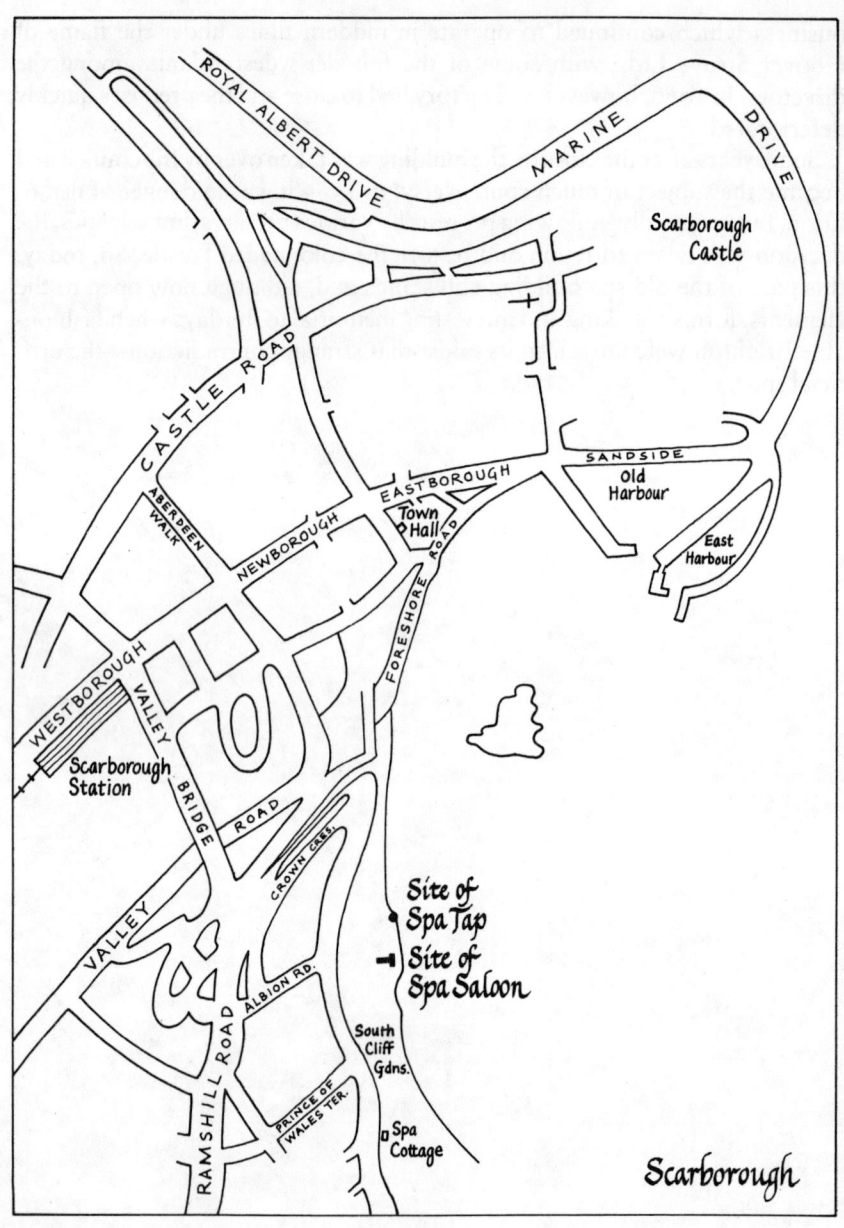

Scarborough

AS A REGENCY seaside spa resort, Scarborough on the north Yorkshire coast never achieved the reputation that Brighton did, but, in origin, it was much earlier. In fact the whole idea of the combined sea and mineral water 'cure' exploited by Dr Richard Russell at Brighton may well have originated here amid Scarborough's fine sandy bays, with their high dividing rock plateau.

The story of the Scarborough spa began as early as 1620 when an observant lady called Mrs Elizabeth Farrow discovered the first of two mineral springs on the foreshore at the foot of the cliffs. As the chalybeate water welled up, she noticed that it turned the pebbles brown and she decided to taste it. The taste was sufficiently unpleasant to convince her that she had found a medicinal spring.

Scarborough now awaited its first spa promoter and, in due course, he appeared in the person of Dr Robert Wittie of York. Dr Wittie confirmed Mrs Farrow's conclusions and added his own personal recommendation on the grounds that the chalybeate waters were 'capable of drying up superfluous humours'. He also pointed out the pleasure of sea-bathing from Scarborough's fine beaches and in 1669 even went so far as to express himself poetically:

'Let Epsom, Tunbridge, Barnet, Knaresborough be,
In what request they will, Scarborough for me.'

After a time, Dr Wittie's promotional activities were strengthened by those of another doctor called George Turnstall and, despite its northern situation, Scarborough was soon on the way to becoming a thriving spa. In 1690 it was even visited by Celia Fiennes, who described it as 'a spaw well on the beach at Scarborough covered by the sea at high tide, leaving a brackish saltiness which makes it purge pretty much'. Whether or not these observations were intended and accepted as a useful recommendation, by 1716 elegant society was here in strength. It was said that there were now 'earls, marquesses and dukes as thick as berries on hedges' and, according to Defoe, the company was not only from the north of England but from Scotland as well.

Nor was the 'spaw well' the only attraction. In 1720, some years before Dr Richard Russell introduced his sea-water 'cures' at Brighton, visitors to

Scarborough were already taking to the sea in a big way—though perhaps not always for therapeutic purposes. It had now become the custom for sea-bathing parties to gather on the beaches (normally in the shelter of tents or awnings) and for the men to row themselves out to sea before jumping naked into the water, while the women demurely submerged themselves clad in gowns—a custom which established sea-bathing at Scarborough probably earlier than anywhere else.

The provision and maintenance of facilities for mineral water-drinking, on the other hand, were proving more difficult. In 1737 the old Spaw House, which consisted of two rooms, was destroyed by a landslide and for a short time the waters were actually lost. However, the building was replaced in 1739 by the more pretentious pump-room later described by Smollett in *The Expedition of Humphry Clinker*, in which he wrote: 'At the other end of Scarborough are two public rooms for the use of the company who resort to this place in the summer to drink the waters and bathe in the sea: and the diversions are pretty much on the same footing here as at Bath.'

The diversions may have been on the same footing as those at Bath but the spa building certainly was not and, after a further landslide, yet another spa saloon had to be built.

This time there was a hall in the Italian-Renaissance style, a theatre, refreshment rooms and a promenade protected by a sea wall. The premises were opened in 1800 and soon gained in popularity, especially after 1827 when a bridge was constructed over the ravine that separated the spa from the town. By the following year, additional recreational interest became available to the visitors through the appearance of a museum in the shape of a Roman-Doric rotunda, but in 1839 disaster struck yet again and the spa saloon was blown out to sea in a gale.

By now Scarborough had become accustomed to making good the losses inflicted by the sea and, within a few months, a new castellated Gothic-style spa building appeared on the site. It had a saloon with windows looking out to sea, a promenade room and a small sunken court at the end of the terrace from which the waters of two springs—the original chalybeate known as the north spring and a saline known as the south spring—issued from lion-mouthed spouts.

So popular did the spa now become that by 1840 it was said that anyone who was not to be seen at Scarborough was out of fashion and of no account. Ambitious construction programmes for the building of expensive hotels and marine drives were already under way and in 1858 Sir Joseph Paxton was

Scarborough: *Scarborough New Spa, from an illustration of about 1840.*
Built on the sea wall in 1839, this castellated Gothic-style edifice replaced three earlier spa buildings, the first two having been destroyed by landslide, the third by storm. Waters from two springs—one saline, the other chalybeate—issued from lion-mouthed spouts in a small sunken court at the end of the great terrace. The room with the windows looking out to sea was the saloon, or promenade room, used especially in rainy weather. The bridge (built 1827) across the ravine linked the spa to the town but the cliffs had not yet been planted out with shrubs.

In 1858 the spa building was transformed and added to by Sir Joseph Paxton, whose work included a fine music-room and gardens. However, in 1876 a disastrous fire destroyed most of it and, when eventually the present-day buildings began to emerge, the waters were obtainable only from a tap. Today they are no longer available.

called in to remodel the spa building. The Paxton extensions included a fine music hall and garden.

Yet, extraordinary as it may seem, in 1876 the greater part of the building was destroyed by fire. It was as if the ancient elements of earth, air, fire and water were determined that the spa at Scarborough should not endure.

Eventually, to the designs of Thomas Verity, there emerged the Grand Hall, with seating for two thousand people and with a surrounding promenade, gallery and theatre. This was followed in 1913 by a new bandstand, colonnade and café and, later still, by the present-day roof garden and ballroom. But none of these later buildings had anything to do with water-drinking. The spring that Mrs Farrow had discovered way back in 1620 was now hidden away under a manhole and even a spa tap provided in Edwardian times had disappeared.

By transforming itself into a large seaside resort, Scarborough had lost its water-drinking image but it had won for itself an important place on the map—a very different fate from that of some other spas of greater architectural distinction, whose names and fame are now sadly forgotten.

Dorton

THE STORY of the spa at Dorton and its disappearance into the realms of the forgotten or the unknown is perhaps one of the saddest in spa history. The spring, which was chalybeate, stood in a wood belonging to a Jacobean mansion called Dorton House (now in use as a preparatory school). Although the meaning of the name Dorton ('the place of the waters') suggests that the spring had been known since Saxon times, no attempt was made to exploit it until early in the 19th century, when ambitious and extensive plans were devised to create spa buildings 'to the elegant designs of Mr Hakewill'.

Not all of the plans materialised, but many did, and the result was a splendid pump-room in the Regency classical style with an entrance on the eastern side consisting of a semi-circular portico supported by nine Corinthian pillars. Perhaps the most impressive feature of all was the tower, which was built to resemble the Winds of Athens. There were also fancy glades, a natural woodland stream and well laid-out gardens with flower-bordered footpaths.

For a time this elegant little Buckinghamshire spa flourished and cures were claimed, but its shortcomings soon became apparent. On the one hand, it had come too late to be blessed by Beau Nash and, on the other, it could not provide the facilities now being offered by its nearby rival, rapidly growing Leamington. As a parliamentary witness pointed out many years later, at Dorton there were no houses or hotels locally where people could reside, and few were impressed by advertisements declaring that accommodation and amusements could be had at the nearby hilltop village of Brill. Brill itself could only offer one or two inns anyway.

In 1835 efforts were made to revive the spa at Dorton and an advertisement was placed in the *Promenade Musical*. But little came of it and a grand fête held the following year for the benefit of Buckinghamshire Infirmary fared no better.

After these failures, the pump-room fell rapidly and ignominiously into ruins and, today, all that remains of the classical buildings is a decorative stalactite built into the water-garden of Dorton House and two broken pillars lying abandoned at the side of a marshy track through the dense undergrowth of the wood—a track that was once a flower-bordered drive designed to carry people of rank and fashion on their way to drink the 'health-giving' waters.

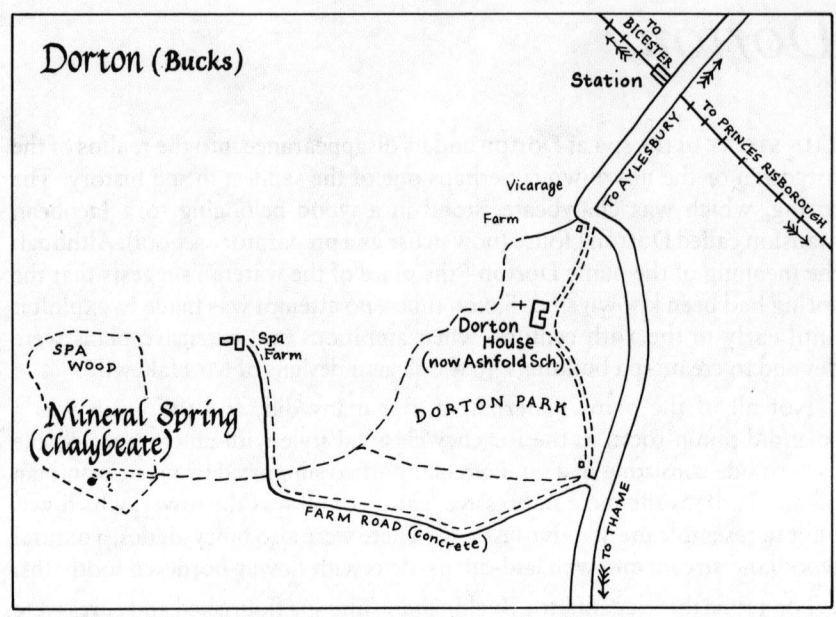

Dorton: *The Pump Room, from an early 19th century engraving.*
This is the eastern entrance to the pump-room of a once elegant and impressive Buckinghamshire spa, whose chalybeate water was said to have effected many cures. Set under a semi-circular portico supported by nine Corinthian columns, the early 19th century building was a replica of the Winds of Athens. It formed a small part of an ambitious and extensive plan which never came to fruition. Among the causes of failure was the absence of houses and hotels in the vicinity where visitors could be accommodated and, perhaps even more important, was the patronage bestowed by the Princess Victoria in 1836 on rival Leamington.

After this date, despite strenuous efforts, Dorton Spa found itself unable to compete and decay was rapid. Nevertheless it seems extraordinary that today, on an undeveloped woodland site, virtually nothing remains but the spring itself.

Dorton: *The chalybeate spring, as seen today.*

Lying hidden away in Spa Wood, this small brick enclosure now provides the only visible sign of the spring which once attracted people of rank and fashion to the small Buckinghamshire village of Dorton. Today, even the clues to the spring's whereabouts are no more than two broken-down columns at the side of a marshy overgrown track leading through the wood. Gone are the flower-bordered footpaths and fairy glades beside the stream, where visitors to the splendid Grecian-style pump-room could stroll and relax. The only known surviving relic of that bygone era is a decorative stalactite built into a water-garden in the grounds of neighbouring Dorton House (now a preparatory school). All other vestiges of Dorton's early 19th century spa have been swallowed up by the wood.

Perhaps the sorriest spectacle of all is the rudimentary circular brick enclosure with its wooden door, built at a later date and just big enough to protect the chalybeate spring. Surrounded by bramble and nettle, this final relic of Dorton's Regency spa still stands hidden away in the wood.

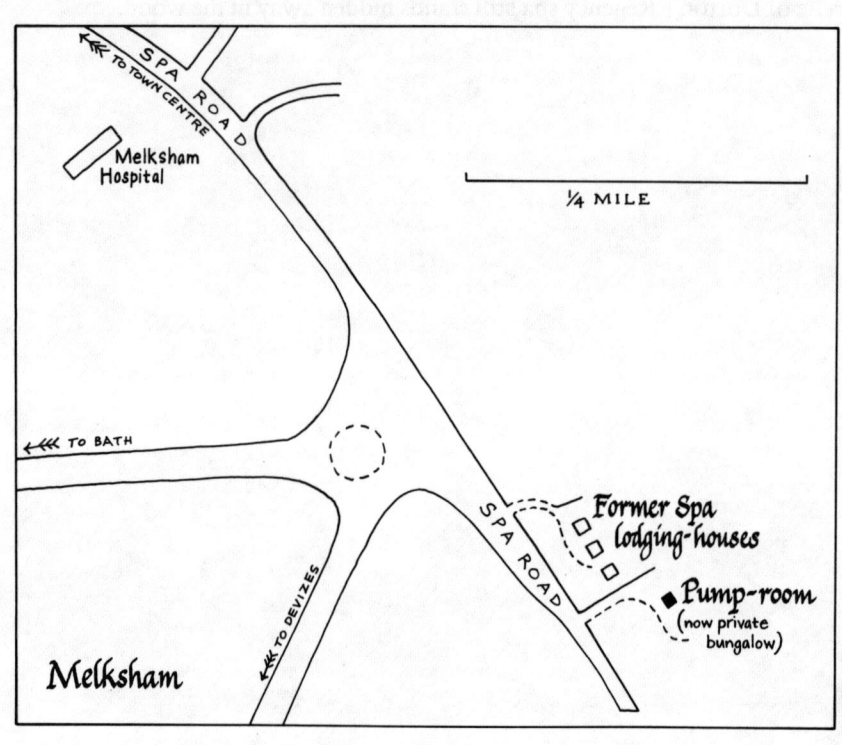

Melksham

ANOTHER MINOR spa of the Regency period with a brief life span stood on the south-eastern outskirts of the now semi-industrialised country town of Melksham in Wiltshire.

About 1815, saline and chalybeate springs were discovered here in a field beside the road to Devizes—a road still known as Spa Road but now reduced to a cul-de-sac separated off from the new highway. The pump-room was a small stone single-storeyed building which cannot be compared with the fine pump-room at Dorton, but spa visitors were well catered for in an adjacent row of handsome square pedimented villas, each four storeys high, which still survive. These one-time lodging-houses are now divided up into smaller residential units for modern living, but, as a landmark, they still bear witness to an age when almost any newly discovered mineral spring was considered worthy of some architectural effort.

In spite of Melksham's efforts, the little country spa was too close to Bath to have much chance of success and, in due course, the wells had to be filled in. The pump-room has now been converted into a residential bungalow and is painted over to match the small group of modern bungalows surrounding it. But the waters of this small Wiltshire spa still have to be reckoned with when, from time to time, they bubble up through the grass on to the piece of land facing the old pump-room.

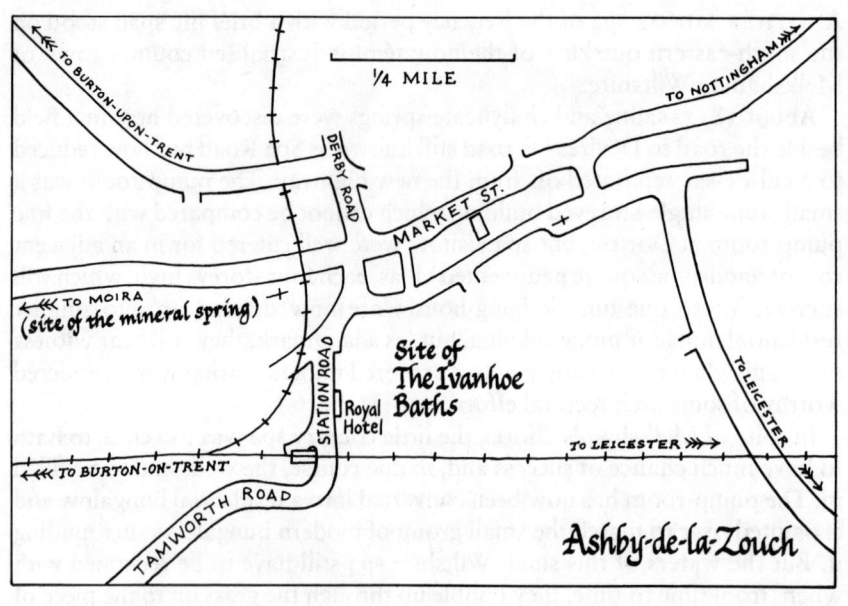

Ashby-de-la-Zouch

ANOTHER INTERESTING example of a spa of this period which failed to stay the course was the one at Ashby-de-la-Zouch, a small Leicestershire town south of Derby, where a sulphur spring was discovered at the Moira coal mine.

Moira, where the water was struck at 700 feet below the surface, was three miles distant from the town, but this did not deter the townspeople. Anything which was good for skin diseases, including scrofula, was worth fetching and, in the early days, before arrangements were made to transport the water in carts or tanks to boats on the canal and thence by truck to the town, there were regular pilgrimages out to the mine.

Twenty years later, in 1819, the commercially minded first Marquess of Hastings decided to set up a proper spa at Ashby-de-la-Zouch by pumping the water to a reservoir in the town and providing a bath-house, hotel, theatre and several elegant terraces for the accommodation of visitors.

Designed by the town architect, Robert Chaplin, the bath-house was completed by 1822 and named the Ivanhoe Baths in honour of Sir Walter Scott, whose novel *Ivanhoe*, based on Ashby Castle, had just been published. It was a handsome single-storey structure built in local stone with a frontage of more than two hundred feet and a central pump-room approached by a temple-like portico of Doric columns. Originally it was surmounted by a dome and linked by colonnades of six baths at each end, with extensive spa gardens at the back. Adjacent to it stood the Hastings Hotel (later renamed the Royal Hotel), built in similar style by the same architect.

Once the spa had been set up, the Ashby waters were recommended not only as a cure for skin complaints but also for 'full-neck, nerve-ache, green sickness and ringworm', as well as for the more common complaints such as gout. Yet even a list as impressive as this failed to achieve a fashionable status for the spa and, as seaside holidays grew in popularity, it slowly petered out.

Today, the Doric-pillared hotel still stands beside the Tamworth road, near the station, but the Ivanhoe Baths have gone. In the early 1970s and to the regret of many of the townspeople, this neglected but distinctive building was pulled down.

152 Ashby-de-la-Zouch

Ashby-de-la-Zouch: *The Ivanhoe Baths, from an old photograph.*
This handsome single-storey building, with its central temple-like portico of Doric columns, was designed by a local architect, Robert Chaplin, and completed in 1822. Originally surmounted by a dome, the building had long colonnades at the two ends, each leading to six baths. Behind were extensive spa gardens. The promoter of this small but unusual Leicestershire spa was the first Marquess of Hastings who, in 1819, arranged to bring the waters from a sulphur spring discovered some twenty years earlier in the nearby coal mining village of Moira. Named after Sir Walter Scott's newly published *Ivanhoe*, the buildings stood behind and adjacent to the Hastings Hotel (still surviving in Station Road as the Royal Hotel), built in similar style to accommodate the visitors.

When seaside holidays came into vogue, the Ashby spa petered out and the buildings gradually fell into a state of decay. Finally, in the early 1970s, they were demolished.

Admaston, Sutton and Saltwell

Some fifty miles or so the the west of Ashby, the small spas of Admaston, Sutton (near Ludlow) and Saltwell were all marked on Dr Granville's spa map of 1841, though only Admaston achieved any sort of fame.

Situated about two miles north-west of Wellington in Shropshire, Admaston had the advantage, like Ashby, of possessing a handsome hotel built in the Doric style, though its waters, known since Georgian times, were of the chalybeate type and remained in local demand well into the present century. In fact the Admaston waters were bottled and supplied to a chemist in Much Wenlock right up to the 1920s. Today, the hotel is in private residential use but the spring is still there, bubbling up into a large basin in the backyard and leaving its characteristic rust-coloured deposit on the recently re-pointed brickwork. Efforts are now being made to preserve it.

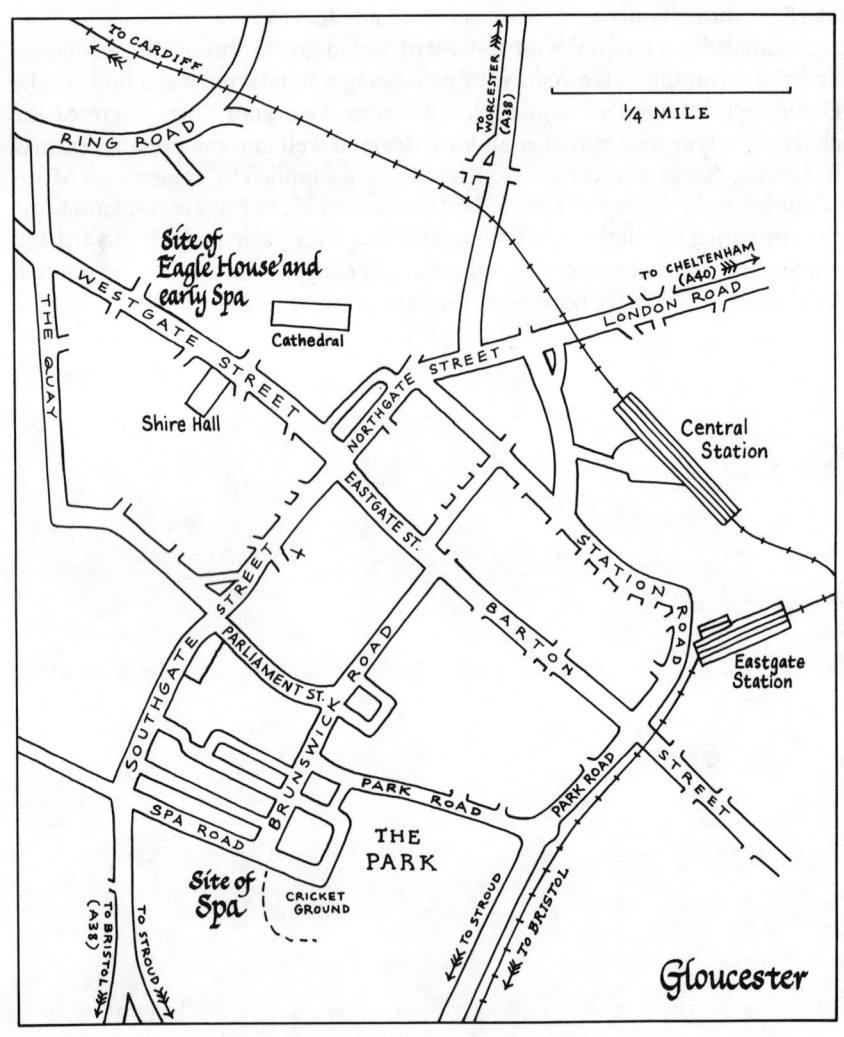

Gloucester and Tewkesbury

ANOTHER WEST country spa of early 19th century origin but one with the advantages of an important geographical situation was that of Gloucester some sixty miles to the south.

Standing on the southern outskirts of the town, Gloucester's small and simple but attractively sited pump-room represented a second attempt to join in the spa boom. The first had been made a quarter of a century earlier, in 1788, when an elegant dwelling called Eagle House changed hands. (Later known as the Duke of Norfolk's House because the duke sometimes stayed there, this old house stood in Westgate Street near the cathedral and was demolished only a few years ago.)

Unlike his predecessor, who had ignored the spring in the garden, the new owner of Eagle House became intrigued by the unusual properties of its water. He learnt that when used for washing, it spoilt the clothes; when employed in tea or beer brewing, it ruined the product; and even when mixed with brandy, the result was far from satisfactory. There was, however, a brighter side to the picture for it was reported that people suffering from a variety of complaints actually benefited from drinking the water.

In a spa age, few could ignore the implications of such reports and the new owner, having arrived at the inevitable conclusion, lost no time in having pipes laid for the conveyance of the water to a small room convenient for visitors.

The initial response to advertisements proclaiming the virtues of Gloucester's first discovered mineral water—it was specially recommended for 'dejection of the spirits, languor, scrofula and all nervous disorders'—was very encouraging and, after a garden long room had been constructed, it was estimated that '400 persons assembled of a day'.

This early success, however, was short-lived. People soon realised that the cloudy unpleasant looking water with the offensive taste and smell compared unfavourably with that which could be had not far away at neighbouring Cheltenham, where recently the water had actually been drunk by the King. So, within a year, Gloucester's first attempt to establish a spa had failed and no further attempt was made until 1814, when another sulphur spring was discovered at what was then known as Rignum Stile grounds.

Gloucester

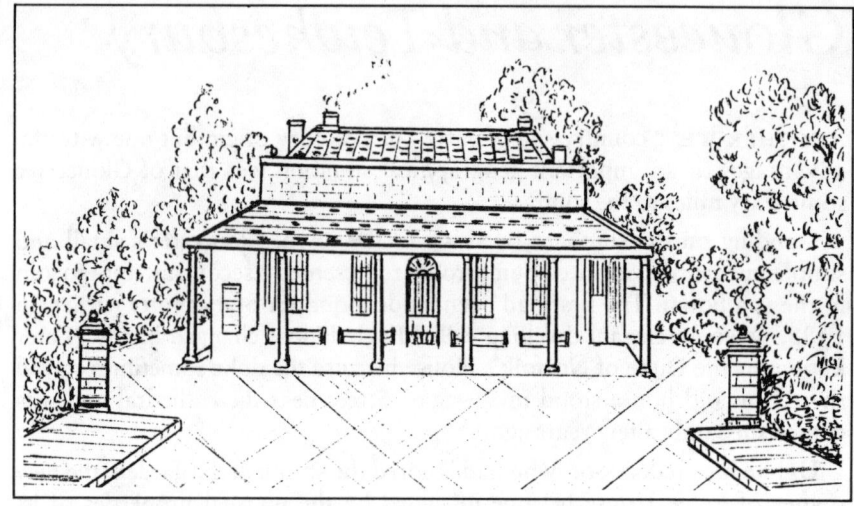

Gloucester: *The Pump Room, from an old drawing.*

This plain but pleasant little building, which included hot, cold and vapour baths, was opened on 1 May 1815, following the discovery the previous year of a sulphur spring in a nearby field. There were now three known springs in the immediate neighbourhood, one of them chalybeate and one strongly saline, and all were given their own special spout in the pump-room. The promoter and owner of the land was Sir James Jelf, a local banker and mayor of Gloucester, whose bank failed just as the spa scheme was completed. Spirited efforts to rescue it finally resulted in its becoming the property of a stock company.

Approached by a widened road (now Brunswick Road) and laid out with shrubberies and wide gravelled paths arranged in serpentine fashion, the spa was patronised by W. E. Gladstone, who used to join his father here. But by 1862, when a tap was placed outside for free use by the public, it was obvious that it could not compete with Cheltenham and with the increasing industrialisation of the town. Little was spent on maintaining the pump-room and about 1900 the original baths were removed and not replaced. With local limelight captured by the activities of the adjacent county cricket club, the spa building succumbed to dry rot and, in 1960, to the dismay of the conservationists, it was demolished.

Apart from the gardens, the only reminder of it today is one of the large stone acorn vases which, accompanied by some stone lions, once adorned the parapet. Partly obscured by shrubbery foliage, they now stand beside a small plaque which marks the spot.

Gloucester 157

Tewkesbury: *Spa building at Newtown, from an old drawing.*

Early in the 19th century, this small pump-room stood over a saline spring about a mile to the east of Tewkesbury on what is now an industrial housing estate. The first of the so-called Walton group to be discovered, the spring appears to have attracted notice and local attention in about 1746, when it was provided with a pump. Forty years later, after the appearance of a pamphlet by the Worcester physician James Johnstone, an attempt was made to popularise the neglected well and others of its kind by encouraging the principal inhabitants of the area to provide suitable accommodation for visitors. New buildings, including Walton House (originally called Walton Spaw and now a children's home), were erected or planned, accompanied by glowing descriptions of the location—'on the finest plain in the world, at the conflux of the river Avon and the Severn'.

But, despite all such inducements, it soon became clear that the would-be spa was too near to Cheltenham, with its almost identical waters, to succeed. The Cheltenham waters also possessed traces of iodine and bromine and were equally well endowed with salts with the same 'salutary qualities'! The result was that the little pump-room near Tewkesbury quickly fell into neglect, while another pump-room erected almost opposite Walton House never came into use at all.

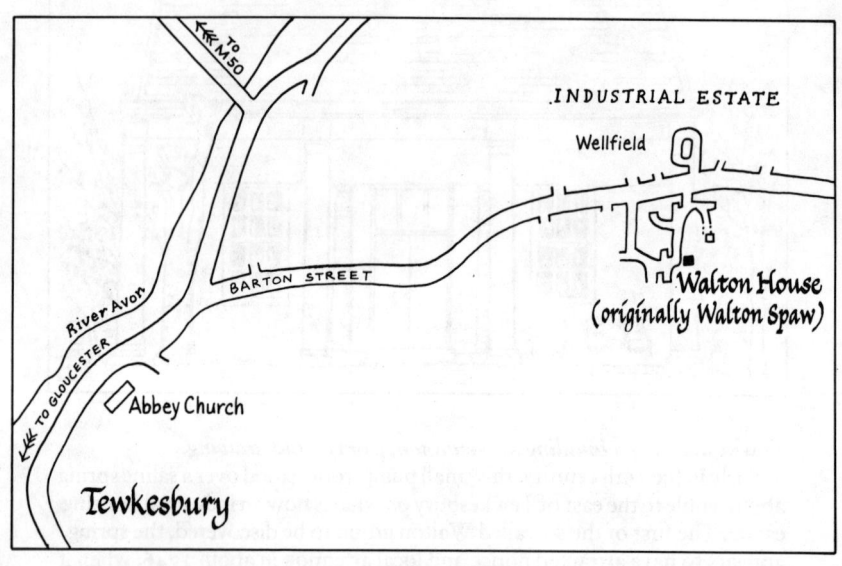

Rignum Stile grounds adjoined what is now the county cricket ground and, close to it, were two other springs already known to local residents. Since one of these springs was strongly saline and the other was chalybeate, the new discovery spelt opportunity—opportunity which did not escape the notice of the owner of the land, a local banker and mayor of the town called Sir James Jelf, who promptly decided that the time had come to take action.

The land-owner's first move was to set up a temporary building with a proper pump, sink new wells and make a 'handsome approach' by widening Parker's Row (now called Brunswick Road). After this he embarked on the foundation of a new and permanent pump-room, forty feet long by twenty feet wide, equipped with hot and cold vapour baths at the rear.

Among the subscribers to the project were Lord Somerset, the Duke of Norfolk and many local worthies, and the opening ceremony took place on 1 May 1815. According to the reports, it was an occasion when several thousand people drank the water and 'all testified to the beauty and gaiety of the spectacle'.

The running of the Gloucester spa was placed under the direction of a Mr A. Clark and all appeared to be well until a few weeks later, when the news suddenly broke that Jelf's bank had crashed. Jelf himself claimed that he had been stabbed in the back by his creditors but this did nothing to restore confidence and soon it was realised that the newly created spa had very little financial backing and that nobody was willing to rally to its support. Within weeks, the new pump-room, together with walks and grounds, was up for sale.

Buyers for Gloucester's fallen spa were not easy to find and eventually the whole of the area was sold for only £7,500 to a Mr Philpotts, before being taken over in 1816 by a newly formed stock company with twenty-six shareholders.

In an urgent attempt to make the spa viable, the company laid out additional walks, engaged a band to play at least once a week and put forward ambitious plans for developing the whole district with hotels and houses. By 1829, at least some of the proposed developments had materialised in the shape of Sherborne House (later to become the Spa Hotel) and Ribston Hall, and, during the years up to 1850, the little spa just about managed to hold its own. But already one of its chief medical promoters had left town and the new breed of business men, busily occupied in turning expanding Gloucester into an industrial city, had too many other matters on their minds to take much interest.

So, once again, the future of the spa was in jeopardy and in 1860 the proprietors offered it to the City of Gloucester with a view to the whole area being laid out as a public park. After much wrangling among all concerned, the Board of Public Health finally acquired the property and in 1862 a tap was placed outside the pump-room for the benefit of the public.

Yet none of these measures could save the spa from decline and in 1900 the original baths were taken out and not replaced. Nothing came of a suggestion in 1905 that the spa should be revived on a municipal basis and the last mention of it in *Kelly's Dictionary* was in 1931.

Meanwhile the pleasant little pump-room, with its distinctive parapet adorned by carved stone lions and acorn vases, continued to succumb to the ravages of woodworm and other forms of decay until finally, in 1960, the council decided to demolish it, leaving only a solitary acorn vase and a small plaque as a reminder of Gloucester's early 19th century bid to become a spa town.

Ten miles to the north of Gloucester and even more overshadowed by what neighbouring Cheltenham could offer was a small spa at Newtown, about a mile east of Tewkesbury. Known as the Walton Spa, this was a somewhat insignificant affair centred around a saline spring discovered in 1746 but largely ignored until forty years later when a physician of the Worcester General Infimary published a pamphlet suggesting that its waters, which contained traces of iodine and bromine, were of value in diseases of the lymphatic glands. Shortly afterwards, a house called Walton Spa (later renamed Walton House and now in use as a county children's home) was built. Most of the visitors who came seeking health cures at the primitive little pump-room erected over the well stayed here.

Despite claims that the water increased strength, spirits and appetite and that Tewkesbury was situated on the finest plain in the world, this tiny spa was doomed to failure almost from the start and today the only reminders of it are the names given to one or two streets in the new housing estate which covers the area where it once stood.

Leamington

FAR MORE fortunate and lasting was the spa established in the tiny Warwickshire village of Leamington Priors on its beautiful finely sheltered site beside the River Leam. It is now believed that the rock strata underlying Leamington was once covered by a primeval sea and that the saline spring waters, confined for countless centuries, finally forced their way through fissures to the surface. That being so, Leamington possessed, in addition to its many other advantages, a spring water that could never dry up.

In 1784, the little village began discovering, or rediscovering, its seven saline springs and it built baths around some of them. However, it was not until about 1810 that it recognised its full potentiality and set about transforming itself into the handsome Regency spa town that was to become the resort of almost every ailing aristocrat in the country.

The existence of the original well, which once stood on a site near the parish church (a much smaller church than it is today), had been recorded as early as 1586 by a man called Camden, but it was left to Benjamin Satchwell, the local postmaster, shoemaker and poet, to rediscover and proclaim its virtues nearly two hundred years later.

A small stone well-house erected over this well in 1803 by the fourth Earl of Aylesford was replaced in 1815 by a more solid structure provided by his successor, the fifth earl. With its old stone inscription to Benjamin Satchwell and its clanging chained metal cup, this single-storey rectangular building became known as the Aylesford Free Well and remained one of Leamington's central landmarks until it was demolished (allegedly because of vandalism) in 1961. Sadly, all that remains of it today is a memorial stone on the pavement to mark the spot.

In 1784, Satchwell also discovered a spring in what was to become known as Bath Street and here, two years later, his friend the land-owner opened Abbott's Saline Baths, later known as Smith's Baths. These premises were demolished in 1867 and a store (Francis's) now stands on the site.

In 1790, after a third spring had turned up in the High Street, thirteen baths originally known as Wise's Baths and later as Curtis's Baths were built and became sufficiently well established to survive for sixty years. But by the time a fourth and a fifth spring were discovered and still more baths were built, it was less easy for such low-capital concerns to prosper, especially as a magnifi-

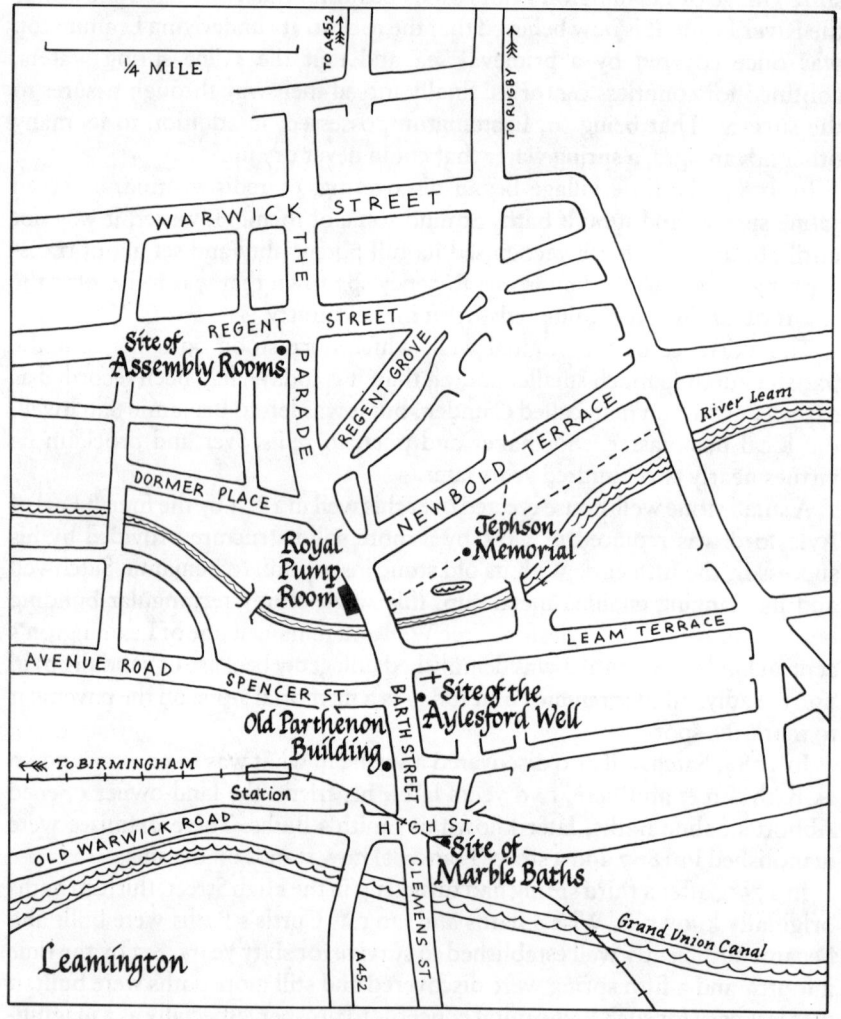

cent pump-room was now about to appear on the site of the latest discovery—the sixth spring.

Leamington's sixth spring was discovered in 1810 on land belonging to a Mr Greatheed and, by 1813, a small syndicate had been formed to erect a fine two-storeyed building in the classical style. With its long Doric colonnade, the new building cost about £30,000 and was opened in 1814.

One of the smaller spa establishments to face the daunting competition of the new pump-room was Smart's Marble Baths, also known as the Imperial Fount, built in 1819. These premises stood on the site of Leamington's seventh spring, at the corner of the High Street and what is now Clemens Street. At that time, Clemens Street was a continuation of the very fashionable Bath Street, and the new Marble Baths were probably as good as they claimed to be—four in number, all made of marble and exquisitely fitted. But, as Bath Street declined, so did Smart's Marble Baths and by 1850 the building had been turned into a carriage works. Today nothing is left except part of an old wall, still just discernible beneath the railway bridge.

To cater for the amusement needs of a growing clientèle, the Upper Assembly Rooms had been built in 1812. Standing where a department store now stands at the corner of Regent Street and The Parade, the building contained card, billiards and reading rooms as well as a ballroom and, until faced with serious competition from the Lower Assembly Rooms, opened in Bath Street in 1821, was well patronised. Through various stages of decline, it survived for fifty years.

So splendid, both externally and internally, were the new and competing Lower Assembly Rooms in Bath Street and so well did they cater for the ebullient leisure activities of the visitors that the building became known as the Parthenon. Not surprisingly perhaps, its owner Robert Elliston is believed to have lost a fortune on it and, when its Parthenon days came inevitably to an end, it was used for a multitude of purposes before finally relinquishing its lower half for use as shop premises. Most of the neighbouring balconies, porticos and pediments, amid which it once stood, have now vanished and the building itself can hardly be described as reminiscent of the glories of ancient Greece but the upper storey is still worth looking at.

Fortunately, the architectural decline of Bath Street was not echoed elsewhere and much of Leamington soon began to bear witness to the presence and influence of the aristocratic visitors who came not only to find cures for their gout but also to find accommodation suitable for continuing the social life to which they were accustomed. Even today, the willingness with which

Leamington Spa: *The Aylesford Well, from an old print.*

This building was erected in 1813 by the 5th Earl of Aylesford over a saline spring discovered in 1784 by a postmaster, shoemaker and poet called Benjamin Satchwell. The earl refused to grant a building lease of the site on the grounds that the water should not be locked up from the poor. A memorial stone now marks the position of the well-house, demolished in 1961.

Leamington Spa: *Smart's Marble Baths, also known as the Imperial Fount, from an early drawing.*

This building was erected in 1819 at the High Street corner of Clemens Street, at that time an extension of the town's most fashionable thoroughfare, Bath Street. It stood on the site of the seventh spring to be discovered in Leamington. As the owner was pleased to emphasise, the waters on offer were similar to those at Harrogate and the four baths, all exquisitely fitted, were made of marble. In addition, there was a library and an arcade, at the end of which stood three urns, each containing samples of the different waters.

Yet, despite all the luxury, the Marble Baths went into decline about 1850 and eventually the building was turned into a carriage works. Part of its old wall is still visible beneath the railway bridge but, like so much at this end of the town, now due for a facelift, it is hardly reminiscent of Leamington's palmy days.

Leamington Spa: *Upper Assembly Rooms, from a drawing of 1826.*
Designed to cater for the growing number of spa visitors, the Upper Assembly Rooms were opened in 1812 in Regent Street (at the corner with The Parade) on a site now occupied by a department store. The building possessed a ballroom, card- and billiard-rooms and also a reading-room. Although it found itself, in 1821, in competition with the new and splendid Lower Assembly Rooms known as the Parthenon in Bath Street on the southern side of the town, it survived for nearly fifty years. In the early days it provided traditional amusements for what was predominantly an aristocratic clientèle, while later on, after the beaux and rakes had departed, it became a popular venue for concerts and public meetings.

the little village on the Leam responded to these demands is still reflected in some of the fine streets and the names which were given to them.

With so much to recommend it, Leamington was ready for the visit of the Princess Victoria in 1836—a visit so successful that it persuaded the young queen two years later to allow the town to call itself Royal Leamington Spa, an advantage which helped it to weather some of the more difficult years ahead.

Once the beaux and rakes had left and the Victorian way of life had asserted itself, Royal Leamington Spa forgot its frivolous past and became quite a sober place. Most of the new water-drinkers, many of whom were beginning to arrive by train—the first station, Milverton, was opened in 1844—were of a different breed from their predecessors. Their maladies were generally unconnected with dissipation and their entertainment requirements were relatively modest. They liked the atmosphere of Leamington's spacious crescents and terraces and enjoyed listening to music in the Pump Room and in the beautifully laid out gardens. They wanted comfortable apartments but otherwise demanded so little that no more ambitious building programmes, other than those concerned with providing houses for the growing residential population, were needed.

There was, however, one major development in 1846. This was the acquisition by the town of the Newbold Meadows out of which was created the famous Jephson Gardens, with its impressive lodge gates immediately opposite the Pump Room and Parade. Until this time there had been very little provision for outdoor relaxation either for the visitors or for the local inhabitants and the new pleasure ground was an immediate and lasting success. Dr Jephson, after whom the gardens were named, was one of Leamington's most popular physicians. He had arrived in the town in 1819 and won general approbation because of his devotion to his patients and the contribution he made to the spa. A memorial statue of this celebrated figure, sitting within a Corinthian temple, is still a familiar feature of the gardens.

Of course, once its heady Regency days were over, Leamington experienced the ups and downs common to other spas and, by 1860, the popularity of the waters had waned. At this time the Pump Room had a private owner who announced his intention of closing it down and selling it for redevelopment purposes—a disaster only narrowly averted by the townspeople, who formed a new company to carry out the extensive reconstruction work required.

In 1882, after passing through that curious phase in spa history known as the hydropathic age, the Pump Room experienced another crisis which again

168 Leamington

Leamington Spa: *The Royal Pump Rooms, as seen today.*

This impressive building was started by a small syndicate in 1814 and was narrowly saved from demise in 1860. In 1882 a newly formed public company took over the building and carried out extensive reconstruction work. In the 1960s urgent structural repairs and renovation of the frontage were undertaken by Leamington corporation which, in conjunction with the Regional Hospital Board, continues to finance the spa and to offer a wide range of treatment. The saline water is still available to the public for drinking.

entailed a struggle for survival. But perhaps the biggest struggle of all was in the 1960s when, after two world wars and declining fortunes, the problems of rehabilitation looked almost unsurmountable.

This time, in order to save it, the famous Regency building had to be given almost a complete face-lift, but finally this was achieved and it emerged triumphant into the modern world with a new status—that of a medical centre able to provide patients with a wide range of spa treatments under the aegis of the National Health Service, the Regional Hospital Board, and the long established British Spas Federation.

Today the Royal Pump Room also provides the public with free access to the famous saline water. The scene around the basin in the fountain room next to the restaurant can hardly be compared with the corresponding scene in Regency times, but it is interesting to reflect that the taste and composition of the water is probably just the same.

6
Early Hydropathic Spas

EARLY IN the 19th century, Vincenz Priessnitz of Graefenburg in Silesia (later Jesenik in Czechoslovakia) startled the world with his hydropathic 'cures' and it was not long before the message reached Britain.
By the time it did, most of the Regency spas were fading and, with one or two exceptions such as Leamington, which was subsequently able to join the hydropathic league because of its abundant supply of water, there was little chance of revival. As the spas closed down, people with health problems and sufficient money and leisure to spend on 'cures' found themselves facing a growing vacuum and were only too ready to welcome the arrival of a new therapy.

The new therapy was quite different from that provided by the old spas in that it depended on special methods of applying water to the body rather than on simple bathing and drinking. The procedures were often elaborate, by no means always pleasant, and usually very costly. Also very costly were the imposing, specially designed buildings in which the patient was expected to reside while undergoing treatment, so, in the early years at least, hydrotherapy was not for the poor.

In general, this new kind of spa, catering for an exclusive section of the population, mainly the upper middle classes, was dominated by a new kind of man. Often he was a member of the medical profession who saw himself in the vanguard of 'progress' and was undeterred by the strictures and opposition of more orthodox colleagues. One of his notable characteristics was the highly autocratic attitude which he extended to patients and colleagues alike and which was frequently reflected in the establishments over which he presided. Unlike the proprietors of the old spas, he did not depend on royal or aristocratic patronage but, in order to succeed, he still needed, and usually possessed, certain entrepreneurial gifts.

One of the people who brought the message of hydrotherapy to England was Dr James Wilson, an impulsive but talented and impressive looking man with curly silk whiskers who believed in the enforcement of stern regimes and strict rules. Having spent a year as Priessnitz's patient and pupil, Wilson arrived in Malvern in 1842, found a partner to help him in his new venture and promptly wound up his orthodox London practice.

James Wilson's chosen partner was Dr James Gully, a short, stout, urbane man with a staid manner, who was already a popular and well-known practitioner in Malvern. Although quite different in character and appearance from Wilson, James Gully recognised the opportunities, accepted the challenge and joined in the campaign to provide Britain's unsuspecting health-seekers with a new way of life, with Malvern as the pioneering centre.

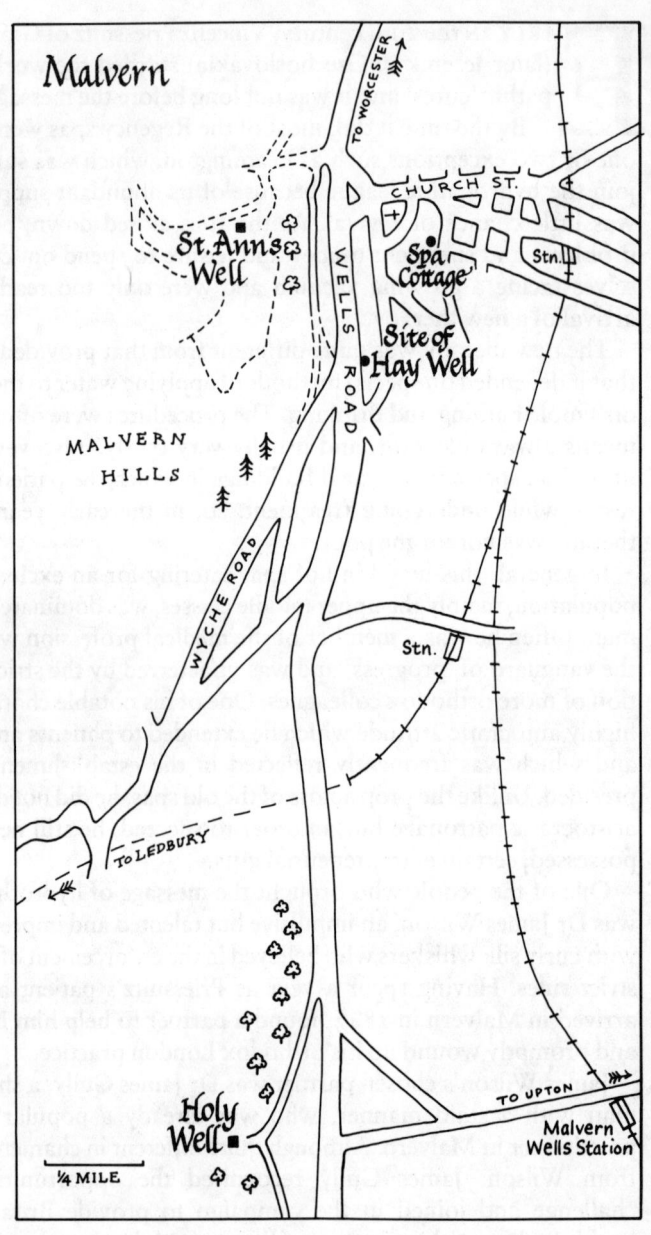

Malvern

MALVERN HAD everything the two physicians needed. Not only was it beautifully situated on the Worcestershire-Herefordshire border with plenty of hills to provide the patients with exercise, but the seven villages strung out along the road encircling the hills were blessed with numerous springs. Admittedly they were *pure* water springs but two of them already had important spa reputations.

The fact that these springs were already well known by the time the hydropathic age dawned was due mainly to the activities of a very astute 18th century spa promoter called Dr John Wall. Building on the ancient traditions associated with Malvern's holy wells, John Wall had overcome the 18th century preoccupation with *mineral* springs and had managed to persuade people that water with little or no mineral content could still possess healing qualities. As he pointed out, the Malvern water had been used for therapeutic purposes since at least the 16th century.

One historian thinks the first spring in the area to acquire a healing reputation was one at Little Malvern. Variously called Ditchford's, Mary's or Nancy's Well, it was presumably named after the women who used to draw the water and carry it on horseback to Worcester. But neither this nor the ancient Hay Well (built over in 1886 by the Baptist church at Great Malvern) were destined to achieve any lasting importance. It was the Holy Well at Malvern Wells and St Ann's at Great Malvern that were to acquire that distinction.

Together with the surrounding lands, the Holy Well had been granted by Elizabeth I in 1558 to a certain John Hornyold and, from 1622 onwards, the water was not only drunk but it was also bottled—as was the water from the Eye Well a few feet higher up the hillside.

'A thousand bottles there,
Were filled weekly,
And many costrils rare,
For stomachs sickly;
Some of them into Kent,
Some were to London sent,
Others to Berwick went,
  O praise the Lord.'

So went the Malvern Song, but it was not until John Wall decided to analyse the waters and to publish his findings in 1745 that either Malvern Wells or Great Malvern (nearly three miles to the north) became known as spas.

The son of a well-to-do Worcester tradesman, John Wall had been born in Powick in 1708 and educated at the local grammar school and Oxford, from where he went on to become one of the original physicians of Worcester Infirmary. It was when he was thirty-five that he decided, with the help of a colleague, to analyse the waters of the Holy Well and those of two wells at Great Malvern—St Ann's up on the hillside and the chalybeate spring that existed on the lower slopes of the village below the Priory church. After that, things were never quite the same again.

Referring to the Holy Well and St Ann's, Dr John Wall concluded that 'the efficacy of this water seems chiefly to arise from its great purity' and, after mentioning many miraculous cures, he added the recommendation that, to be successful, it needed to be drunk on the spot and to be taken regularly over a long period.

It was not a world shaking statement and, as can be seen from a verse written by one of the wags, some people were less impressed than others:

'The Malvern water, says Dr John Wall,
Is famed for containing just nothing at all.'

Nevertheless, just as the idea of *artificial* mineral water coupled with frivolity had caught on at Brighton, so the idea of *pure* water coupled with austerity caught on at Malvern.

One of John Wall's more laudable aims in promoting the Malvern water was to raise funds to improve the primitive and overcrowded conditions at the Holy Well and in 1757 he built a bath-house on the site. The number of visitors began to increase and in 1761 Well House (today a boys' preparatory school about half way up Holy Well Road), was opened as a lodging-house and was enlarged eight years later by the addition of a long room.

After John Wall's retirement to Bath in 1774, there was a temporary decline in popularity but eventually the Well House became so well patronised that Rock House, adjacent to the well, was built in 1812 (in 1770 style) to provide extra accommodation in the form of private apartments. This was followed by several other early 19th century houses near by and also by Essington's Hotel lower down the hill.

When the first visitors' guide book appeared in 1796, the centre of the water-cure was still the Holy Well, but by 1820 it was shifting to St Ann's

Malvern: *The Holy Well, from an old print (probably 1869 or 1875).*

Situated high up on the wooded slope of the hills above Malvern Wells, this mid-19th century building houses an ancient spring of pure water renowned for centuries for its miraculous and curative properties. Water from the spring and from the Eye Well (behind the building) was bottled on the site as early as 1622.

The first bath-house, known as Wells House (now a school), had been established about 1757 lower down Holy Well Road by Dr John Wall, the local physician responsible for turning the village of Malvern into a spa town. Also preceding the Holy Well building was Rock House (just off the picture on the left), built in 1812 (in 1770 Gothic style), to provide extra lodging accommodation. At these, as at later and more ambitious establishments in neighbouring Great Malvern, the spa regime remained extremely austere both before and throughout the hydropathic era introduced in 1840 by doctors Wilson and Gully.

With the ending of the boom around 1880, the Holy Well buildings began to deteriorate and for many years were used as a commercial bottling plant for 'Malvern Seltzer' water before being abandoned in the 1960s. In 1970 they were saved from demolition by the Civic Trust and associated organisations, who made it possible for them to be privately renovated on condition that the well-house was re-opened to the public. By 1970 this had been achieved and now, once again, water from the Holy Well can be drunk on the site.

Malvern: *St Ann's Well, as it is today.*
The older part of the well-house (on right of picture) dates back to 1813. It was built for the use of visitors who used to either climb the steep zigzag path with its 99 steps (now only 95) or ride up the hillside on a donkey, as the Princess Victoria regularly did in 1831, to drink at the famous spring 800 feet above Great Malvern.

Discovered in 1086 by a monk named Aldwyn, the spring became well known in the mid-18th century when it was named after St Ann, the patron saint of springs. This was the time when Dr John Wall was promoting Malvern as a spa town, proclaiming that the absence of mineral salts, with their disagreeable taste and associated effects, was in fact an advantage. If his patients were too ill to travel, the versatile physician arranged for the water to be sent to them, thereby starting the bottling industry which, by 1850, had grown into a flourishing export business. Despite the witticisms about the water being 'famous for containing nothing at all', the spa shared in the Victorian boom and St Ann's acquired the extension now used as shop and café.

Inside the original cottage, spring water still issues from a dolphin's spout into a marble basin presented in 1892 by the lady of the manor, who also commissioned the verse inscribed above it.

Well for the simple reason that more accommodation and amenities were becoming available at Great Malvern.

Perched high up on the wooded hillside above Malvern Priory church, St Ann's Well had been mentioned as long ago as 1282 by the Bishop of Worcester but, until the 19th century, it had been little used except by the local population. Now, in 1813, a small well-house was built over it in the cottage ornée style (the style briefly popular in late Regency and early Victorian times as an expression of the fanciful wish to return to the simple virtues of country living). Here the invalid could rest, obtain glassfuls of the water or put the affected part under the spout, assisted by a woman attendant who was described as 'neat and clean and with great civility'. Not until about 1860, after the hydropathic boom had brought increasing numbers of visitors, was a small bath and pump-room extension added, thereby completing the well-known venue that still persuades many a visitor to undertake the steep hillside climb today.

In the early days, the familiar zig-zag path up the hillside started in the gardens of the Crown Hotel next to Mount Pleasant on Belle Vue Terrace and was used by donkeys as well as by humans. A donkey ascent was the method of travel chosen by the twelve-year-old Princess Victoria when she came with her mother, the Duchess of Kent, on a visit in 1831, and also by the Dowager Queen Adelaide in 1843.

At the time Doctors Wilson and Gully started their hydropathic practice, Malvern possessed a number of stately homes such as Holly Mount, where the Princess Victoria and her mother had stayed, a few lodging-houses and some half-timbered cottages hidden away among the woods on the hillside. But it was still a village of only two streets and, as the two doctors realised, some changes were needed.

At the beginning of their reign, it was James Wilson who took the lead. He knew that before there could be any expansion, the confidence of the local population for the new cure had to be won and, to this end, he began by accepting a most unpromising patient. The local carrier was an elderly gout-ridden drunkard but Dr Wilson managed to cure him within a matter of ten days and, when two more spectacular cures followed, he was off to a good start.

Wilson's next move was to obtain the lease of the Crown Hotel, which he converted into a hydropathic centre called Graefenburg House—a venture which attracted more and more people wanting to try out the new remedies. Yet despite the demands on his time and energies, within two years Wilson had written two books on the water-cure and had also laid the plans for a major hydropathic centre to be named after his master, Priessnitz.

Priessnitz House was built in 1845 at a cost of £18,000. This is the building which, with its hugh extensions of later date, eventually became the County Hotel and is now a students' hostel known as Park View belonging to the Royal Radar Establishment. Originally it was a house renowned for the splendour of its appointments and the rigours of its treatments.

Dr Gully was also busy. He had two rival establishments built—Tudor House for the men and Holyrood House for the ladies, with a linking bridge between them which soon became known as the Bridge of Sighs. But, sighs or no sighs, it was the urbane Dr Gully with the ready and charming smile who attracted most of the *famous* visitors to Malvern. Among the distinguished names were those of Gladstone, Macaulay, Dickens, Carlyle, Tennyson, Florence Nightingale and even the celebrated scientist Charles Darwin, who arrived with wife, children and servants after reading Gully's *The Water Cure in Chronic Disease*, published in 1846. With all this acclaim, Dr Gully's income at the height of his fame was of the order of £10,000 a year.

In addition to the major hydropathic establishments, several smaller ones sprang up, including the new Well House which T. C. Hornyold built over the Holy Well after he recovered ownership of the land in 1843. This is the building which, after long years of use as a table water manufactory, was finally rescued from oblivion during the 1970s and, with the help of the Civic Trust, privately restored and re-opened to the public in 1976.

Another small but notable establishment was Spa Villa, built beside the chalybeate spring in Priory Road. This little spring had been noticed as early as 1540 but had remained obscure until Dr John Wall analysed its waters two hundred years later. Although it was the only spring mentioned in Malvern's first guide for visitors, within twenty years it had fallen into neglect and nothing more was done to exploit it until Wilson and Gully arrived on the scene. Then a cottage ornée (later extended to produce the agreeable house it is today) was built, followed by Spa Villa (now called Oakdale) on the adjoining site.

Spa Villa was equipped with some of the latest hydropathic devices including, as structural evidence in the kitchen area still shows, a device for pouring cold water through a three-inch pipe from a height of twenty feet on to the hapless patient waiting naked below. But its fame did not last because in 1846 a quarrel with his partner induced James Wilson to buy up the little

Malvern: *Spa Villa and the Chalybeate Pump Room, from an early drawing.*
These buildings still stand in Priory Road, just below Swan Pool and within sight of the Abbey Church. Now known as Spa Cottage, the little ornamental pump-room was erected in the early 1840s, with a gabled portion added later. The spring which supplied it, originally called the Dog Well, had been noticed as early as 1540 but it remained obscure until Dr John Wall analysed its water in 1745. In 1796 it was the only spring in Great Malvern to get a mention in the first guide book for visitors but its popularity never became really established and by 1822 it was neglected and almost forgotten.

Nevertheless, in 1825, a General Buchanan laid out an approach and designed walks around it—a move which no doubt led to the building of the cottage pump-room, followed by Spa Villa where patients could stay and receive the somewhat drastic hydropathic treatments meted out by the pioneer doctors, Wilson and Gully. Then, in 1846, after a quarrel with his colleague, Wilson bought the little spa and kept it locked to exclude Gully's patients. To make matters worse, the death of a major land-owner later that year precipitated the sale of the surrounding estate for development and by 1860 the spa premises were deserted.

Today Spa Villa, re-named Oakdale, is privately occupied. So too is the one-time pump-room where the old iron-impregnated spring now lies buried beneath the concrete of the back-yard.

spa and to keep it locked in order to prevent Gully's patients from using it. After that, it never recovered.

The quarrel between the two pioneer doctors arose as a result of one of Gully's publications in which he subtly criticised his partner and gained more popularity for himself. These clashes of personality inevitably caused divisions but they did not affect the way in which the hydropathic establishments were run and any patient coming to Malvern could still expect to be subjected to the same stern routine and discipline.

A typical day at Priessnitz House began at 5 a.m., when the patient was called from his bed, stripped by a bath attendant, wrapped tightly in a cold wet sheet and further encased in blankets. After being immobilised in this manner for about an hour, the patient was released and required to sit in a small portable bath so that a pitcher of coldish water could be poured over him. He was then allowed to dress and to meet his fellows before being despatched with a Graefenburg water flask in his pocket to one of the hillside springs. During the season, a German band from Wiesbaden would be waiting at St Ann's Well to cheer or encourage him whilst he refilled his flask, as directed, for the return journey.

Back at Priessnitz House, the patient was at last allowed to break his fast with bread and butter, treacle and more water, after which he took orders for the rest of the day from the doctor in attendance. Normally this meant more baths, sometimes of an ingenious nature, followed by more exercise, with no excuses allowed, before dinner at 3 o'clock. Dinner was the main meal of the day and invariably consisted of boiled mutton and fish, but, here again, encouragement was on hand, this time in the persons of Dr and Mrs Wilson who nearly always sat, one at each end, of the long table.

After the meal, the patient was allowed a measure of free time, though he was usually advised to use it wisely by taking more walks in the hills before returning for the social event of the day—a general assembly in which he could meet his fellows whilst the attendants prepared more baths. Finally, there was supper at 8 o'clock consisting of bread and butter, milk and biscuits and still more water. So to bed!

In spite of this demanding day, many of the male patients who were suffering from overwork, over-eating and the stresses and strains of town and city life appeared to benefit and, complain though they did, they stayed on. As for the hydrotherapists, they had to face persistent opposition from the rest of the medical profession as well as the caricatures of the cartoonists but they, too, stayed the course—and flourished.

By 1851 other doctors, including the bearded temperance and social reformer Dr Ralph Grindrod, had joined the happy throng and expansion was still the order of the day. In 1862 the Imperial Hotel (now the Girls' College) was built to help accommodate more out-patients and other visitors, thereby creating a need for more entertainment which, in its turn, led to the building of the Assembly Rooms in Grange Road in 1884. (Still looking like a miniature Crystal Palace, this is the building that now houses the tourist office: it was enlarged in 1923 and bought by the council in 1927 for part conversion into a theatre and ballroom.)

Despite the attractions of the Assembly Rooms, by the mid-1880s, Malvern's once fabulous spa was obviously well past its peak and, when Priessnitz House was reconstructed in 1890–99, it was soon seen as the last remaining stronghold of 'the cure'. An outbreak of typhoid fever in 1905 fuelled the growing mood of scepticism and, by 1908, there was only one water-doctor left in Malvern.

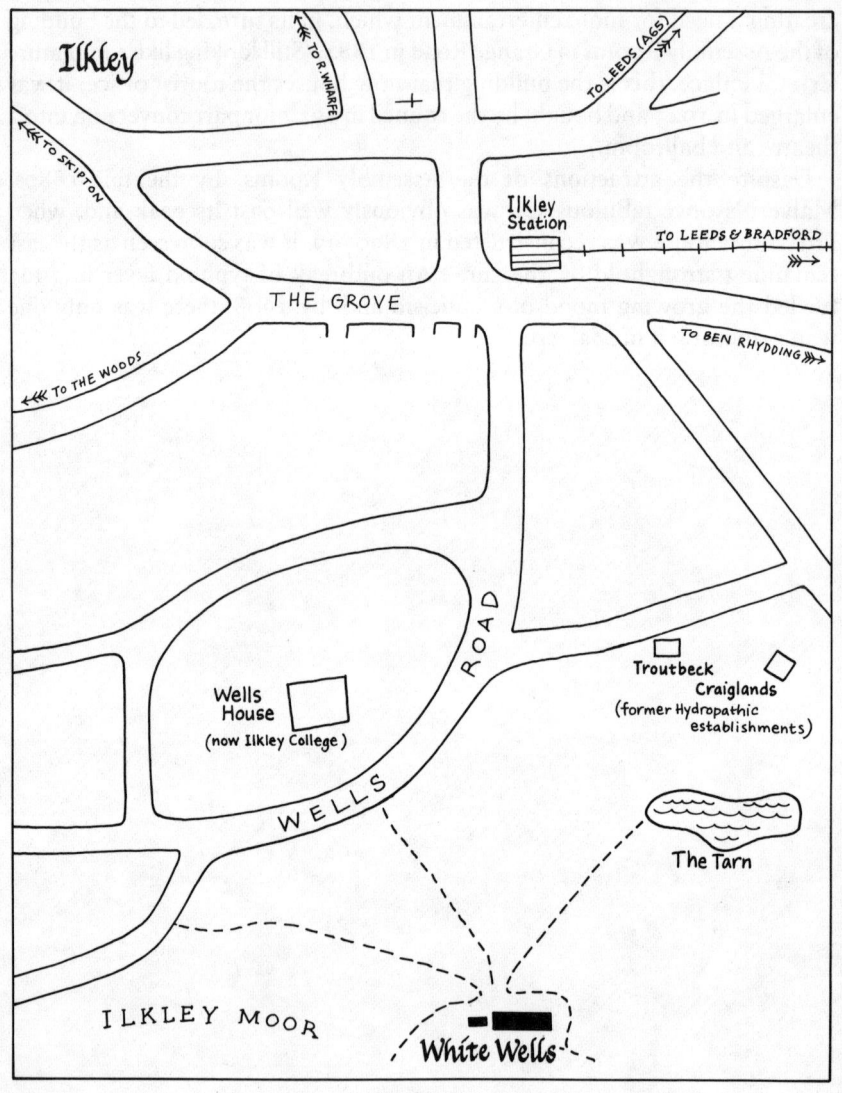

Ilkley

NEWS OF the benefits of hydrotherapy was not, of course, confined to Malvern. Its spread was rapid and far reaching and, probably as early as 1843, a group of cottage buildings standing on a knoll about half way up the moorside overlooking the little Yorkshire town of Ilkley suddenly acquired a new importance.

Known today as White Wells, these moorside cottages contained three baths, one of them a deep circular plunge bath hollowed out of the rock and constructed as early as 1760 by a disciple of the 'cold water cure' called Squire Middleton. It other words, Ilkley was a pioneer of the first order and, understandably, it now considered it had a special right to join in the 19th century water-cure boom.

There was even a suggestion that Ilkley's water-cure history went further back still, to the time of the Romans. Roman legionnaires had certainly been stationed in the area and there was some evidence to suggest that they had channelled some of the moorland streams towards the White Wells site for their own use. The Roman addiction to bathing was well known and the manner in which the water still trickles endlessly down into the 18th century plunge bath appears to support the theory.

But whether or not the Roman invaders had played any part in the story, Squire Middleton had built his two baths and had later added a small 'charity' bath housed in an adjacent cottage (now converted into toilets). The baths were run by a certain William Butler and his wife and were patronised by the gentry of Ilkley, who used to come as far as they could in their carriages and then walk the rest of the way in order to bathe in the 'mellifluent, diaphanous luminous waters'.

Alluring as this description may sound, the Ilkley water was, and still is, icy cold and devoid of any medicinal or buoyant salts. According to a 1977 analysis, it is simply a clear, colourless spring water of moderate hardness, organically pure and free from metallic contamination and coliform organisms.

But, as at Malvern, such minor deficiencies did not deter Victorian enthusiasm for the water-cure and, while the developers hurriedly set about planning their grand hydros on more accessible plots of land at the edge of the moor, this well-known Ilkley landmark continued to attract visitors. As the donkey shelter in the passage under the building still bears witness, special provision was made for those who could not cope with the steep rough paths.

Thus, White Wells helped to transform the little Yorkshire town of cottage industries into a thriving spa centre and it was not until water-cures in general began to lose their appeal that the buildings were adapted for use as a moorland café and eventually allowed to decay.

By 1974, after more than half a century of neglect, White Wells was in a state of collapse and was only saved from oblivion by the interest of a 75-year-old ex-business man from Bradford, Eric Busby. As a last gesture before the whole of Ilkley was incorporated into the Bradford metropolitan area, Ilkley council allowed Mr Busby to rent White Wells and gave a grant to help renovate the building. With the help of the grant, one of the baths was boarded over to provide extra floor space for a small caretaker's cottage and the other was restored—a happy outcome which means that not only has the famous plunge bath been rescued from oblivion but it can now be viewed by the public on certain days of the week during the summer.

Among the 19th century hydropathic establishments that sprang up in and around Ilkley were Craiglands, Troutbeck, Rockwood House and Wells House. All were successful in their day and both Craiglands and Troutbeck still survive as hotels, while the Italian Palazzo-style Wells House, built as a sanatorium in 1855 on a terrace overlooking the town, is now in use as a college of further education (Ilkley College).

The most notable of the hydropathic establishments, however, was that of Ben Rhydding, founded in 1844 by Hamer Stansfield, a former mayor of Leeds. Like Dr James Wilson of Malvern, Stansfield received his inspiration and ideas from a visit to the Graefenburg spa in Silesia and, almost immediately on his return, set about building a massive castle-like establishment with windswept Ilkley moor on its doorstep. Built at a cost of £30,000, it became variously known as the 'Northern Graefenburg' and the 'Yorkshire Malvern'.

As at Malvern, the Ben Rhydding regime involved early rising, diet, exercise and an assortment of 'kill-or-cure' treatments such as wrapping the patient in wet sheets and subjecting him to alarming procedures with cold douches. Although discipline was of the strictest and patients had to conform, there was at least one concession to comfort at Ben Rhydding in the form of luxurious and sophisticated refinements. These included private bathrooms, a bowling alley and a 'fresh air bath' consisting of a closed room into which moorland air was pumped.

Ilkley: *White Wells, as seen today.*
This well-known group of white-washed cottages high up on the moorside overlooking the small Yorkshire town of Ilkley houses a deep circular plunge bath hollowed out of the rock in about 1760 by a certain Squire Middleton. An early believer in the cold water 'cure', Middleton built two adjacent baths, both fed by pure spring water and patronised by the neighbouring gentry. A separate cottage housed a third 'charity' bath for the use of poor people.

With the approach of the Victorian hydropathic age, White Wells became generally popular and donkeys were used to bring visitors up the steep paths to bathe in the icy cold spring water. (The passage underneath the house where the donkeys used to wait is still there.) Although by this time the developers had taken their cue and were busy building their giant hydros on more accessible slopes around the edge of the moor, White Wells retained its local clientèle. Early in the 20th century, however, it fell into a state of neglect and eventually the building was used as a tea-room, then boarded up and left empty and derelict.

Rescue finally came in 1974 when an ex-businessman from Bradford took it over from Ilkley council and, with the help of a grant, began the task of restoration. The famous plunge bath is now fully restored, while the second is boarded over to provide caretaker's accommodation.

Ilkley: *Ben Rhydding Hydropathic Establishment, from an old print.*

Situated near Otley in Wharfedale on the edge of Yorkshire's Ilkley moor, this romantic looking building with castle-like turrets and battlements dated back to 1844. It was founded by a former mayor of Leeds called Hamer Stansfield on his return from a visit to the Silesian spa, Graefenburg.

Ben Rhydding hydro was luxuriously equipped with private bathrooms, a bowling alley and a 'fresh air bath' or closed room into which moorland air was pumped. Yet the regime, which included treatments such as 'wet-sheeting' and 'cold douching', was regarded as one of the strictest and most austere in the country. An early patient who helped to establish its fame was John Smedley, a wealthy Derbyshire textile manufacturer who emerged from his spartan experiences declaring himself a new man!

Between the wars the hydro became a golf hotel and during the Second World War it was taken over by the Wool Secretariat. Finally, with the war over, this notable Victorian building, once a flourishing spa centre, fell to the demolition squads.

Whatever its merits, this curious mixture of luxury and Spartan austerity attracted ever increasing numbers of patients, in fact so many that, when the railway came in 1865, a special station had to be built for their use. Both the station and the village that grew up around it adopted the same Scottish sounding name as the hydro—a name which in fact had evolved from a bean field that had once stood near the site and was marked on an old map of the district as Bean Ridding.

Ben Rhydding reached the height of its fame following a visit by the Derbyshire textile manufacturer, John Smedley. In spite of his newly acquired fortune, Smedley had returned from the Grand Tour of Europe physically and mentally exhausted and, as a last resort, had finally acceded to his wife's persuasions to try a course of hydrotherapy—a decision which was to have a far reaching effect both on the future of Ben Rhydding and on the popularity of the 'water-cure' throughout the country.

When John Smedley finally left Ben Rhydding, he declared himself not only recovered from his mental depression and other ailments but also spiritually converted and determined to spread the message. Such unsolicited publicity was the dream of every spa proprietor and it was more than enough to carry the giant Yorkshire hydro successfully through the Victorian age and well into the Edwardian. Only when declining faith and the new social pressures that followed the First World War began to take their toll generally did this famous establishment, perhaps the strictest of its kind, finally renounce its mission and convert itself into a golf hotel.

During the Second World War, the building underwent a spell of duty as the Wool Secretariat but, by now, the end was in sight and, when peace came and the size and cost of upkeep had to be reckoned with demolition squads moved in and the last curtain came down on the great pile.

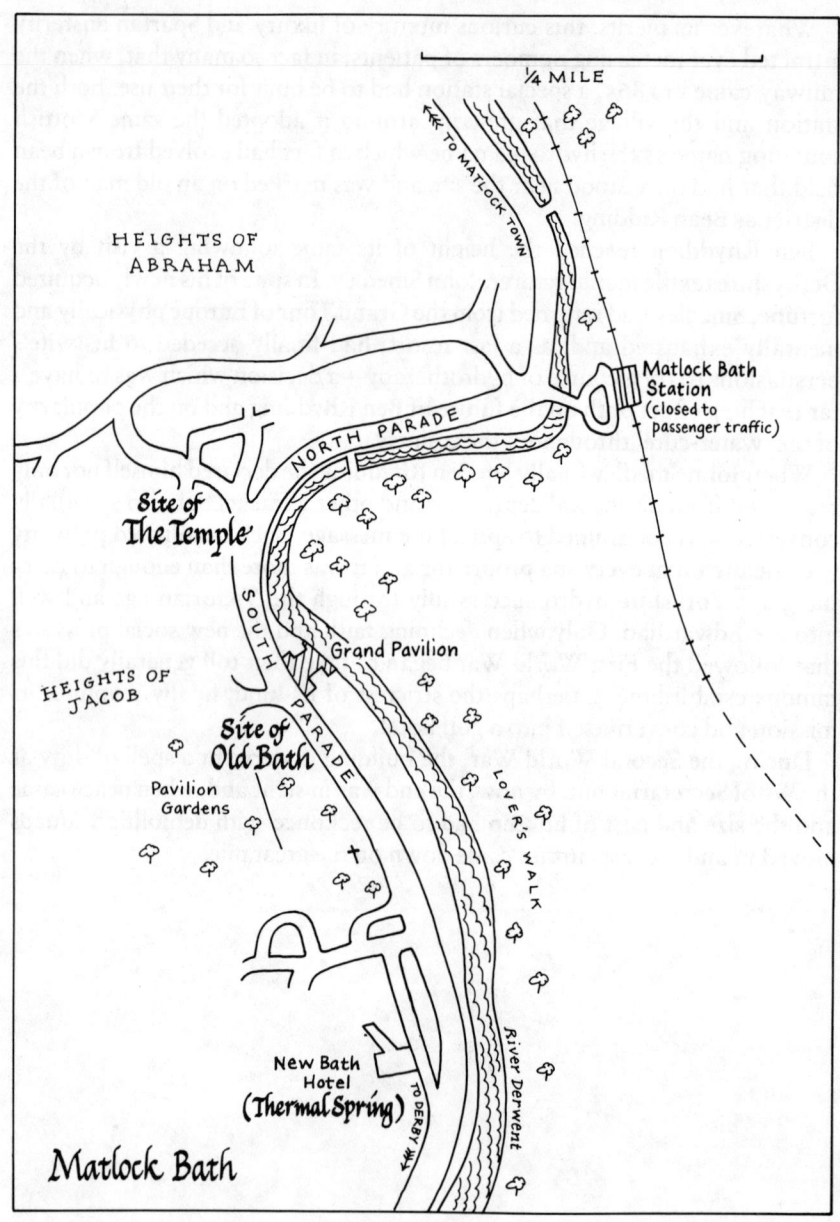

Matlock

WHEREAS YORKSHIRE'S famous hydro disappeared completely, the imitative establishment built by John Smedley on the steep 'bank' near the centre of Matlock still survives. The building is now in use as Derbyshire county's administrative headquarters but its sheer size and solidity still bears witness to the faith and aspirations with which the wealthy industrialist emerged from the wet sheets and cold douches of Ben Rhydding declaring himself 'a new man'.

John Smedley's choice of his home town as the place in which to repay his debt by advancing the cause of the 'water-cure' was both understandable and fortunate. The area was extremely scenic and, due to adjoining Matlock Bath's long and interesting history as a spa village, there were already certain facilities available for visitors.

According to some evidence, the thermal springs of Matlock Bath had been known to the lead-miners of the area as far back as the time of the Roman occupation. Certainly by the 17th century, the warm weakly saline waters were being used by the lord of the manor and his family for bathing and eventually a small bath was dug.

It was the building of this small bath in about 1698 that aroused the interest and attention of two neighbouring and enterprising freeholders, who promptly built a similar bath for public use a short distance away. The management of the new bath was entrusted to a third freeholder called George Wragg, who succeeded in obtaining a long lease on the land at a small rent and, after making a few extensions, began turning in high profits.

Not surprisingly this success did not escape the notice of the trustees of the manor and demands for a revised lease and a higher rent soon had to be met. But by this time the water, which was quite palatable, had achieved a reputation as a cure for colic, consumption, gout, rheumatism and cutaneous complaints, and, in about 1727, George Wragg was able to sell out to the Nottingham firm of Smith and Pennell for £1000.

In 1734 Smith and Pennell added an assembly room and private rooms for visitors, thereby creating a small complex of buildings which became the nucleus of the spa. Later known as the Old Bath, these buildings stood on the hillside opposite the present-day Grand Pavilion and, in due course, were joined by the Old Bath Hotel.

The next step taken by the Nottingham developers was the improvement of the track from Matlock Bridge—an undertaking achieved by blasting a new road (the line of the present A6) through the rocks. This was followed by the erection of an elegant annexe to the Old Bath called The Temple. The Temple stood a little higher up the hill but it was linked by a promenade and proved a tremendous success. According to the records, the little spa with the splendid scenery was now attracting 'persons of quality'!

In terms of noble patronage as well as in terms of architectural merit, Matlock Bath could not of course compete with its larger and more accessible neighbour, Buxton, but at least it won a reputation as a 'select spa, better suited to a contemplative than a dissipated temper of mind'—a very good recommendation indeed in Victorian times.

The main expansion occurred between the late 1790s and the 1830s, by which time Matlock Bath had plenty of well laid out gardens and romantic walks. By now there were also several new hotels up on the hillside, while down on the main road was Hodgkinson's, a once noted posting-house which continues to exist today as a public house. Added to all this came the discovery of a new spring only a short distance away to the south—a discovery that led to the opening of the New Bath Hotel, also still surviving, with its large internal plunge and swimming bath supplied by the spring.

There were some big changes, of course, when the railway arrived in 1849. By opening up the spa to the newly prosperous middle and upper working classes from Manchester and other nearby industrial towns, the railway brought about a general exodus of the gentry. But this did not worry the new visitors and soon the little resort became known as the 'Switzerland of England'. One of the main needs now was for a station worthy of the name.

The station was duly designed, probably by Sir Joseph Paxton, gardener's boy turned architect and railway entrepreneur, who appears to have decided that even the humblest day tripper should be given the opportunity to alight at Matlock Bath in style. The result was the Swiss-style building in chequered yellow brick which still stands today, though the line is now closed to passenger traffic.

So this was the scene to which John Smedley returned from his experiences at Ben Rhydding. Now converted both to hydrotherapy and to religion, the Derbyshire mill-owner's original and first intention was to save his own textile workers from the evils of their unhealthy lives. However, as he soon discovered, this was not as easy a task as he had imagined. Most of the Lea Mills workers preferred their own way of life and resisted both the 'water-

Matlock 193

Matlock Bath: *The Pavilion and Royal Hotel, from an old photograph.*
Situated on an elevated plateau on the steep, richly wooded hillside above the deep ravine carved out by the River Derwent, the old Pavilion was opened in 1844. It was linked by descending paths and terraces to the Royal Hotel opened six years earlier, in 1878, as a hydropathic establishment on the site of the Old Bath complex. Hotel and pavilion both owed their existence to the weakly saline thermal springs which welled up from deep sources in the hillside rocks at a constant temperature of 68°F—springs recognised for their healing qualities since the late 17th century.

By late Victorian days, the case for incorporating the bath-house of 1734 and the antiquated Old Bath Hotel into a 'magnificent Gothic structure', complete with swimming and hydropathic baths, had looked reasonable enough. Yet neither the new hotel nor the plate-glass-fronted pavilion, with its central concert hall, assembly room and promenade side annexes, were ever a financial success. The hotel ran into trouble even before it opened and, following the closure of the Pavilion in 1925, ended up as a semi-derelict building which was burnt down in the 1930s. By this time, the post-war slump had shattered any hope of recovery.

Matlock Bath: *The Grand Pavilion, as it is today.*

Recently restored and standing prominently beside the narrow main road (A6) with the River Derwent behind, the Grand Pavilion was built in 1910–11 by a German company for the old Matlock Bath, Cromford and Scarthin council. Originally known as the Kursaal, it came too late to have much impact on the declining spa and was used simply as the council's administrative headquarters. After 1956, when the Derbyshire County Council established itself in the premises of John Smedley's old hydro at Matlock Bank a few miles away, the Pavilion was put to a variety of uses and became increasingly neglected. By the 1970s it was threatened with demolition but rescue finally came and restoration was completed in 1978.

Part of it is now in use as a tourist office and the rest as an entertainments complex. The adjacent fishpond is fed by water from one of the thermal springs up on the hillside and is able to support some of the more exotic varieties of fish throughout the winter. There is now some talk of providing the Pavilion with at least a spa tap for the use of visitors. At present only the fishes have the privilege of being able to sample the water.

cure' and their employer's own brand of Methodism. Fortunately for Smedley, the middle classes proved more receptive, at least on the first score, and it was for them that he built the great hydro at Matlock Bank.

Opened in 1852, Smedley's hydro proved such an enormous success that similar establishments began springing up throughout the area and, within the year, the group of villages known as the Matlocks had become a major centre of the hydropathic boom. In fact by 1862, Smedley had amassed an even bigger fortune than that which he had given away at the time of his conversion.

In the light of this encouraging situation, the case for replacing the Old Bath and its somewhat antiquated hotel at Matlock Bath looked reasonable enough and in 1866 a company was formed for the purpose. However, by this time the initial excitement was over and a shortage of finance caused long delays. So it was 1878 before Matlock Bath's 'magnificent Gothic structure', later known as the Royal Hotel, was finally opened.

Six years after the opening of this new hydro with its huge dining-room, a hundred bedrooms and, eventually, a suite of hydropathic baths and a swimming bath, yet another spa structure appeared. Standing on the hillside just above the hotel, this was the 228-foot-long iron and glass Pavilion. But soon both establishments were in financial difficulties and in 1889, after a resolution to wind up the company, the Pavilion passed into private hands and only with difficulty managed to survive until 1925 before finally closing down.

By now the Royal Hotel was also semi-derelict and in the 1930s it became the victim of a fire, leaving only the Grand Pavilion and the New Bath Hotel in Matlock Bath as reminders of the old spa days. Still standing on its prominent site beside the main road, the Grand Pavilion was built in 1910–11 by a German company and was originally known as the Kursaal. In recent years successful efforts were made to save this massive and distinctive building from a similar fate to that of its predecessors and in 1977 the restored building was opened as a tourist office and an entertainments complex.

Now that the Matlocks have taken a new lease of life, both on the tourist and on the industrial front, there are hopes that the famous thermal waters of Matlock Bath might once again be made available to the public. At present that privilege is reserved only for the exotic fishes that inhabit the roadside pond (fed by water from one of the thermal springs before it flows into the River Derwent) just outside the Grand Pavilion.

The story of more distant hydropathic centres, including the successful 'Scottish Graefenburg' at the Bridge of Allan, the Strathearn at Crieff and the famous hydro at Peebles, followed much the same pattern as that of the Matlocks and Ben Rhydding. Once the railways could transport people easily and comfortably over long distances, the remoteness of a spa was no longer a deterrent—indeed it was sometimes seen as an asset—and, by 1855, there were massive castellated Gothic-style hydropathic establishments to be found in almost every corner of the country.

As time went on, increasing numbers of Queen Victoria's more affluent subjects decided to avail themselves of what these remarkable establishments had to offer. Whether they set out primarily to improve their health, to establish their social status or merely to widen their horizons was a purely personal matter. What was important was that hydrotherapy had become an accepted part of the Victorian way of life.

7
Rural and Provincial Spas

IN SPITE of the increasing number of hydropathic establishments, many of the rural and smaller provincial spas made only minor concessions to the new craze and some resisted it altogether.

To be commercially viable, the new 'cure' needed the support and promotional activities of local practitioners and by no means all country doctors were prepared to subscribe to what they saw as new fangled ideas emanating from the Continent. Many still preferred to prescribe a good old-fashioned course of treatment at the local spa. It might no longer be regarded as orthodox medicine, any more than hydrotherapy was, but in some cases it still appeared to be the only answer to some of the countless afflictions affecting mankind.

Some of the rural and provincial spas were, of course, very rudimentary affairs indeed, often consisting of little more than a pump or spout housed in a tiny well-house, with an inn or other accommodation close by for the convenience of visitors.

Many such spas had faded out at the first signs of the industrial invasion but others, further away from the smoke of the factories, were actually managing to improve themselves and to develop considerable reputations.

Strathpeffer: *Pump Room interior in the early 20th century.*
Beautifully situated near Dingwall and the Cromarty Firth, the four sulphur springs of Strathpeffer were known and used as early as the 1770s. A pump-room was built over the 'strong' well in 1819 but the spa made little headway until after the railway arrived in 1885 and a certain Dr Fortescue Fox from the London Hospital became resident physician. This father-founder of the Victorian and Edwardian spa wrote a book extolling the virtues of the Strathpeffer climate and its pump-room waters, including those from an ancient chalybeate spring known as the Saints' Well three miles away.

The first British spa to introduce peat baths, Strathpeffer began to attract fashionable people from all over the country and in 1909 the new pump-room, as seen in the picture, was built. Yet within ten years decline had set in and the spa buildings were allowed to deteriorate. In recent years, amid much protest, the main building was demolished, leaving only a small pump-room in the Pavilion Spa Gardens as a reminder.

Strathpeffer and Moffat

EVEN AS far north as the highlands of Scotland there was a spa ready to welcome all who could reach it. Strathpeffer (meaning 'the valley of the radiant river'), with its unique and beautiful situation amid mountain scenery, plus a mild and sunny climate, possessed four sulphur springs, all renowned for their exceptional purity, as well as chalybeate spring.

The spa at Strathpeffer dates back to 1772 when a London physician declared that its sulphureous waters were among the strongest in Britain. But at that time, neither the impressive list of complaints which the waters were claimed to cure, nor the building of a pump-room in 1819 could overcome the transport problem and Strathpeffer had to wait until the railway arrived in 1885 before it rose to fashion and popularity.

After that, this well-known Scottish spa, owned by the Earl of Cromartie, remained active and viable until about 1919, when decline rapidly set in. Eventually and for reasons unknown, the main pump-room building which contained the sulphur baths was pulled down and, today, only a small pump-room in the Pavilion Spa gardens remains open for members of the public who wish to sample the sulphur waters. Due to corrosion in the pipes, the chalybeate water is no longer available.

The spa at Moffat in Dumfriesshire also had a reputation for fine scenery and it was more accessible. Its saline-sulphur spring had been discovered in 1630 about one and a half miles from the village and had been enclosed in a small stone building with two Latin inscriptions on the walls. In translation, one of them read: 'It does good alike to the poor and the rich.'

Additionally endowed with a chalybeate spring discovered in 1633, Moffat developed into quite a fashionable 18th century spa. Robert Burns came regularly and even James Boswell was sent here for the cure. In 1829 a bath-house was built and, at the end of the century, a hydropathic hotel. In 1921, however, when the spa was already in serious trouble, the hotel, like many kindred establishments, went up in flames and this spelt the end of Moffat's spa days. Today, the springs still exist but the bath buildings have been converted into council offices.

Spas of northern England

Among the more isolated spas of the north were also those of Edlingham and Gilsland in Northumberland, Shap in what is now Cumbria, and Houghton-le-Spring in Tyne and Wear. The one that held out the longest was the spa at Gilsland where the sulphur and chalybeate waters were still available as late as 1920, even though the large hotel which once catered for the visitors had been burnt down in 1859 and replaced by a convalescent home. At Shap, the original spa hotel (now enlarged and modernised) still stands.

Croft-on-Tees

IN THE Darlington area, sulphur springs were discovered during 19th century coal mining operations at several villages, notably Dinsdale, Gainford and Middleton, and attempts were made to exploit them. But the only spa in this area really worthy of the name was at Croft-on-Tees where, according to folk lore, the first of four mineral springs was discovered in 1669 and where there was no coal to mar the landscape. Even today the Spa Hotel, built in 1808, still stands on its prominent corner site facing the wide road over the river—evidence of the one-time importance of Croft as a spa centre.

The original well at Croft became known as the Old Well. It stood in a field where Spa Farm now stands to the south-west of the village, the story being that it came to light during rock boring operations by the lord of the manor, the first Sir William Chaytor. Sir William, it seems, recognised the nature of the find and ordered a pond fed by the spring water to be made for the benefit of two colts suffering from skin disorders. After the horses had been made to stand in the water and had been encouraged to drink, both animals recovered and news of the cure quickly spread.

By the following summer it was reported that men were bathing naked in the pond, and, since this was considered indecent, action was taken: '. . . thereupon Sir William caused it to be enclosed and made into a cold bath, since which time many have received wonderful benefit by it.'

According to later reports, by 1692 crowds of people were flocking to Croft and, as time went on, long lists of credibly attested cures were published, among them that of a drugster from the Strand. Reputedly suffering from the symptoms of consumption, it was reported that the drugster rode all the way from London in 1713 in order to bathe in the bath and drink the water, after which he returned home fat and jolly!

Such reports, coupled with an advertisement in *The Postman* brought fresh fame to Croft and it was not long before sealed bottles of the water were being sold on Ludgate Hill at the exorbitant price of half a crown a bottle. Even so, the village continued to suffer from a lack of suitable accommodation, which caused people to go elsewhere. It was for this reason that eventually, in 1808, the Spa Hotel was built—an event which brought about a minor revival and led to the construction of a new bath-house in about 1814.

In 1826 yet another chapter in Croft's spa history opened when the lord of

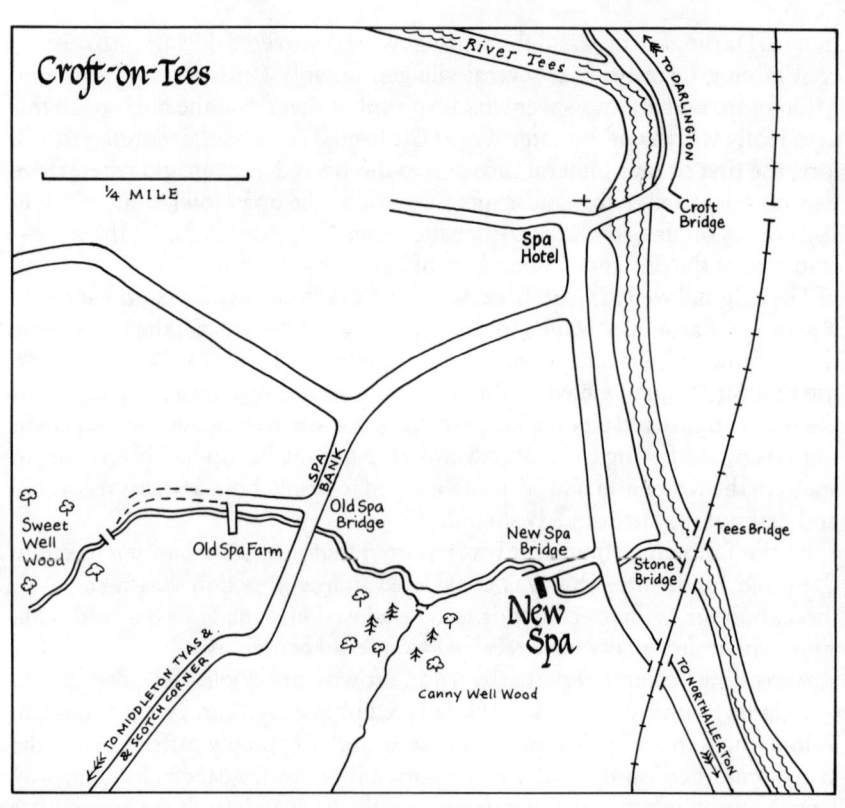

the manor uncovered some information among his grandfather's papers pointing to the existence of another mineral spring. The following year rock boring operations were started on the indicated spot and ended with the discovery at twenty fathoms of the sulphur spring subsequently known as the New Well.

The water of the New Well, which stood less than half a mile from the Old Well and was within easy reach of the Northallerton road, was found to be exceptionally 'strong'—'the strongest in the country', claimed the promoters, who lost no time in creating what was to become known as the New Spa and Baths.

The newly built premises consisted of a pump-room thirty feet long, equipped with three cut glass taps set in freestone, and twelve other rooms containing cold and steam-heated baths. Although a modest looking building, there was a broad verandah, rose-covered trellises, rustic seats and an approach drive from the Northallerton road, taking in a bridge over a stream. It was flanked by gardens, shrubs and walkways. Today the bridge is still there but the gardens have reverted to their woodland state and all that remains of the spa building is the concrete platform on which it once stood.

Shortly after the opening of the New Well at Croft, the Canny Well was discovered in the wood behind and its weaker sulphur water was piped to the building for use in a five-foot plunge bath. After the Canny Well came the discovery of Croft's fourth mineral spring—known as the Sweet Well because it was mildly saline and free of sulphur. The Sweet Well was discovered some distance beyond the original Old Well south-west of the village.

But it was the strong sulphur water of the New Well that continued to capture the public's attention. When freshly pumped up from the ground, it had a constant temperature of 52°F and was described as having a very peculiar dull blue tint almost like the colour of a jelly fish. Not the most encouraging of descriptions one would think, but of those who came seeking health or the preservation of their youth, none were deterred.

The recommended dose for drinking was half a pint three times a day before meals—a dose claimed to make the patient feel like 'a giant refreshed'! To help matters further, patients of Victorian times could have their souls soothed by a rendering of *Whisper and I Shall Hear*, obtainable by placing a penny in the musical box at the end of the counter. Or, if they felt the need to keep their spirits up, there was *The Boys of the Old Brigade*.

During the 1920s, nearly every house in Croft took in spa visitors and there were daily excursions from neighbouring towns. But sadly, the inevitable

Croft-on-Tees: *New Sulphur Spa and Baths, from a 20th century photograph.*

This simple building, opened in 1829 and demolished in the late 1960s, was typical of many of the smaller rural spas. It stood just off the Northallerton road (nearby landmarks: railway bridge and stone road bridge) at the south end of the attractive village of Croft on the Durham-Yorkshire border. Built by the lord of the manor, Sir William Chaytor, over a newly discovered well, it claimed to have the strongest sulphur water in the country—stronger even than Harrogate water and surpassing that of Croft's Old Well, discovered earlier, in about 1669.

The New Spa was approached by a long drive and small stone bridge, flanked by extensive wooded grounds laid out with shrubs and walkways. The pump-room, which originally opened out on to a verandah adorned with roses, was equipped with three cut-glass taps set in freestone. Twelve other rooms contained various types of bath. There was also a plunge bath, 5 feet deep, supplied by a weaker sulphur water from the Canny Well discovered some time later in the wood behind.

The New Spa's quiet but regular clientèle lasted well into the present century and the baths remained open until 1958, when the proprietress died. By 1967, however, the building had become unoccupied and fell into a state of decay which led finally to its demolition.

decline was drawing near, hastened by two world wars and the introduction of the National Health Service. The final episode in the Croft story occurred after the New Well building was taken over by a tennis club for use as a pavilion. To begin with it was put to good use but later it was left unoccupied and finally, in the late 1960s, after vandals had removed lead from the roof, decay was rapid and the Chaytor family decided to have the building demolished. Today only three cottages remain to mark the spot and they are scheduled for future demolition.

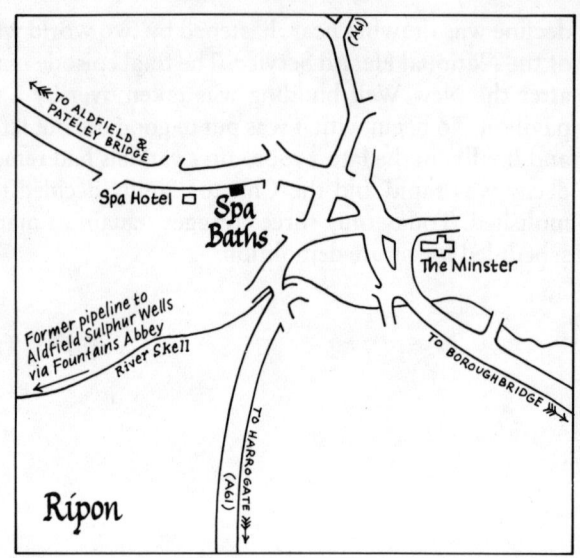
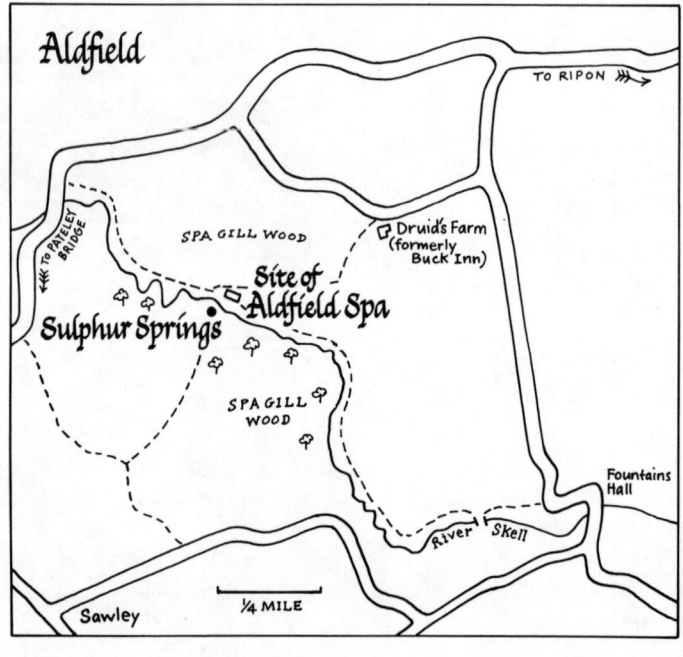

Ripon and Aldfield

BY MID-VICTORIAN times, the British Spas Federation's northern membership list had grown to include several new coastal resorts such as Whitby, Filey and Bridlington, together with a whole string of small spas within easy reach of the Great North Road (the old A1) and the main-line railway that followed roughly the same route.

Among the interesting but less successful of these was a late Victorian spa at Ripon in Yorkshire where today a large red-brick Edwardian building known as the Swimming Baths (now supplied with corporation water) and the equally conspicuous Spa Hotel near by bear witness to a grand scheme which never quite made it.

Although ideally situated at the confluence of the Rivers Ure, Skell and Laver at what is now called 'the gateway to the Yorkshire dales', Ripon had the disadvantage of depending on a sulphur spring three miles away at the village of Aldfield. The date of discovery of the Aldfield spring is not known but the two small wells stood (and still do) in Spa Gill, a sequestered part of the valley of the River Skell, about a mile and a half to the west of Fountains Abbey. It is believed that the monks, who probably followed the footpath alongside the stream, once used the water.

The shortest route today from Aldfield is across the fields and through Spa Gill Woods from Druids Farm (built as the Buck Inn in about 1846) where, despite attempts by pheasant shooters to discourage walkers and sightseers, the footpath remains a right of way. For anyone with a good sense of smell, the two small sulphur wells, contained within a small wired enclosure on the south side of a wooden bridge over the stream, soon make their presence felt.

An additional clue to the whereabouts of the springs is the derelict cottage standing near by on the north bank of the stream. This may have been the cottage mentioned by Dr Granville in 1841 when he wrote: 'By the kind permission of my Lord de Grey, on whose property the well is, people from all parts are allowed to have access to the spring at all times, and to make use of its water. He has permitted a room in an adjoining cottage to be fitted up with the necessary conveniences for either a warm or a cold bath of the mineral water, and has appointed a goodly dame at the cottage to attend and perform all such services as the use of the water may require.'

Dr Granville also noted that the sulphur water of Aldfield kept a constant level with the upper part of the well at a depth of four or five inches and that, like the principal sulphur well on the bog lands of Low Harrogate, it was transparent and colourless, with a constant temperature of 52°F. He observed that the succession of air bubbles rose to the surface every two or three minutes and that the taste was one of 'pleasing freshness'—a view unlikely to be shared by many people today, though some of the villagers still go down to the wells to fetch water for animals suffering from skin complaints such as eczema.

It was in 1899 that the proposal to convey the Aldfield water to Ripon by means of a three-inch pipe across the fields first began to occupy the minds of the local community. By the following year, 'to bring or not to bring the sulphur water from Aldfield' was a major issue dominated, of course, by problems of finance. The mineral water had now been declared equal to, if not superior to that of Harrogate and the idea was to transform Ripon into a spa worthy of it. Not only were spa baths and a hotel to be built, but also the ambitious 'West Ripon Estate'. It was a venture to which a Mr Robert Williamson and six other optimists, all about three score years and ten, eventually agreed to put their names.

In July 1904, on the strength of good reports on designs for the Ripon Spa Baths and confirmation by Sir Herman Weber that the water was of benefit in cases of gout, rheumatism, skin diseases and gall-stones, the corporation also finally gave the scheme their blessing. Possibly the outcome would have been different if the building speculator had acted more promptly and if the spa age had not been almost at an end, but, as things were, the new pump-room and spa baths attracted only a small clientèle and those who had plunged deeply into bricks and mortar lost their money. Even the local poet failed to rally sufficient support when he wrote:

'Go to the wells and find repose
In draughts that stink but never pall,
For sulphur water this good purpose serves,
It soothes your stomach and restores your nerves.'

Perhaps there were not enough stomachs and nerves in need of attention in this part of Yorkshire, or perhaps, as one distinguished observer said later, 'experience shows that spas are of slow growth, their curative value is established by generations of opinion'. No doubt he was right, though, judging by the experience of some country spas, not even age could guarantee survival.

Malton and Hovingham

AMONG THE oldest of the Yorkshire spas was one at Malton on the York–Scarborough road. The Malton 'spaw' spring was discovered by two doctors called Lister and Simpson and a layman called King in the time of James II and was described as having waters similar to those of Scarborough.

According to early treatises written in 1669 and 1732, the spring stood in Longster's garden under the hill on the west side of Malton, about twenty-five yards north of the river (Derwent) and sixty or seventy yards south of the road. (Part of the Longster premises, originally a coaching inn but later used by the family for their seed and corn business, still survives as a radio and television shop at the corner of Yorkersgate and Railway Street.) The 'iron and salt' water, which was said to flow in a very copious stream, was reputedly good for 'afflictions of the liver, indigestion and general languor of the system', the traditional dosage being one to four half-pints at short intervals.

In about 1816 the presence of this saline-chalybeate spring at Malton inspired the lord of the manor, the Earl Fitzwilliam, to erect a pump-room described some twenty-five years later by Dr Granville as 'a handsome pagoda standing prettily in the gardens adjoining the hotel'. As Dr Granville saw it, the hotel offered very superior and extensive accommodation and he expressed surprise that the Malton spa had already ceased to be a resort of 'persons from a distance'. Today the hotel building still stands, but nowhere on the desolate stretch of river bank behind it are there any traces left of the old spa.

During the 19th century, the attractive village of Hovingham (childhood home of the present Duchess of Kent) some eight miles north-west of Malton also possessed a spa. It was centred around three sulphur springs about a mile's walk from the village in the direction of neighbouring Cawton. However, judging by Dr Granville's description of a 'miserable looking wooden hut in which were two baths', it was on an even more modest scale than the spa at Malton.

Thirty years after Dr Granville's visit, the 1870 edition of the *Imperial Gazetteer of England and Wales* reported the existence of a 'neat bath building in pleasant grounds' at Hovingham, but even this presumed improvement was not enough to save the spa from oblivion and all that remains of it today is the privately occupied Spa House (marked Spa Villa on the Ordnance Survey map), once used for the accommodation of visitors, and a trickle of sulphur water emerging from a pipe in the back garden.

Skipton

FURTHER OVER to the west at Skipton, the story is perhaps a little sadder because here the tiny stone-built spa-house has long since disclaimed its heritage by calling itself the Toll House. Yet the sulphur spring at Skipton had been known since time immemorial and might have remained in continuous use but for disputes over its ownership. It was not until the 1820s that the problem was finally resolved by the agents of the Earl of Thanet in favour of their employer, who promptly offered the lease of the spring free of charge to a local doctor of moderate means called Dodgson.

An enthusiastic devotee of the 'dissemination of sanitary truth', Dr Dodgson had arrived in Skipton in 1822 and had quickly earned the admiration of the townspeople. Delighted with his gift, he immediately erected a pump-room and 'some neat baths' on the site and began devoting himself to their management as well as to the promotion of two other springs—one called Broughton Spaw on the road between Skipton and Colne, where Spa Cottages still mark the spot, and another called Crickle Spaw about a mile further on. As the doctor frankly put it, his intention was to provide some profit for himself and some benefit for others.

Alas, Dr Dogdson's plans did not work out as he had hoped and soon the old problem of economic viability raised its ugly head. In 1866, at the age of seventy-four, this well-meaning and philanthropic physician died in very poor circumstances and the Skipton spa was quickly forgotten.

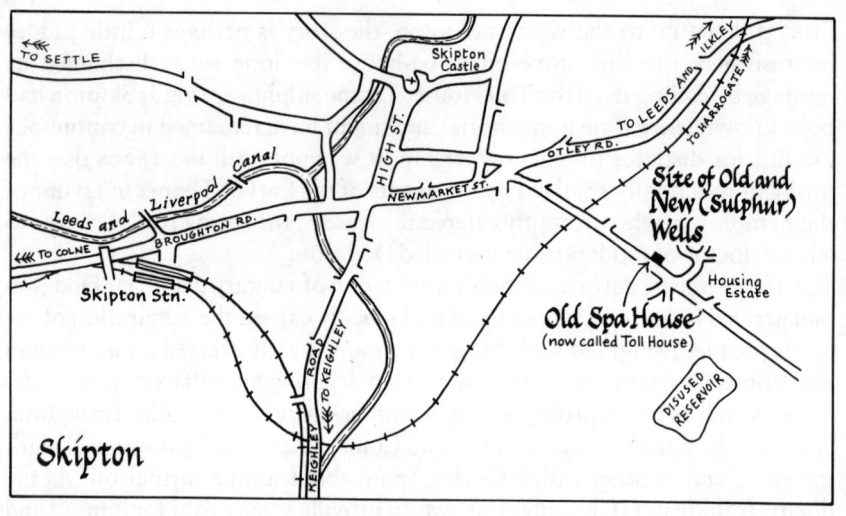

Skipton: *Pump-house (converted into private residence), as seen today.*

Now known as the Toll House (an obvious misnomer since the minor road on which it stands was never a highway), this distinctive single-storey building was originally the pump-house for a sulphur spring. The spring had probably been known and used by the villagers during the 18th century or before but had fallen into disuse due to disputes over its ownership. In the late 1820s, the right of ownership was settled in favour of the Earl of Thanet, who promptly offered its use to a local physician called Dodgson.

An enthusiastic lecturer on health, Dr Dodgson accepted the offer with enthusiasm and erected 'some neat baths' and pump-room in the expressed hope of making a small profit for himself and of benefitting others'. Alas, the project, in company with two others known as the Broughton Spaw and the Crickle Spaw further out on the Colne road, failed to prosper. Dr Dodgson died a poor man in 1866, by which time all three spas had ceased to function.

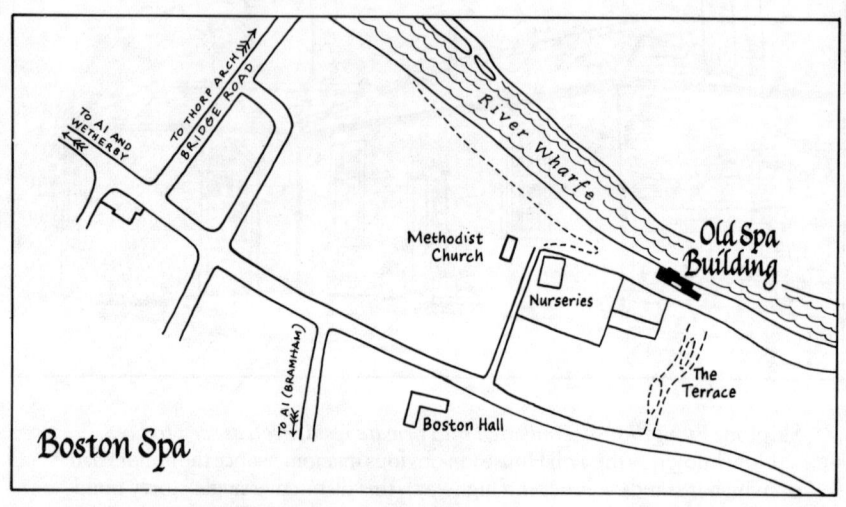

Boston Spa

EVEN MORE scenically situated than Skipton was Boston Spa, three miles east of Wetherby, off the Great North Road (A1). Here the story began in 1744 with the 'best of all worlds', namely the discovery of a saline-chalybeate-sulphur spring at the foot of a steep river bank in the wooded gorge through which flowed the delightful River Wharfe.

The discoverer of the Boston spring was a labourer called John Shires from the nearby village of Thorp Arch (now the home of the National Lending Library). John Shires noticed water issuing from the base of the rocky limestone cliff on the south bank of the river and saw that it was discolouring the stones below. He decided to try it out, first on himself and then on fourteen other men, apparently with such impressive results that samples of the water were carried all the way to York, where an analysis report duly pronounced them strongly purgative.

According to this early account, the news brought at least three hundred people to the tiny village on one Sunday alone and the decision was taken to build a wall to contain the river bank and make the spring easier to reach. In 1753 a house was built for the accommodation of visitors, probably from stone quarried from the cliff, and in 1767 local subscriptions enabled a covered-in pump to be erected.

By 1770 the fame of Boston Spa, or Clifford Spaw, as it was sometimes called, was spreading rapidly but, since the lord of the manor considered it beneath his dignity to make money out of it, it was left to his successors, who had no such scruples, to build baths and found the so-called Bath Company. With the foundation of the company, local people, including the discoverer of the spring, John Shires, were employed as attendants to collect what money they could.

By about 1800, hotels, lodging establishments and many of the elegant houses that still survive in Boston Spa today were beginning to appear and were followed by the building of new spa baths equipped with hot and cold showers. The village now had at least six hundred inhabitants and in 1819 its growing reputation received a further boost by a visit from a distinguished Leeds physician called Dr Adam Hunter who obligingly declared that, in addition to its previously recognised properties, the Boston water was a mild diuretic which operated 'with considerable certainty'.

Boston Spa: *Riverside Spa building, from an old photograph.*

Built on the steep wooded south bank of the River Wharfe, about 3 miles east of Wetherby and the A1, the old stone spa building (now in use as a refreshment hut), with a sulphur pump still surviving in the cellars, is a relic of the days when Boston Spa was a popular watering-place.

The saline-chalybeate sulphur spring was discovered in 1744 after a labourer called John Shires had drawn attention to water issuing out of the bottom of the cliff and discolouring the stones below. After a wall had been built to strengthen the river bank and provide easier access to the spring, a covered-in pump was erected in 1767 and baths were built in 1770. By 1800, the tiny hamlet had grown into an attractive village, renowned both as a spa and as a beauty spot, with elegant lodging-houses and inns lining the main street.

When the spa went into decline later in the century, most of the houses were converted into private dwellings and many of them remain today. The site of the old spring is now a haunt of anglers.

In 1828–9 the celebrated Dr Granville visited Boston Spa but his report suggests that he was more impressed with the beauties of the riverside than with the 'humbler looking building and still humbler bathrooms'. Perhaps his remarks contributed to the emergence of the new Spa Bath Company formed in 1834 with seven shareholders, and the improvements which followed.

According to Dr Granville's account, the pump-room stood at an elevation of about fifty feet above the spring and water was pumped up to it. It is now assumed that the building he referred to was one later converted into three houses which stands opposite the Methodist church. Until filled in in 1962, a fine well stood in the garden leading down to the river.

Apart from the fine houses in the main street, there is now little left of Boston's early 19th century spa. The old stone spa building (some of which now forms part of a refreshment hut) beside the river is in very poor condition, though the old sulphur pump is still there in the cellar. The stretch of river bank where the water-bibbers once strolled and waited is now the haunt of anglers.

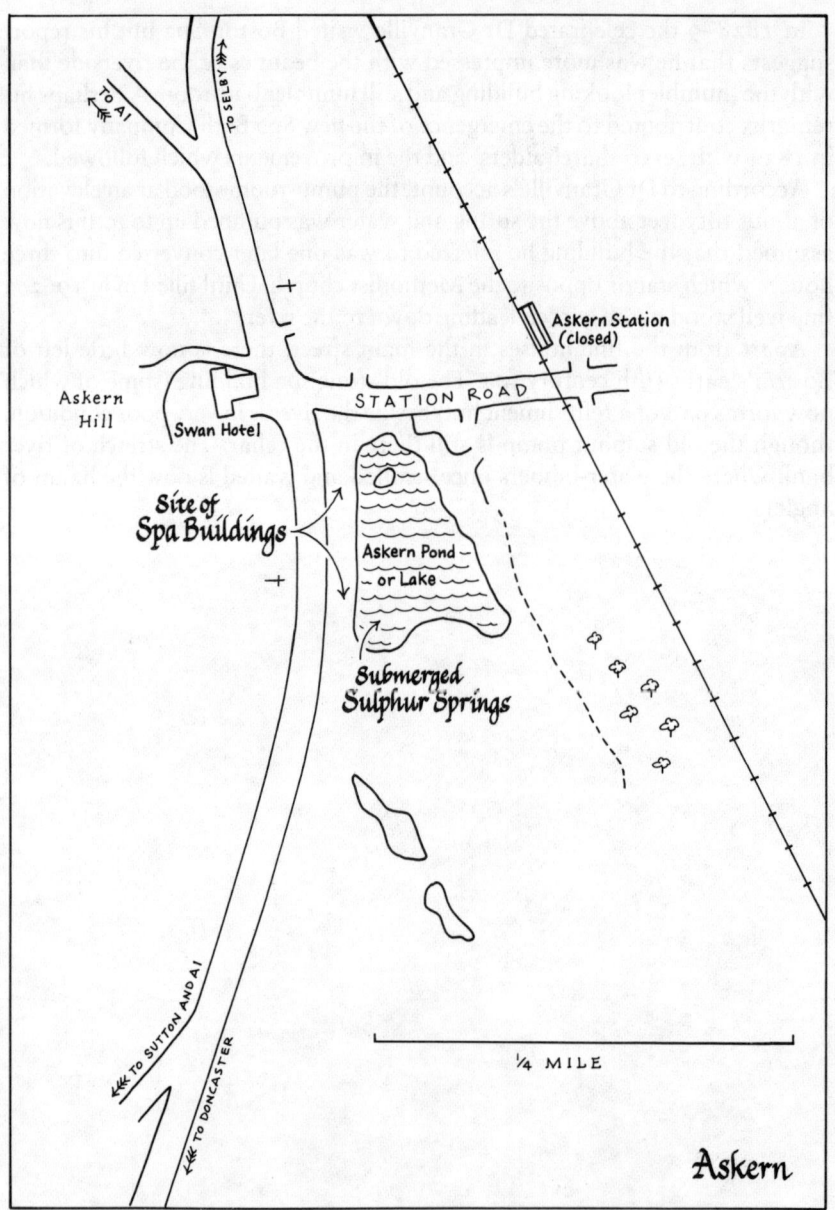

Askern

ATTRACTIVE WATER scenery also played a part in the growth of the spa at Askern in South Yorkshire. Few people know what a charming place this mining village between Pontefract and Doncaster, some four miles east of the A1, once was or that several saline-sulphur springs existed (and still do) beneath the deep waters of its natural lake.

The spa waters of Askern were known as early as 1734, when it was noted that 'they possess an unpleasant odour'. By 1786, visitors were coming to bathe in the waters and the first bath-house, consisting of a straw shed, was erected. This was replaced in 1794 by a 'neat stone building' and followed in 1815 by the much more ambitious Manor Baths at a cost of £1000.

By this time Askern had developed into an attractive spa retreat, well wooded and with several hotels, including the Swan which still survives at the foot of Askern hill in the main street. Here the gentry used to arrive in their landaus to spend days or even weeks drinking and bathing in the sulphur water which bubbled up to the surface near the edge of the lake and was piped to the baths and pump-room close by. Today, all the spa buildings have gone, but, when the wind carries whiffs of the escaping gas to the boat-house and café on the far side of the lake, it is still possible to visualise the scene that once inspired an old Doncaster physician in the early 19th century to write:

'The devil when passing by Askeron
Was asked what he thought thereon;
Quoth Satan—"Judging by the stink,
I can't be far from home, I think."'

Health-seekers of those days, however, were not deterred by quips and cranks and, when a railway station was opened in the mid-19th century, special trains to Askern did a brisk trade during the summer months.

Nor did Askern miss out on the hydropathic boom. In 1894 two large houses on the slope overlooking Askern Pool, as it used to be called, were joined together and converted into a 'splendid palatial hydropathic establishment' with views over the countryside. It is said that on a clear day even Doncaster seven miles away could be seen from the terrace, and so could Goole harbour. After successfully sinking its own sulphur well, the hydro became virtually self-sufficient and so popular that in 1906 even the boat

Askern

Askern: *Lakeside spa, from an old print.*
In the early 1890s, twenty years before Askern became a mining village, this attractive lakeside spa in south Yorkshire ranked quite high in the spa league. Situated in heavily wooded country about 4 miles east of the present A1 between Pontefract and Doncaster, its deep natural lake contained several sulphur springs, known since at least 1734.

In 1815 the Manor Sulphur Baths, costing £1000, replaced an earlier stone bath-house at the water's edge. Hotels were also built and the spa became well patronised by the gentry. In the middle of the century, Askern Spa railway station was opened, heralding further expansion. In 1894, the two large lodging-houses to the right of the picture were joined up and extended to form a 'palatial' hydropathic hotel, with gardens leading down to the 'Pool'. So popular was the spa by 1906 that even the Harwich Express began stopping here.

But in 1911, after coal was discovered on the hillside, the scene changed: deserted by visitors, the spa buildings were allowed to become derelict and were eventually swept away. Today, efforts are being made to recapture some of the old atmosphere by redeveloping the lakeside area for recreational purposes.

train known as the Harwich Express to and from Liverpool and Manchester used to stop at 'Askern Spa'.

But in 1911 everything was changed. In that year the coal industry arrived and the village was rapidly transformed from a watering-place into a small mining centre, with little to remind people of the past apart from the lake and the wooded plain. Today there are plans for rehabilitating Askern and, to this end, a group of derelict spa buildings which stood near the water's edge beside the main road were recently demolished. The plan is to landscape the lake and its surroundings into a recreational area for boating, fishing and associated leisure activities. The water is deep and fish such as carp appear to be unperturbed by the presence of the old sulphur springs.

Other Yorkshire spas

The displacement of the spa at Askern by streets of terraced houses was, of course, no more than a repetition of an old story. By the 19th century, a whole string of north-country spas had already succumbed to the industrial invasion, and none more rapidly and completely than those of the embryo towns. Difficult though the old scenes may now be to visualise, there were once spas at Leeds, Holbeck, Wakefield, Barnsley, Ossett and Clitheroe (Lancs).

As at Leeds, where the Eyebright Spaw, described in 1715 as a 'sovereign remedy against sore eyes', now lies buried under the Majestic Cinema in City Square, most of these early provincial spas vanished beneath the foundations of developing town centres. Even those in outlying areas such as Calverley near Leeds, Tadcaster between Leeds and York, Addingham near Ilkley, Holywell Green near Halifax, and Slaithwaite and Lockwood near Huddersfield eventually followed suit and disappeared into oblivion.

This remarkable concentration of one-time spas was, however, mainly a Yorkshire phenomenon. Once over the border, in Lincolnshire, very few mineral springs were discovered and, apart from the well-known Woodhall Spa, the whole 19th century complement consisted of little more than a minor spa at Gainsborough and an even more insignificant one at a village called Monkswell near Lincoln.

Lying east of the present A1, the spa at Gainsborough stood almost on the site of the King's Theatre (a late 19th century building known until 1904 as the Albert Hall and now used as a bingo hall) in Trinity Street, on the road to Lincoln. People suffering from rheumatism or weak eyes used to come to the low-built pump-room, with dwelling attached, to draw the gypsum (calcium sulphate)-charged water but, partly perhaps because the spa had the misfortune to be associated with a ghastly 18th century crime in which the body of a murdered man was thrown into the bath, Gainsborough never really achieved popularity.

Woodhall Spa

FAR MORE fortunate was Woodhall Spa some twenty miles south-east of Lincoln. Here, following an unsuccessful search for coal, the famous 'iodine' waters were discovered in 1819 and growth was rapid.

The search for coal had begun eight years earlier, in 1811, when John Parkinson, steward of a large wooded estate belonging to a family called Hotchkin, decided to try his luck by sinking a shaft. During the operations, water-bearing rock was struck at five hundred and forty feet but it was dismissed as a nuisance that caused flooding and imposed an additional financial burden. In fact the financial burden was now such that, if it had not been for the deception of the workmen, who began smuggling coal into the shaft in order to keep hope alive and the work going, the enterprise might well have been abandoned. As it was, the speculator continued drilling to a depth of a thousand feet before finally accepting defeat—and eventual bankruptcy.

After the work had ceased, the shaft was covered over and, until the forest estate changed hands several years later, was almost forgotten. It was during this interval that some of the clear salty water released from the rock found its way into a neighbouring brook, where it gradually became known among the local people as a healing water, particularly beneficial for complaints such as gout and rheumatism.

Rumours of the water's curative properties soon reached the ears of the new lord of the manor, Thomas Hotchkin, who tried it himself, found that it relieved his gout and decided to investigate further.

Having traced the source of the water, Thomas Hotchkin sent samples of it for analysis—with spectacular results. Not only did the analysis reveal, as expected, a high concentration of common salt, but it showed that Woodhall possessed a very pure bromo-iodine water unlike any other so far discovered in the country. What was more, it was a water that could be used for both drinking and bathing. It was a signal for action that could not be ignored.

In 1830 Thomas Hotchkin built a small pump-room and bath-house over the Woodhall well and, as public interest grew, decided to sink a new well. The well was completed in 1834 and followed in 1839 by a modest inn—a building described the following year by Dr Granville as 'a neat and unostentatious edifice which serves as an hotel honoured with the name of Victoria Hotel'.

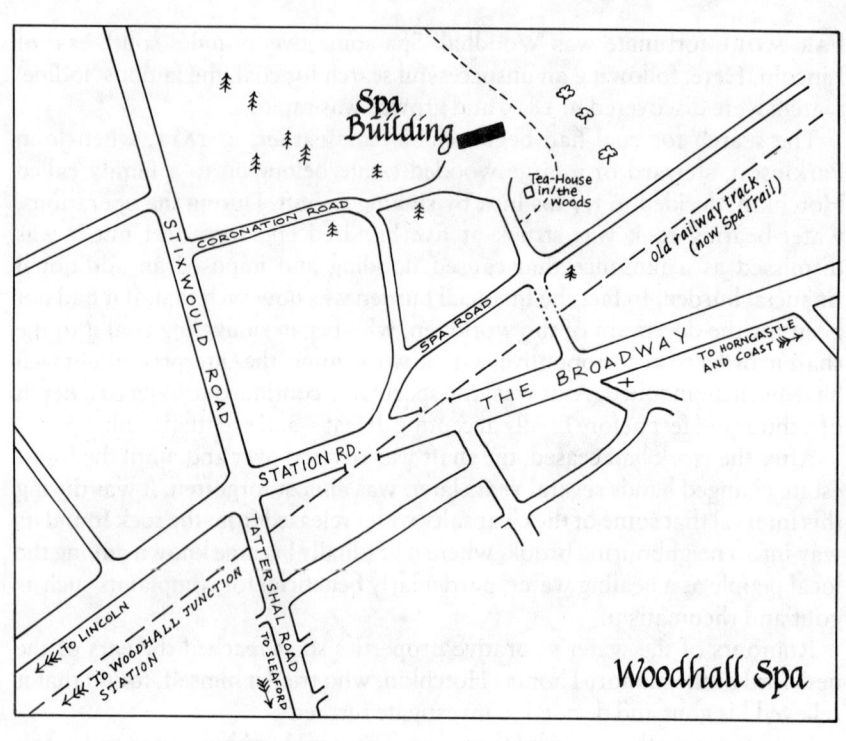

It was obvious, however, that in Dr Granville's estimation, Woodhall was well down on the social scale and, as usual, he made no effort to conceal his views. After consulting the hotel's register of visitors, he wrote: 'Judging from the names, I should imagine that the majority of visitors were farmers and people belonging to the industrious classes. Indeed, neither the bathroom accommodation nor the pump room are calculated for very superior classes of persons.'

But whatever its social shortcomings by Dr Granville's mid-Victorian standards, Woodhall was now an established embryo resort and when Stafford Hotchkin succeeded as lord of the manor, it did not take him long to recognise the fact.

In 1849 Stafford Hotchkin replaced the buildings put up by his predecessor with a large commodious hotel set in grounds of a hundred acres and a much more extensive bath system and pump-room (the core of the existing Spa Baths)—improvements which, as things turned out, were just in time to meet the demands of a fresh influx of visitors brought by the railway in 1855.

One of the leading lights in the early days at Woodhall was a Dr Cuffe, a resident medical superintendent to whom both the baths and the hotel were leased between 1862 and 1883. He was a man specially remembered because of the small cottage hospital he built for poor patients and it was not until after his 'reign' had ended that the Hotchkin family decided to sell off the spa property.

In 1887 all the buildings were acquired by a syndicate which promptly set about updating them in accordance with the notions of the hydropathic age. One of the major changes was the reconstruction of the hotel and its re-equipment with some of the more exotic types of bath such as the 'needle' bath (a device which was supposed to stimulate the patient's system by means of high pressure showers).

As a result of this fresh burst of enterprise, Woodhall Spa witnessed a further increase in the number of spa visitors and more hotels, houses and sporting facilities (including a championship golf course) were laid out in the town. Yet, despite the growing prosperity, Lincolnshire's unique 'iodine' spa never achieved any sort of glamour or even architectural distinction and it remained essentially a rural spa largely dependent on the attractions of its beautiful pinewood setting.

By the time the First World War broke out, Woodhall possessed five hotels but in 1914 one was abandoned by its German owner and in 1920 the Victoria went up in flames. To help counteract these disasters, Sir Archibald

Woodhall Spa: *Hotel with adjacent bath-house and pump-room, from a print of about 1868.*

Scenically situated amid the pine woods of a Lincolnshire estate, these buildings were erected in 1849 by the land owner, Stafford Hotchkin. They replaced a modest inn and bath-house put up in 1830–4 by his predecessor, Thomas Hotchkin, whose interest had been aroused by stories of the clear salty water which, in 1811, had flooded a shaft excavated in an abortive attempt to find coal.

The flood water contributed to the eventual bankruptcy of the coal speculator, an estate steward called Parkinson, whose many problems included deception by the workmen who smuggled coal into the 1000-foot shaft in the hope of keeping their jobs. But it was the water appearing at 540 feet which had interested Thomas Hotchkin and, when analysis showed that it contained iodine, bromine and other mineral salts, he sank a new well.

Equipped in due course by a steam engine for raising the water in buckets, this well became the focal point of the so-called 'iodine spa', quickly acclaimed by sufferers from gout and rheumatism and rising to fame under the expansionist efforts of the second Mr Hotchkin. The commodious hotel was one of two such establishments catering for spa visitors up to the time of the First World War. The war caused one to be abandoned by its German owner and the other was later destroyed by fire. Yet, despite these setbacks, the spa partially recovered and managed to carry on far longer than many of its less isolated contemporaries.

and Lady Weighall lent their finely furnished low timbered house called Petwood (now an established hotel) for the accommodation of visitors.

But this did not solve the problem of the spa's future and, after witnessing a series of unsuccessful ventures by speculators, the Weighalls decided to purchase the whole of the spa centre and to offer it free of charge to the local council. Surprisingly the offer was turned down on the grounds that there was no by-law authorising expenditure on such a concern and, the Woodhall Spa Baths Trust had to be formed to take over and administer the property.

Under the aegis of the Trust, the spa limped on until 1930, when doctors stopped prescribing the water. By this time the town had begun to see itself more as a tourist centre than as a health resort and acted accordingly. At the time of King George V's Jubilee, pleasure gardens were laid out and a swimming pool constructed, followed later by the building of the 'Kinema in the Wood' all of which helped to eliminate the old image and establish the new. During the Second World War the spa premises were used by the R.A.F for ablution purposes and emerged without any serious damage, but the subsequent introduction of the National Health Service quashed any hope of re-establishing the spa.

Under the N.H.S the regional hospital board finally agreed to convert the pump-room and the rest of the premises into a rheumatism clinic but declined to take over the establishment completely. A lump sum was paid towards the running costs while responsibility for the upkeep of the buildings was left in the hands of the Trust. There was no question, however, of using the original spa waters: all the therapies employed at the clinic depended on ordinary tap water and eventually the old well in the boiler room was covered over and the steam engine, once used to draw up the water in buckets, was despatched to the Lincolnshire Life Museum in Lincoln, where it underwent restoration before being placed on display as an interesting 19th century relic.

Although still clearly recognisable, the central spa buildings of Woodhall, in their vast woodland setting, bear witness to the many changes of the past fifty years. The once open verandahs are now enclosed and there is a modern portico to the one-time pump-room, now converted into a patients' reception centre. The small musicians' gallery facing the entrance is hidden away behind a wall and the long mahogany counter from which the natural mineral water was once dispensed from two taps is no longer there. But at the back of the building some of the old Georgian chimneys still stand.

In recent years doubts have been voiced about the future of the N.H.S rheumatism clinic and there has been some talk of closure. Perhaps this is the reason why there are renewed and lingering hopes in some quarters that one day Lincolnshire's famous 'iodine' clinic may yet come back into its own.

Spas of eastern England

Compared with Woodhall, the few spas which sprang up on the eastern side of the country south of the Humber were of little account and all were destined to obscurity.

At Thetford in Norfolk, a chalybeate spring was discovered near the Mills in 1746 but no immediate attempt was made to exploit it and it was 1819 before the grounds were laid out and a small pump-room built—an enterprise which proved to be on too small a scale to turn this interesting old market town, with its Priory remains, into a popular resort. Nevertheless, Thetford's old pump-room survived and still exists today as a private residence.

Even less fortunate than Thetford was Mistley in Essex. Standing on the Colchester road overlooking the Stour estuary near Manningtree, Mistley might well be described as the marine spa that never was. It was the brainchild of a friend of Horace Walpole called Dr Richard Rigby who, as a patron of the arts, commissioned Robert Adam to design the necessary buildings. Alas, with only part of the work completed, financial misfortune overtook the Rigby family and today only a few relics of the projected health resort remain. They include the twin cupolas of an Adam-designed church (the body of which was knocked out by the Victorians), one of the two lodges built as an entrance to the spa, and the statue of a large swan. The swan, believed to have been made originally for the spa, now dominates a great basin in the village centre.

Another Essex failure was the spa at Hockley, some five miles north of Southend-on-Sea. Here a well was discovered in 1838 and immediate attempts were made to exploit it by building a pump-room, baths and a hotel. The pump-room was described by one historian as big enough for Bath—which may explain why it quickly became a white elephant. After a spell of duty as a Baptist chapel, it was finally converted into a factory.

Maybe the little spa at the village of West Tilbury on the marshy north bank of the Thames should have done better because it possessed two mineral springs, one with distinctly unusual properties. Discovered in 1724 by the owner of West Tilbury Hall and originally used for domestic purposes and later as a palliative for gout and colds, the water of this particular spring was eventually sent for analysis by a Dr Andree. In marked contrast to most other

Woodhall Spa: *Bath-house and pump-room, from an old drawing.*

This is the building, part of which dates back to 1849, which was to become the core of the present-day premises known as the Rheumatism Clinic. In the old days, the spa tap was situated on the rear wall behind a mahogany counter in the central area and above it stood a small recessed musicians' gallery (now filled in and plastered over). The rest of the building contained baths for hot bathing, as well as high pressure showers known as needle baths, used to stimulate the patient's system. There were also rest rooms and a reservoir for extra spa water. Major alterations made by the Spa Baths Trust from about the year 1900 resulted in the replacement of the verandah by a single-storey extension and the erection of a central brick portico, but the premises are still recognisable and the pre-Victorian chimneys at the back remain.

In 1969 the spa was finally closed and the steam engine, once used to draw up the water, was later removed to the Lincolnshire Life Museum in Lincoln for restoration and exhibition. When the building became a rheumatism clinic under the N.H.S., the simple old pump-room was turned into a patients' waiting-room. As for the original bromo-iodine water, once highly prized and reputed to be the strongest in Europe, that now languishes in its deep well, boarded over in the old boiler room. It is no longer drunk and, for bathing purposes, its place has been taken by ordinary tap water!

natural mineral waters, the Tilbury water was declared *anti*-purgative and was bottled and advertised as such by a doctor who dedicated his pamphlets to Sir Hans Sloane. For a time at least, the response was very satisfactory and a second spring, found in the rectory garden in 1783, was given similar publicity—again with encouraging results. However, no assembly rooms were built and, since there were virtually no entertainments to be had in the village, decline and eventual demise were inevitable. Today nothing remains of either well, though the kitchen of West Tilbury Hall marks the site of the original discovery.

South of the Thames, the famous Tunbridge Wells was too close at hand to give Canterbury much of a chance, though a chalybeate spring had been discovered here as early as the 18th century. According to Celia Fiennes, who visited it, the spring was properly railed in and had steps leading down to it, with a small pavement for the company to stand on. Apart from this, however, Celia's observations can hardly have helped matters for not only did she find that the water ran too slowly but, according to her report, it caused one gentleman in the house where she was staying to develop numbness in his limbs. One of the few redeeming features appears to have been the 'fine walk and Seates and places for the musick', but that was not enough to keep Canterbury on the spa map for very long.

Droitwich

COMPARED WITH the eastern counties, the Midlands were well supplied with mineral springs. They were not as plentiful as in Yorkshire but, as the population began to increase in the early 19th century and people became aware of the benefits to be gained, more springs came to light. When this happened, even a little town such as Bakewell, half way between Buxton and Matlock, was tempted to make its bid for fame.

Predictably, as at Bakewell, most of the attempts ended in early failure and it was left to the fortunate few to reap the rewards. With the exception of Leamington, Buxton and Matlock, the most successful 19th century spa in the Midlands was probably the one at Droitwich, the town with the huge underground brine lake formed by subterranean streams passing over beds of rock salt.

Droitwich had been known since Roman times and its salt industry dated back even further. However, the value of its brine as a therapeutic agent—it is ten times stronger than sea water and as buoyant as the water of the Dead Sea—was not recognised until 1830, and then only by chance due to a cholera outbreak. The story, with variations, is that a worker in the salt industry became a victim of the disease and was ordered to take an immediate hot bath. To save time, the man either jumped into or was dipped by his fellow workers in one of the hot brine vats—and recovered.

As news of this and similar incidents spread, the demand for hot brine baths increased dramatically and bath-houses with deep pumping systems—the brine lake lies between two and three hundred feet below ground—were hurriedly erected. When the brine was found to be good for rheumatic complaints as well as for cholera, Droitwich rapidly developed into a spa.

Unlike some spas, at Droitwich the emphasis from the beginning was on health rather than on fashion and there were few social pretensions. The Royal Brine Baths were opened in 1836 on a site now occupied by a block of offices called the Royal George at the corner of the present A38 with the Hanbury road and were followed four years later, in 1840, by the old Saline Baths which stood in the centre of the town on the site now occupied by the converted St Andrew's Brine Baths building.

A leading light in Droitwich's transformation from a small industrial salt-producing centre to a well-known Victorian spa was John Corbett, an

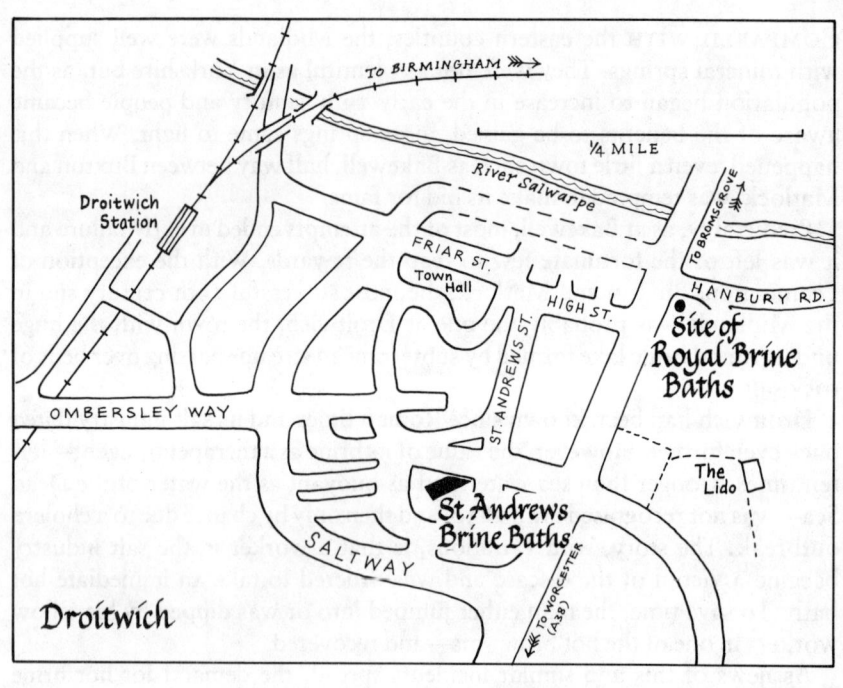

Droitwich: *The Saline Baths and Hotel, from an early print.*
This building stood in the centre of Droitwich on part of the site later occupied by the St Andrew's Brine Baths. Like the Royal Brine Baths built four years earlier, in 1836, on the north-eastern side of the town, the Saline Baths owed their existence to the 1830 cholera outbreak. During the epidemic, doctors had recommended their patients to take frequent hot baths, so when a worker in the salt industry contracted the disease he was hurriedly dipped in the nearest vat of hot brine. The victim recovered and, as the news spread, wealthier residents began demanding brine bathing facilities for themselves—a demand quickly met by enterprising doctors who immediately recognised the value of the town's underground brine lake, two to three hundred feet below the surface. Since the lake contained the strongest salt water known, some ten times stronger than sea water, all that was required were suitably equipped baths with deep pumping systems.

As these began to appear and it was noticed that warm brine bathing also benefited rheumatic sufferers and those with skin disorders, invalids began flocking in from other parts of the country, bringing with them a new prosperity and a new role for Droitwich—that of a 'brine spa'.

Droitwich: *St Andrew's Brine Baths, as seen before their closure in 1975.*
Situated in the centre of the town, part of this building stands on the site of the old Saline Baths of 1840 and dates back to 1875. Largely as a result of the work of John Corbett, a local salt manufacturer turned philanthropist, the premises were gradually altered and extended, thereby replacing the older brine bathing establishments and completing the town's transformation from an industrial salt producing centre into a well patronised spa. The baths were supplied with brine from the natural springs via the pumping station in the High Street and, as time went on, were equipped with the most up-to-date therapeutic facilities, including a heating system for raising the temperature of the water to around 90°F.

In later years the baths were administered by a medical trust which catered for a wide variety of patients. After the 1975 closure on economic grounds, the building was leased to an engineering firm and converted into offices, but the local authority is now considering the possibility of re-establishing brine therapy in the town. Meanwhile the famous brine continues to be pumped to the open lido in Droitwich Park, where it is diluted to the strength of ordinary sea water.

energetic mid-19th century salt manufacturer who made himself responsible for many of the initial borings. (Unfortunately, like his successors, Corbett failed to keep proper records of the exact whereabouts of the wells and, although it is known that thirty-two were in operation at different times, by 1922 when the salt works were finally closed by the Salt Union, most of the locations had been lost.)

Among Corbett's more notable contributions to the town was a model self-contained village outside the industrial centre which he established for the benefit of his salt workers, and also a mansion called the Chateau d'Impney which he had specially designed for his French wife. An interesting feature of the mansion, which still stands about a mile out from the town on the Birmingham road and is now in use as a hotel, is that it provides one of the two remaining outlets for the famous brine. The other outlet is at the modern lido in Droitwich Park where today the water is diluted and used for ordinary swimming purposes.

But it was the salt magnate's foundation of the St Andrew's Baths on the site of the original Saline Baths which provided the town with its major spa facility. Complete with boilers for heating the water to temperatures around 90°F, the original part of the building was opened in 1877 and proved an immediate success. It was followed by several extensions, including the major one containing a large brine swimming pool known as the Big Swim (to distinguish it from the earlier Little Swim), used in the treatment of a whole new range of complaints from rheumatism to the after-effects of nervous disorders. In order to ensure that the hot brine, with its stimulating effect on the skin and circulation, remained available, the baths were eventually taken over and run by a non-profit making organisation called the Droitwich Medical Trust which in due course extended its services to the National Health Service.

By 1971, however, there were financial difficulties and the building was taken over by the council. In 1975 the decision was taken to close the baths down and the premises were leased to an engineering firm who, converted them into offices. Although the chances of restoring them to their former use now look slim, Droitwich still possesses its basic commodity. The huge underground brine lake is still there and there are growing demands on both medical and historical grounds for a revival of the once famous spa.

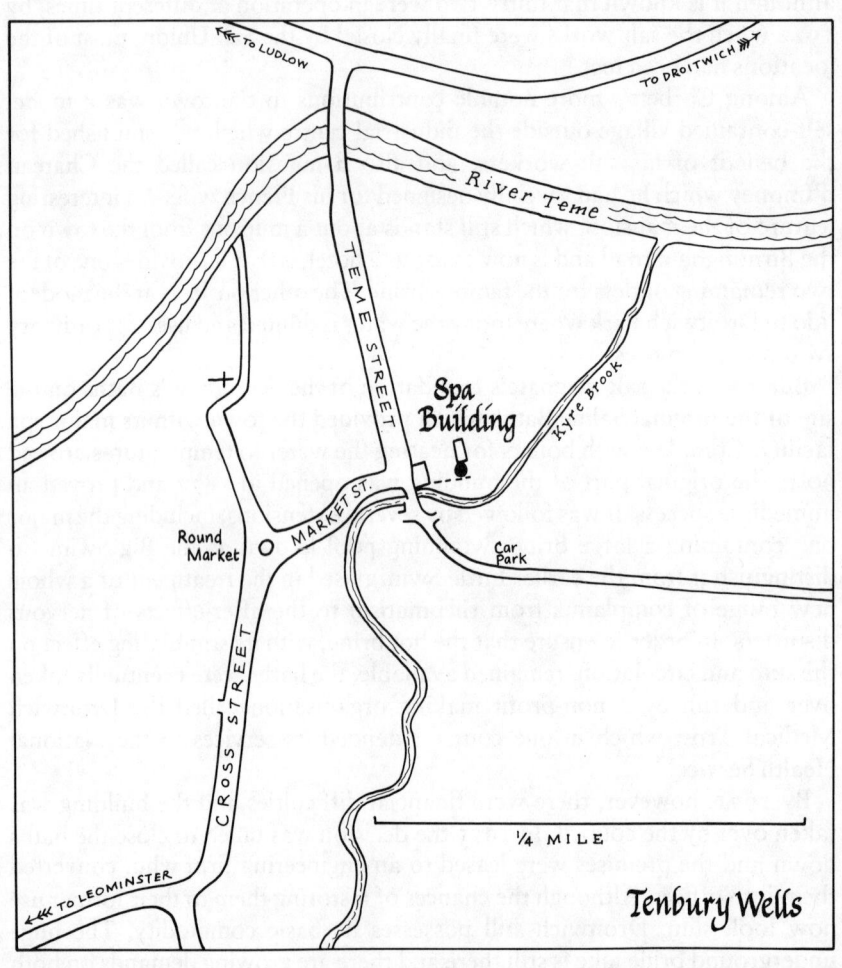

Tenbury Wells

ABOUT TWENTY miles to the west of Droitwich, approaching the Welsh border country, Tenbury Wells has also been faced in recent years with a dilemma and its curious little 'pepper-pot' spa building made of glass and iron is now in such a dismal state of decay that even its continued existence is in doubt.

A small market town in the Teme valley where the London coach used to stop on its way to Wales, Tenbury became a spa in 1839 following the accidental discovery of a saline spring during a search for ordinary drinking water in the back garden of a house near the Kyre brook. The discovery led to the construction of a brick-lined well, three feet in diameter, news of which soon reached the ears of Dr Granville.

When Dr Granville arrived to inspect the new spa, he was enthusiastic about the presence of iodine in the water and even recorded its effects philosophically, namely that 'upon swallowing half a tumbler of the Tenbury water, a disturbance, or rather commotion, is set up in the abdomen'. But he looked with disfavour on the apathy of the local inhabitants who appeared to have done nothing to promote the spa apart from running up some temporary baths on an unsatisfactory site. In the doctor's own words, they had taken no steps at all 'to render Tenbury habitable for people of consequence'.

Perhaps Dr Granville's censorious remarks had some effect because a small red-brick bath-house eventually appeared and the water was acclaimed as being good for 'glandular swelling, congestion of the liver, scurvy and scrofula and, when used for bathing, as a relief for gout and rheumatism'. The metal-clad pagoda-like building known as the 'pepper-pot' which now stands in such dilapidated condition over the site of the old well at the side of the brook behind the Crow Hotel followed in 1862.

In the early days, Tenbury advertised itself as 'a spa for middling and working classes' which offered 'every convenience at the lowest possible price'. It was hardly a description calculated to produce an exciting image but no doubt it satisfied an important need and in later years the image improved when Tenbury became known as 'the spa in the orchard'. Nevertheless it was 1911 before any serious attempt was made to bring the spa up to date by installing plunge and steam baths, and by that time it was too late. The First World War was only three years away, bringing with it the inevitable decline.

Tenbury Wells (Worcs): *The Pump Room, as seen in about 1970.*

Shaped like a small oriental temple, some say like a giant pepper-pot, this unusual looking metal-clad pump-room was built in 1862. It stands at the rear of the Crow Hotel close to the bridge over the Kyre Brook in the centre of the town on the site of saline springs discovered in 1839 during a search for a domestic water supply.

Once known as 'the spa in the orchard', Tenbury Wells lacked the frivolities and diversions of pre-Victorian spas, claiming instead to be 'for the middling and working classes' with 'every convenience at the lowest possible price'. With its small red brick bath-house for brine bathing, it was reasonably well patronised in the late 19th century but, despite some renovations and the addition of plunge and steam baths made in 1911, decline set in after the First World War.

Various propositions for rejuvenation were put forward as late as 1931 but the spa was finally closed in 1939 and the wells filled in. Since then the building has been used by a brewery, as a tea-room and, lastly, as a meeting-place for the Women's Institute. By 1978 it was in such a bad state of decay that it was bolted and barred and threatened with demolition—though not without protest from local residents.

Propositions for rejuvenating the Tenbury spa were made as late as 1931 but nothing came of them and in 1939 the pump-room was closed and the wells filled in. Since that date, the premises have been used for a variety of purposes. For many years they were leased to a brewery, then used as a café and, in recent times, as a meeting place for the Women's Institute. Finally, in 1978, they were bolted and barred pending the council's decision on their future.

So today, covered in rust, Tenbury's curious Victorian relic awaits its fate. No doubt it could be renovated to become a tourist attraction, or maybe it will simply find its way to the scrap metal yard.

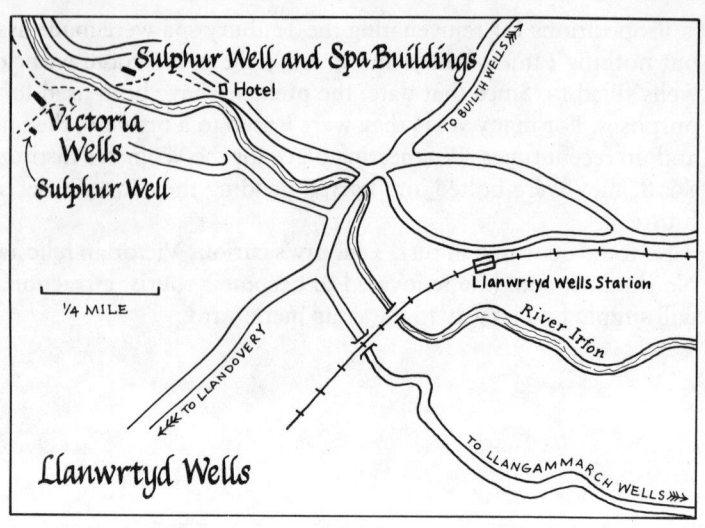

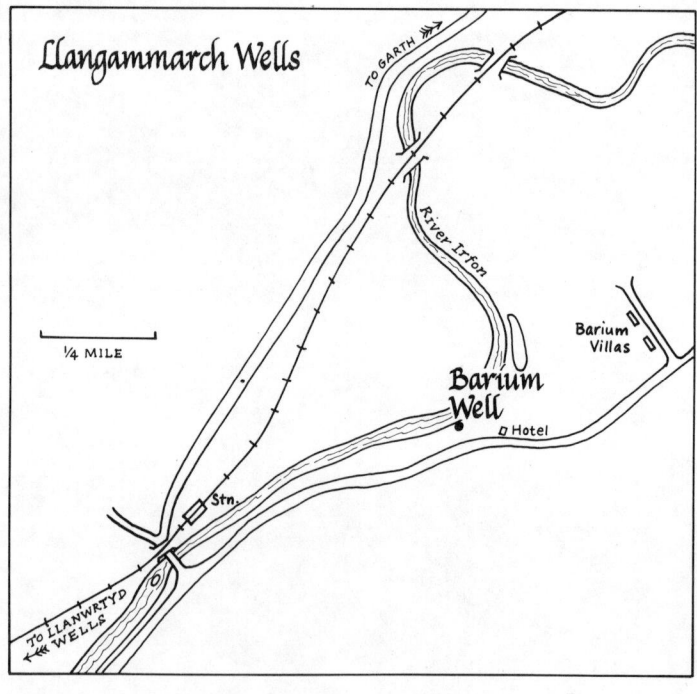

Minor Welsh spas

ALTHOUGH LESS accessible than their English counterparts, most of the Welsh spas with their even finer scenery professed to offer 'complete' health cures rather than limited ones. But only those which survived long enough for the railways to reach them achieved lasting reputations.

Such a spa was the one at Trefriw ('place of healing') in Caernarvonshire on the west bank of the River Conway which, at one stage, claimed to possess water with the highest sulphur content in the world. History does not relate whether or not the claim was ever substantiated but no doubt anything seemed possible in circumstances such as these where the water rises in a cave cut out of solid rock and where there were rock-hewn basins reputedly dating back to the time of the Romans.

Until mine debris closed the cave, it is believed that invalids in the 18th century were familiar with the Trefriw waters. However, it was 1833 before they became freely available and 1863 before the owner, Lord Willoughby d'Eresby, had the first bath-house built. Later the Trefriw wells were leased to a company, who erected a picturesque pump-house and baths and began advertising the waters. It was claimed that they were extremely beneficial in cases of rheumatism, anaemia and skin diseases and, during the late 19th and early 20th centuries, there was no shortage of visitors. After that, however, the spa was allowed to run down and eventually the buildings fell into decay. Today the Trefriw water is seldom drunk at the well but it is still bottled and commands quite high prices.

Like Trefriw, the remote Breconshire (now Powys) village of Llanwrtyd on the banks of the River Irfon was also beautifully situated and it, too, was soon making some big claims. A spring had been discovered here in 1732 by the Reverend Theophilus Evans who suffered from scurvy, the story being that the sight of a frog gambolling in the water of what was locally known as the 'stinking well' made him decide to see if the water could do as much for him as it appeared to be doing for the frog. After drinking it over a period of a few weeks, the priest found himself cured and spread the good news.

The source of the 'stinking well' proved, of course, to be a sulphur spring which, like others before and after it, was duly acclaimed as having the highest sulphur content in the country. With the additional attraction of a chalybeate spring discovered close by, it was only a matter of time before the

Llanwrtyd Wells: *Spa buildings, from a 20th century photograph.*
These simple spa buildings were erected in the grounds of the Dol-y-Coed Hotel in the old Breconshire (now Powys) village of Llanwrtyd. Approached by a long tree-lined walk along the bank of the River Irfon, they provided Victorian visitors with two types of water—sulphur and chalybeate. It is believed that the sulphur spring was discovered in 1732 by the Reverend Theophilus Evans, a sufferer from scurvy whose attention was attracted by a frog frolicking about in what the local people called a stinking well. Attributing the frog's lively antics to the water, the priest decided to try it out on himself—apparently not in vain for within a few weeks he was cured.

Claiming that its springs had the highest sulphur content in the country, Llanwrtyd Wells managed to remain viable until after the First World War before following others into decline. Partly due to vandalism, the buildings are now boarded up and semi-derelict but sulphur water continues to flow into the ornamental blue-tiled well in the old pump-room (seen on the right of the picture) where copious bubbles of hydrogen sulphide gas still fill the air with the characteristic smell.

little Welsh village became a small but popular Victorian spa centred around the Dol-y-Coed Hotel in whose grounds the wells stood, modestly but adequately protected by a group of simple wooden buildings and approached from the hotel by a wide tree-lined promenade along the river bank.

Today these structures stand derelict and boarded up but one of them still contains a large imposing blue-tiled well on a round platform, full of bubbling sulphur water and emitting the characteristic smell.

Both Llanwrtyd Wells and a neighbouring small spa known as Llangammarch Wells four miles further west remained viable until well into the 20th century, partly no doubt because both existed in conjunction with hotels where visitors and patients could be comfortably accommodated.

Standing in the grounds of the Lake Hotel, also on the banks of the River Irfon amid beautiful surroundings, the 'barium spa' of Llangammarch was able to claim a certain uniqueness because its waters contained barium chloride, a substance renowned for its 'noteworthy and important' effect on the heart and circulation.

The 'barium spa' owed its existence to a shepherd who first detected the spring by observing that, even during drought conditions, water went on rising up from the river bed. After the discovery, a simple wooden pump-room with bathing facilities was built close to the river bank and charges were imposed—2d per glass for drinking purposes and four shillings for a barium bath. In the early days the little spa did well but, today, the simple wooden building is in the last stages of decay. In fact, apart from a row of farm workers' dwellings called Barium Cottages about half a mile away (up the hill and just off the main road), there is little left to remind even local people of the unusual nature of the waters of Llangammarch.

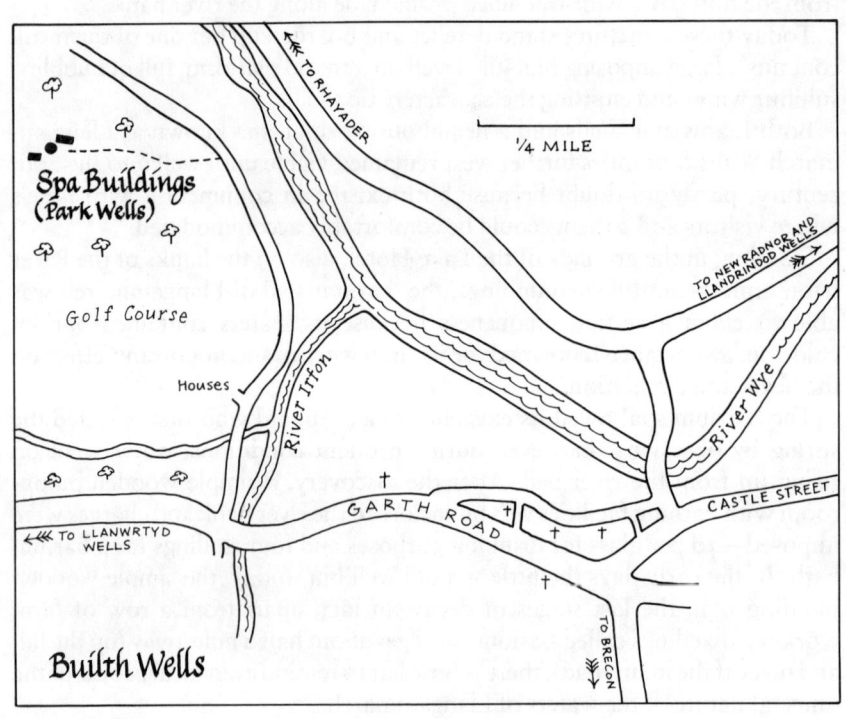

Builth Wells

A LARGER AND considerably more important spa was one at Builth (now in Powys), about seven miles south of Llandrindod Wells. Situated at the point where the River Irfon joins the Wye, Builth originally possessed two spas— Park Wells and Glannau Wells. However, Glannau, with its saline and sulphur waters, had but a short life and is now completely derelict. Park Wells, on the other hand, has still much to show for itself.

Standing on the north-eastern fringe of the town, this attractive Welsh spa had the advantage of possessing three different kinds of water—sulphur, chalybeate and saline—and was once quite fashionable, even in international circles. It was approached by a promenade which, even as far back as 1740, extended all the way from the bridge over the Irfon to the wooded site where a pump-room and ancillary buildings still stand.

The spa at Builth owed much of its early popularity to a visit by a niece of the younger Pitt called Lady Hester Hope and eventually reached its peak about the middle of the Victorian age. After that it began to succumb to growing competition from Llandrindod and became something of a backwater. The decline, however, was relatively slow and it was well into the 20th century before Park Wells was finally closed. The house which was once used to accommodate visitors is now privately occupied while some of the wooden spa buildings, including one used for parties and dances, have been allowed to decay. But the charming little black and white octagonal pump-room, with its four wells now protected by wooden lids, is still preserved in good condition.

Builth Wells

Builth Wells: *Park Wells, from an early 20th century photograph.*
Situated on the outskirts of the Welsh market town, the mineral springs at Builth were known as far back as 1740. During the century that followed, a small spa was established which achieved considerable popularity amongst the local gentry, especially after a visit in 1808 by Lady Hester Stanhope, niece and domestic support of the younger Pitt.

The spa appears to have reached its peak about the middle of the Victorian era, after which it was affected by the exploitation of the springs at Llandrindod. Growing competition from this quarter gradually turned it into something of a backwater but it managed to survive until 1939, when it was finally closed down. The round white-washed building in the picture is the old pump-room which still contains the three tile-lined wells of sulphur, chalybeate and saline waters. The pavilion building on the left was used for parties, while the proprietor's house to the right, now privately occupied, was large enough to accommodate visitors. Although the pavilion has decayed, it is interesting to see how this group of buildings, tucked away in a wood, is still recognisable as a Victorian spa.

Llandrindod Wells

WITHOUT THE arrival of the railway in 1865, Llandrindod would probably never have become the important Welsh spa that pushed Builth into a poor second place. It is thought the place may have been known to the Romans, but by the 17th and 18th centuries it was still no more than a remote Welsh hamlet.

The earliest reference to any mineral water at Llandrindod was in 1696, when one of the saline springs was mentioned as being in use by a family called Vaughan. After that the spring, hidden away in its woodland setting, appears to have been either forgotten or ignored—until it was re-discovered and visited by the occupant of a local farmhouse, a lady by the name of Mrs Jenkins. Mrs Jenkins subsequently discovered a sulphur spring close by and began selling the waters, claiming that they had 'effected some important cures'.

But Llandrindod was still far from becoming the respected spa of Victorian times. There was still only one road over the common, fewer than a dozen houses scattered over a wide area and no real village. In 1749 an ambitious attempt was made by a certain Mr Grosvenor from Shrewsbury to create a spa resort but it ended somewhat ignominiously. With the help of his brother-in-law, Mr Grosvenor began by repairing and extending some of the existing houses and then set about the task of converting a dilapidated mansion near the old parish church into a large and sumptuous hotel. (Known as Llandrindod Hall, it was this mansion that gave the developing village its name.)

Standing in the middle of nowhere, the hotel that emerged had accommodation for several hundred guests and became known as Grosvenor's Hotel. The amenities included the services of hairdressers, milliners and even glovers and it was well equipped with facilities for balls, assemblies, billiards, racing, and all the other entertainments considered necessary to attract fashionable society. No picture survives of this huge establishment but, with its splendid hillside situation looking northward over the lake—one of its dining-rooms stood where Llandrindod Hall Farm now stands—it must have been impressive.

At the beginning the hotel was very successful. According to one account, 'the utmost regularity and systematic management prevailed in the interior of the house; so that attendance, elegant entertainment and a succession of

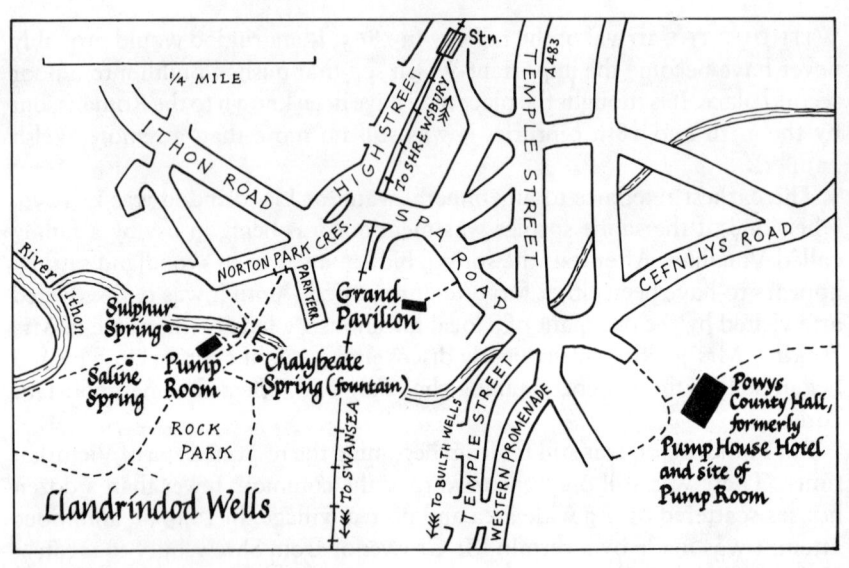

varied amusements gave the place a winning charm or irresistible fascination'. But Grosvenor died in 1757 and, after a few years, the hotel began to acquire an unsavoury reputation for gambling and clandestine love affairs. Understandably, the local people objected and, in due course, the 'fashionable gamesters and libertines' departed, leaving the establishment to decline into a rather pathetic resort for the physically infirm. After 1787 the lease was not renewed and the hotel finally closed in 1790. In its last phase, the building became a 'house of industry'—a sort of weaving manufactory for the ablebodied poor—before finally being razed to the ground at about the turn of the century.

This sad demise did not, of course, mean that people had lost all interest in the springs and in 1805 much smaller premises with an adjacent pump-room were erected about half a mile away to the north, on the site of Mrs Jenkins' farmhouse. Originally described as 'a modern brick sashed dwelling-house', these premises were later given the name of the Pump House Hotel.

With the appearance of the Pump House Hotel, the spa's fortunes began to revive and, on two occasions, the building had to be enlarged. A quaint aspect of spa life in those days was the double-tariff introduced by the proprietor John Cane in 1830. There was one tariff for 'first-class' visitors, who paid £2.10 a week, and another for 'second-class' visitors, who paid £1.60 a week, with lower rates for servants. The two sections of the hotel consequently became known as the 'House of Lords' and the 'House of Commons' but, from all accounts, nobody minded. It was said that the 'Commons' enjoyed themselves very much more than the 'Lords'!

Quite often, however, the problem of choice or allocation did not arise because by this time Llandrindod's popularity was such that many visitors were not even able to obtain admission to the Pump House Hotel. Some went to the ancient Llanerch Inn, some to the Rock House, and others to outlying farmhouses. Sometimes the unlucky ones tried a small neighbouring spa called Llandegley Wells instead, while others went to Blain Edw Farm which stood about three miles away and had its own sulphur spring.

It was about this time that *Cook's Typography of Wales* appeared with details of the various waters and their appropriate dosages, incuding recommendations for the use of the sulphur spring discovered by Mrs Jenkins. This was now regarded as the most important of the springs, its water being described as a purgative of no mean order which 'should on no account be taken in the afternoon'. Possibly to convince people about the water's potency, it was further pointed out that 'when thrown on hot iron, it emits a blue flame and smells like brimstone'.

Compared with these daunting properties, the water of the saline spring appears to have been relatively mild, but there was a warning about the chalybeate spring, the latest of the discoveries. In this case, it was recommended that the water only be taken 'between the hours of six and seven before the sun is too high in the sky' and preferably after bleeding during the period of March to November.

But whatever the limitations and deterrents, the spa at Llandrindod continued to hold its own until the railway's arrival in 1865 heralded the beginning of the boom. After that, expansion was so rapid that by 1888 there were enough genteel hotels and boarding-houses for all who wished to come and it was mainly because of the growing demand for more luxury and the provision of hydropathic facilities that the Pump House Hotel was sold to make way for a more opulent establishment.

A great red-brick structure set in ornamental grounds of nearly a hundred acres, the second Pump House Hotel helped to transform Llandrindod into one of the most popular watering-places in the country. It offered virtually everything, including, by the end of the century, a special parade for the promenaders and a bandstand to enable the early morning ritual of taking the waters to be carried out to the accompaniment of music. One measure of its success was the addition of a new wing in 1900 containing a hundred and fifty additional rooms.

Meanwhile, with expansion still in the air, the town became indebted to a certain Mr Pilot who dreamed, correctly as it turned out, of the existence and location of a saline spring on the west side of the town in what was then known as the Rock House estate—a beautiful wooded glen-like park bounded on its west side by the River Ithon. Exploration revealed not only the existence of the saline spring in a hollow near the Ithon's tributary stream but also the existence of three other kinds of spring—sulphur, chalybeate and magnesia—something which not even Mr Pilot had dreamed of.

The presence of this galaxy of assorted mineral springs, all within a stone's throw of each other, is attributed geologically to the unusual nature of the substrata and it was naturally greeted with enthusiasm by the inhabitants of the spa town, including the owner of the land and promoter of the Central Wales Railway, Sir Richard Green Price.

The task of building a pump-room was immediately undertaken and there emerged the simple black and yellow brick structure with the chequered

Llandrindod Wells: *Old Pump Room and Hotel, from a drawing of 1850.*
These spa premises stood on the site of what is now Powys County Hall where saline and sulphur springs, probably used by the Romans, had been re-discovered in 1736. The old pump-room (on right) with adjacent hotel (centre) were built in about 1805, owing their existence to the demise eighteen years earlier of a much larger spa hotel (originally a mansion called Llandrindod Hall) opened by William Grosvenor of Shrewsbury in 1749 nearer the old parish church and lake. Grosvenor's hotel had succumbed to gamesters and left behind it a somewhat unsavoury reputation which was slow to evaporate. Despite this setback and the remoteness and inaccessibility of the village, the springs still provided opportunities for exploitation and, small though it was, the new hotel, standing where a farmhouse had previously stood, prospered.

From about 1830 its proprietor John Cane operated a double tariff—one for 'first-class' and one for 'second-class' visitors—but not even this unusual degree of discrimination appears to have affected its popularity. Water-drinking began at six in the morning and went on until nine. The spa buildings were gradually enlarged and finally possessed both a parade and a bandstand, but in 1888 they were sold to make way for the large and luxurious Pump House Hotel which nearly a century later, in 1974, was to become the county's administrative headquarters.

Llandrindod Wells: *Pump Room in Rock Park, as seen today.*
On its sloping woodland site near the River Ithon on the west side of the town, this late Victorian pump-room, with its chequered yellow brick, owes its existence to a Mr Pilot who dreamt there was a saline spring near by. The spring was duly discovered and still exists, together with the abandoned pumping machinery, in a shed on the left-hand side of the path leading up towards Arcade Cottages (once part of a small shopping arcade for spa visitors).

With the discovery of three other springs, the pump-room was supplied with four distinctive types of water, all duly dispensed from behind a marble-topped counter. There was magnesia from a spring now buried beneath the tarmacadam at the front; chalybeate from the spring which continues to supply a fountain in the wooded area just beyond; and sulphur from a spring on the bank of the stream at the rear, once reached by a covered way but now lost in undergrowth. The flimsy structure to the right of the picture was originally a covered open area where visitors could sip their water and listen to the band.

Despite its varied inducements, the Rock Park pump-room went into decline after the Second World War and in recent years was leased to an entertainments group. In 1977 this too went bankrupt, leaving the building empty apart from a few surviving hydropathic relics. Its fate now lies in the balance.

design which, although now in its twilight days, still survives. With its picturesque approach by way of the rustic wooden bridge over the stream, the new pump-room was soon attracting a fresh influx of visitors, many of whom used to arrive at the nearby railway station, and it was not long before a covered open-air extension (now boarded up) was built so that people could sit out whilst sipping their water and listen to the band.

In the old days, five distinctive types of water, imaginatively called mild sulphur, radium sulphur, chalybeate, lithium-saline and magnesia, were dispensed from behind the marble-topped counter, while rooms at the rear catered for the patients' hydropathic needs. (A few fearsome looking shower relics were still on the premises in 1978).

A little higher up the hill there was a small shopping arcade built in the same style as the pump-room, while leading from the back of the pump-room there was a covered way down to the sulphur spring on the bank of the stream. According to the boyhood memories of one elderly resident who still lives and works in the park, there was also once a row of sixty rustic toilets lining the upper bank of this leafy walk!

Despite its many and varied inducements, Llandrindod Wells, like most spas, was affected by the First World War and was afterwards left with the task of trying to lure back the visitors. Ambitious plans were drawn up for a fine new pump-room but it did not materialise and some of the other attempts at publicity met with only qualified success. When the Prince of Wales (later Edward VIII) visited the town for the Scout Jubilee in 1926, he was afterwards conducted to the pump-room in Rock Park, given a sample glassful of one of the pleasanter mineral waters and asked what he thought of it. Apparently the royal reply, accompanied by a thoughtful glance out of the window, was: 'You have some beautiful surroundings here'!

However hard the struggle, the Rock Park pump-room managed to remain open throughout the inter-war years but the great Pump House Hotel on the hill at the other side of the town succumbed to a new way of life after being acquired by the Lady Honeywood Hotels Ltd in 1929. During the Second World War its massive late Victorian and Edwardian buildings were requisitioned for use as an officers' cadet training unit and afterwards, in 1947, were converted into a teachers' emergency training college. When the college closed in 1950, the premises were taken over by the educational authorities for use as a school for deaf-mute children, until finally, in 1974, they became, and now look likely to remain, the administrative headquarters of the new county of Powys.

By this time, Rock Park was also council property and, despite all efforts to make it a going concern, the pump-room was near the end of its career. When it finally closed in 1975, the premises were let to an entertainments group which went bankrupt two years later, leaving the fate of the building once again in the balance.

Today Llandrindod's only available natural mineral water is that of a chalybeate spring known as the Rock Spout, which stands in the wooded area facing the Rock Park pump-room. It issues from a fountain given by the lord of the manor in 1879—a time when Llandrindod's star was still in the ascendancy and when the resort was still in process of establishing its lasting and honoured place in spa history.

8
Spa of the North

Harrogate, Knaresborough and Harlow Car

IN THE 16th and 17th centuries, the springs of four neighbouring hamlets known as Knaresborough, High Harrogate, Low Harrogate and Harlow Car within the Forest of Knaresborough laid the foundation of a remarkable group of spas—remarkable because, by the end of the 19th century, there were over ninety known mineral springs within the group. Although a far cry from the fashionable spas of Bath and Tunbridge, this collective 'spa of the north' also had the distinction of being the place where, in 1596, the term 'English spa' originated.

Brought to the surface by the folding and associated faulting of the earth's crust into an anticline running north-east and south-west across Harrogate, the springs that gradually came to light belonged to all three main groups—saline, chalybeate and sulphur—and it is said that no two were exactly alike.

Traditionally the Harrogate area had been associated with springs as far back as the Middle Ages, when a holy well named after a 6th century bishop of Glasgow called St Mungo or St Magnus stood at the top of Cold Bath Road on a site which can still be identified by the inscribed stone wall of a demolished house called St Magnus Villa. (Now the end structure of a row of private garages, the wall survived the demolition.)

Today there is no sign of the holy well and even the mineral springs discovered centuries later lie largely forgotten beneath metal covers in the Valley Gardens and elsewhere. The bath chairs and the water-drinkers have also long since vanished from the scene and Harrogate has been transformed into a conference centre noted more for its flowers and gardens than for its Victorian pump-room (now a museum). Nevertheless, many of the giant hotels erected in the Victorian heyday still stand, reflecting some of the former glory.

The story began with the Tewit Well, which still stands near the south-west corner of the two-hundred-acre Stray (once part of the forest, then a cattle common and now a cultivated tract of open grassland) in the part of the town earlier known as High Harrogate. The Tewit Well was reputedly discovered in 1571 by a nearby land-owner called Slingsby, now believed to have been *Mr* William Slingsby and not Sir William Slingsby as formerly supposed.

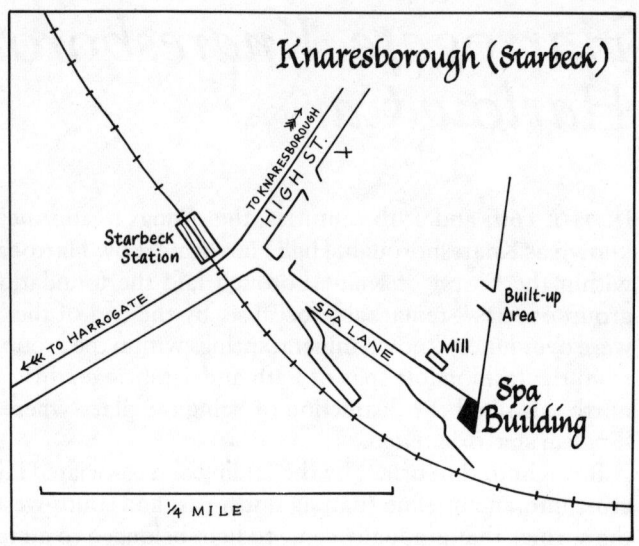

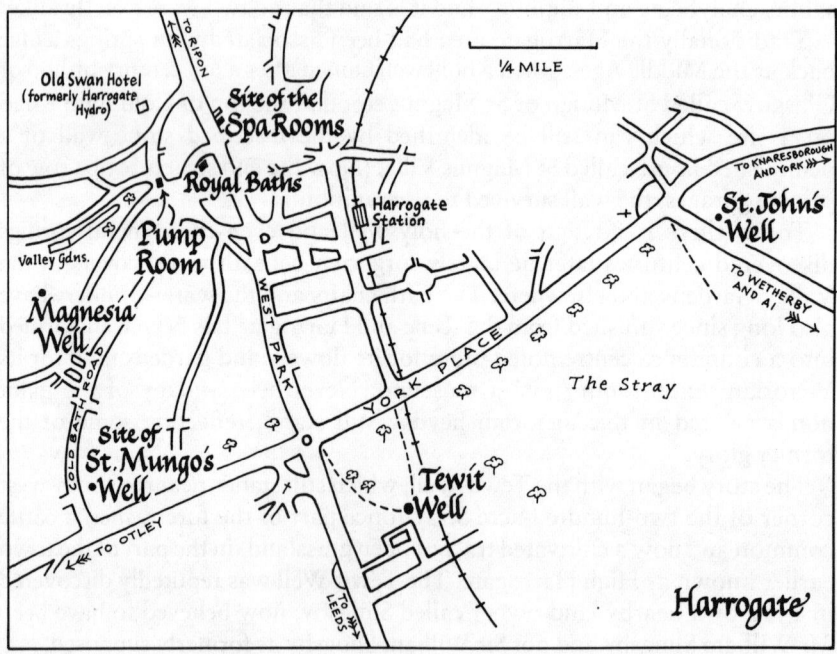

It seems that one day Slingsby noticed the spring and its 'ruddily stained banks', tasted the water and came to the conclusion that it was similar to that which he had drunk the previous year during a visit to Spa in the Belgian Ardennes. Hence the reference twenty-five years later by a physician called Dr Timothy Bright to the 'English spaw' and the subsequent adoption of the term by other writers and by the public at large.

According to the records, Slingsby recognised the potentialities of the chalybeate water almost immediately and had a paved area and a wall built around the well before proclaiming its virtues. Legend suggests that the Tewit Well gradually acquired its name because peewits (lapwings) used to come and drink at it.

The medical profession was soon recommending the bubbling irridescent water of the Tewit Well for complaints ranging from 'melancholic humours' to colic. However, by 1626 the writer of one report was complaining that the well had become dirty and neglected—a reflection perhaps of a maintenance problem due to its situation on what had already been described as a marshy 'rude barren Moore' where gusty winds blew and where there was not an inn in sight.

More favourably situated was the Sweet Spaw, later known as the John or St John's Well, discovered on firmer ground nearly a mile to the east in 1631. Dr Michael Stanhope found this spring beside a path (now the Wetherby road) whilst riding over the common. It was a pure (salt free) chalybeate spring like the Tewit Well but because of its superior situation it soon became the more popular of the two. In the early days it was provided with nothing more than a stone basin but in 1656 a rudimentary walled structure with a low roof was built over it.

Meanwhile the Knaresborough Spaw was growing up around a group of springs only a mile or two east of the John Well. Standing beside a small brook at Starbeck (now an industrial suburb) on the road to Knaresborough, this little spa possessed two alkaline sulphur springs and one chalybeate, which meant that there were waters available for both drinking and bathing. It is known that by 1652, several 'bathing-houses' were already in use at Knaresborough, where people suffering from rheumatism and other muscular pains could enjoy the benefits of heated sulphur water and then relax in a bed of blankets. The bathing-houses were not suites of baths but lodging-houses with a few bath tubs to which the sulphur water was carried in casks from the wells.

After the Forest of Knaresborough was enclosed in 1771, all the Starbeck wells were filled in and were seen no more until the waters began to re-surface of their own accord some fifty years later. Not until then did the Old Spaw rise again and, with the help of public subscriptions, acquire its cottage pump-room of 1828, followed by the later Gothic-style extensions which still survive today as part of an interesting battlemented villa tucked away at the end of a cul-de-sac.

Knaresborough Spaw enjoyed its new lease of life until about the middle of the 19th century, when competition from a new swimming bath in an adjacent field and the rival attractions of expanding Harrogate, with its superior hotels and newly arrived railway, began to take away the visitors. Unable to withstand the loss, the 'old baths' finally closed down in 1890 and the premises became a private residence.

By the middle of the 18th century, several inns catering for visitors who wished to drink at the Tewit and John wells, and perhaps also at the Starbeck well, had established themselves in High Harrogate. There was the Queen's Head (later called the Queen, rebuilt in 1855–61 and now the premises of the Leeds Regional Hospital Board), the Sinking Ship (later called the Royal Oak) and the Granby (rebuilt about 1820), with its long-standing aristocratic connections. There was also the Dragon (demolished in the 1880s to make way for Mornington Crescent), known for its clientèle of wealthy commoners who said they preferred a hotel where they could 'please themselves'.

As well as providing lodgings, the inns became the centre of a developing social life associated with the springs. However, not everyone approved of the way things were going and in 1734 a Dr Short wrote that 'these noble Fountains' were losing 'their due Reputation', that they were 'no longer the Hospital of Invalids, but too often the Rendezvous of Wantonness, and not seldom, of mad Frolicks'.

Although Dr Short's strictures appear not to have affected High Harrogate's growing popularity, there were already signs of increasing competition from the neighbouring sulphur spa of Low Harrogate, which stood about a mile away to the west, in the middle of another common.

Here, down in the valley, was a small group of sulphur springs which had been known and used by the villagers since at least the beginning of the 17th century. The settlement consisted of cottages and lodging-houses, some dating back to a time when they were no more than encroachments on the common. Because it had proved impossible to find any better solution, fines imposed by the Honour court had eventually been converted into annual rents and, by the time a Dr John French published his first treatise on the

Harrogate: *The Tewit Well, as it is today.*

This domed temple-like structure stands above an old chalybeate spring on the west side of the Stray near the Leeds road. Built from a design by Thomas Chippindale in 1804–6, the cover originally stood over the Old Sulphur Well in Low Harrogate and was only transferred here in 1842 when the sulphur well acquired its new pump-room.

The Tewit Well, so named because it used to be frequented by peewits, was the first mineral spring to be discovered at Harrogate. Its discovery is attributed to a certain William Slingsby who had tasted chalybeate water at Spa in the Belgian Ardennes and had noticed the similarity. Although the spring was on a marshy 'rude barren Moore' where cold gusty winds blew and 'there was not an inn in sight', Slingsby decided to exploit it by having it paved and walled in and by proclaiming its virtues. By 1626 the medical profession was recommending it and fashionable society was quick to respond.

The discovery of the John Well on firmer ground nearer the settlement of 'Haregate-head' in 1631 brought serious competition but both wells benefited from the subsequent establishment of local inns such as the Queen's Head, the Granby and the Dragon, all of which had appeared by 1700. It was not until Harrogate's spa activity moved decisively to Low Harrogate that the Tewit Well finally went out of use.

Knaresborough: *Starbeck Spa, otherwise known as Knaresborough Spaw, from an engraving.*

Situated near a small brook a mile or two east of Harrogate, part of these buildings date back to 1828. Records indicate that Starbeck's three mineral springs—two sulphur, one chalybeate—were much used during the 17th century for both drinking and bathing. After the enclosure of Knaresborough Forest in about 1771, however, all the wells were destroyed and it was not until the waters began to make their way to the surface again that interest was re-awakened.

In 1828 the Old Spaw, as it was then known, was rebuilt with the help of public subscriptions and renamed Knaresborough Spaw. Extensions were added in the 1830s and 1840s to provide more bathrooms, and the cottage section seen on the left of the picture was replaced by a double-storeyed Gothic-style building. But already neighbouring Harrogate, with its superior hotel accommodation and new railway connections, was taking away the visitors. In 1870 there was also unexpected competition from the Prince of Wales Baths (complete with swimming bath) erected in the next field. The old baths rapidly declined in popularity and about 1890 they had to close. Hemmed in though they now are by housing developments, the Old Spaw buildings still stand at the cul-de-sac end of Spa Lane, just off the main road.

sulphur water treatment in 1652, the settlement was well established, with some of the houses already possessing facilities for hot sulphur water bathing.

An ardent promoter of the treatment and one who claimed much of the credit for himself, Dr French may well have been responsible for the first defection of patients from High Harrogate. It could even be that some of his remarks about the rival waters of High Harrogate were motivated to this end. 'This water,' he wrote, referring to that of the Tewit and John wells, 'for the most part begetteth a very great appetite, by reason whereof many forgetteth themselves at table'!

But even if the sulphur waters of Low Harrogate produced no such lapses, there were, as Celia Fiennes discovered when she visited the sulphur spa in 1697–8, other problems. The verdict of Celia, who chose to stay in Knaresborough because of a lack of suitable accommodation in Harrogate itself was that 'the Sulphur or Stincking Spaw is not improperly termed for the smell being so strong and offensive that I could not force my horse near the well'.

Whatever the reactions of Celia Fiennes' horse, people still came to the sulphur springs and the trend towards Low Harrogate continued to gain momentum, especially after 1740 when the first real inn, the Crown, appeared beside the main well. (The Swan had existed since about 1700 but it was still just an ordinary tavern with a few nearby cottages.) During or perhaps shortly before 1772, four well-heads were erected over the springs.

Although the relative fortunes of the spas of High Harrogate and Low Harrogate were obviously changing, High Harrogate was still regarded as the social centre of the spa community and, as such, continued to attract a good deal of adverse comment. Even Smollett had his piece to say in *The Expeditions of Humphry Clinker*, published in 1771, when he described the place as 'just a wild common, bare and bleak, without tree or shrub, or the least sign of cultivation; and the people who come to drink the water are crowded together in paltry inns, where the few tolerable rooms are monopolised by the friends and favourites of the house, and all the rest of the lodgers are obliged to put up with dirty holes, where there is neither space, air, or convenience'.

Whether or not these criticisms were prejudiced and exaggerated, they appear to have led to the establishment of a proper routine for all spa visitors so that, by the end of the century, conditions were much improved: 'The company in general rise early and repair to the wells, from whence after drinking the water, they return and breakfast at separate tables as they choose or chance to come in: the time betwixt this and dinner is generally spent in making excursions into different parts of the neighbourhood, which abounds with a variety of places well worth the attention of strangers: when the weather will not permit these excursions, a variety of amusements offer themselves indoors, as reading, playing at billiards, cards, etc. At dinner each person takes their seat in the order they arrived at the place, and ascend gradually as others leave it.'

Another improvement was the construction in 1786 of a small domed well-house over the St John's Well. This was paid for by Lord Loughborough, owner of an adjacent estate, and led shortly afterwards to the digging of ditches to provide a drained enclosure with a 'necessary House for Drinkers'.

By the beginning of the 19th century, there was a similar call for improvements at Low Harrogate, where it was realised that the sulphur springs merited something better than a few rudimentary well-head covers. In 1804 the whole area around the main well was drained and paved and a local man called Thomas Chippindale was commissioned to design and build a proper shelter. The result was an open structure with a cupola roof supported on eleven slender Doric pillars (the whole structure was later transferred to the Tewit Well where it still stands) which did much to attract a more fashionable clientèle. Even Lord Byron came and stayed at the Crown in 1806.

By this time, the chalybeate waters of the Crescent Well discovered in 1783 and of St George's Well (near the present St George Hotel), discovered about 1729, were also on offer in Low Harrogate and a further attraction was the so-called Promenade Room (a building now known as the Old Town Hall or the local Finance Office in Swan Road) which appeared a year later to provide shelter and entertainment for visitors in wet weather. Then, in 1818–19, came the important discovery of a sulphur spring on the east side of the Ripon road and this, together with the re-discovery of St George's chalybeate spring (destined to be destroyed later during the making of a highway drain) was all that was needed to start Harrogate off on a new phase of development.

The waters of the new saline spring were claimed to be virtually the same as those of Cheltenham and in 1835 an entrepreneur called John Williams stepped into the picture. After pulling down the small pump-room which had already been erected, Williams built the Royal Promenade and Cheltenham Pump Room—a building which, in later years, was to become known as the Cheltenham Spa Rooms and then as the Spa Concert Rooms.

Standing on a prominent corner site (now part of the Conference Centre complex, adjacent to the Royal Hall), this was the last of the privately owned spas and, until its demolition in 1939, was probably the most impressive

Harrogate: *St John's Well (seen from the east), from a drawing of 1831.*
Situated on the famous open common (now called the Stray), with Christ Church in the background, this small domed well-house was built in 1786 at the expense of Lord Loughborough, new owner of a nearby estate. It housed a chalybeate spring originally known as the 'Sweet Spaw' which had been discovered by Dr Michael Stanhope in 1631, replacing a rudimentary walled structure with low roof built over a stone basin in 1656. Ditches dug in those early days had helped to create a small drained enclosure beside which 'a necessary House for Drinkers' was eventually erected.

Because the John Well was sited on drier ground and was nearer the inns than the neighbouring Tewit Well, it became and remained High Harrogate's most popular spa throughout the 17th and 18th centuries. In 1842 the well-house was replaced by another octagonal, but this time domeless, building which still stands.

building in Harrogate. Its temple-like structure contained a library, a gallery, a large saloon and various other interesting features and facilities.

With the appearance of John Williams' creation, the Old Sulphur Well was seen as primitive and increasingly unsafe—so much so that in 1838 there was a public outcry. The result was that in 1841 steps were taken to secure an Act of Parliament for the setting up of the Harrogate Improvement Commissioners with powers to safeguard and improve the public wells.

The Improvement Commissioners were made responsible for directing further expansion and for exploiting any future discoveries, but their first task was the construction of a proper pump-room over the old sulphur spring. It was this task which, in 1842, led to the transference of Chippindale's domed and eleven-pillared shelter to the Tewit Well and the erection of a new octagonal building designed by Isaac Shutt, whose family kept the Old Swan, in its place. The octagonal stone building was, of course, the Royal Pump Room, now a museum but still one of the town's focal points and probably its most important historical landmark.

With the appearance of the new pump-room, a daily routine was quickly established. Clients would arrive between 7 and 9 a.m. and, for a small charge, be served with one or more glasses of the water. After that, they would normally join the promenaders outside, where they could concentrate on the music, the fashion and the gossip before returning to their lodgings for breakfast. Except for the genuinely afflicted, who spent most of their time undergoing hot-bath treatments, the rest of the day was usually taken up with shopping, sight-seeing and parties. For the local people and the less well-off, there was a public pump outside the building attended by a well-woman.

Shortly after the Royal Pump Room was built, Isaac Shutt was also commissioned to design a replacement pump-room for St John's Well on the Stray and, once again, he produced an octagonal building, though on a much smaller scale. Although eventually, like other pump-rooms in the town, it had to close, this later version of the John Well still survives beside the road leading into Harrogate from Wetherby. For some years after its closure, the building was used as a café but then became derelict and a target for vandals before finally, in 1981, finding a new use as a flower shop and refreshment kiosk. However the chalybeate water still rises from the original spring and can once again be sampled for a small charge.

In spite of the growing importance of publicly commissioned buildings, most of Harrogate's early Victorian spa fame still depended on private enterprise. In 1835 Joseph Thackwray, owner of the Crown, had built the

Harrogate: *The Sulphur Well of 1806, from a drawing of the period.*
With its cupola roof and eleven Doric pillars, this shelter over the main sulphur spring was designed by a local man, Thomas Chippindale. It replaced a group of rudimentary stone well-head covers. Standing in a freshly drained and paved area, the shelter attracted a more fashionable clientèle to Low Harrogate and remained popular for many years. By 1842, however, it was regarded as primitive and unsafe and the newly appointed Harrogate Improvement Commissioners had it dismantled and transported to the Tewit Well for re-erection there. The level of the land around the sulphur well was then raised and the building later known as the Royal Pump Room was built on the site, with the well located in the basement.

Harrogate: *The Royal Promenade and Cheltenham Pump Room, later known as The Spa Rooms, from an engraving.*

This Doric temple-like building was erected in 1835 to house Harrogate's first purely saline spring, discovered in 1819 by two gentlemen called Oddy and Williams.

After its sulphur-free water had been enthusiastically hailed as similar to that of Cheltenham, the spring and, in due course, the Pump Room were named accordingly. One hundred feet long and thirty-three feet wide, the building was lighted on one side by a series of lofty windows. There was a gallery and small library and in 1870 an iron and glass pump-room and colonnade were added on the garden side. Standing adjacent to the site on which the new Kursaal (re-named the Royal Hall in 1914 and now used as a theatre) was to be built in 1903, it was the last of Harrogate's private spas. It was acquired by the borough council in 1896 and used as a concert hall. For reasons unknown, it was demolished in 1939 and the pillars transported to the Northern Horticultural Society's gardens at Harlow Car. A small car park took its place until 1978, when the site was developed as part of a new conference centre.

Montpellier Baths, set in ornamental gardens on land adjacent to his hotel and, within four years, was witnessing the fruits of his labours in terms of six thousand baths being taken in one session alone. There was also a rival establishment known as the Victoria Baths set up by John Williams in 1832 on the site of the Crescent Gardens, where the saline-chalybeate spring had been discovered in 1783. Both Thackwray's and Williams' premises were destined to be replaced eventually by late Victorian buildings but, in their day, both of these privately owned establishments made big profits and a substantial and notable contribution to the Harrogate scene. Furthermore, they did much to create the climate of expansion which was to carry this vigorous northern spa through the Victorian and Edwardian eras at a time when other spas were faltering and struggling for survival.

In 1868 the Improvement Commissioners embarked on a policy of bringing the whole of the spa area of Low Harrogate under municipal ownership and of expanding its facilities to the point where no other British spa could claim superiority. It was an ambitious programme and, predictably, the money was not always easy to come by, especially for the acquisition of the prosperous privately owned establishments. The first acquisition was made in 1871 when John Williams' Victoria Baths were bought and replaced by the New Victoria Baths (premises which were themselves replaced in 1931 by the present-day Muncipal Offices).

The purchase of the Victoria Baths probably marked the beginning of the expansionary phase which was to follow and which should probably be seen in terms of a spa revival rather than in terms of continuing development. The late Victorian spa which was to emerge, complete with solid 'municipal Gothic' architecture, certainly had little in common with 18th century High Harrogate.

The new identity was naturally bound up with the changing character of Harrogate itself—already a very desirable residential town ready and willing to accept its predominantly middle-class spa clientèle but less than enthusiastic about the day trippers who were now beginning to arrive from the neighbouring west Yorkshire industrial towns, and the Sunday excursionists who refused to be deterred even by exhortations from the pulpit.

This was a time when more and more springs kept cropping up on the marshy stretch of land known as Bog's Field—a field hemmed in by rising land just to the south-west of the Pump Room. Most of these springs were of the sulphur variety but eventually a 'magnesia' well was discovered and provided with its own small 'Gothic' pump-room. (After 1895, the position

Harrogate: *The Royal Pump Room, from a drawing made soon after it was built over the Old Sulphur Well in Low Harrogate in 1842.*

Designed by Isaac Shutt for the newly formed Improvement Commissioners at a cost of £3000, it replaced an earlier shelter of 1804–6. (The earlier shelter, consisting of cupola and pillars, was removed to the Tewit Well about a mile away, where it remains to this day.) Originally the Old Sulphur Well was protected by nothing more than a low stone cover, but it had been in use by villagers for the treatment of skin diseases since at least the beginning of the 17th century.

The new Pump Room provided a focus for the emerging spa town, enabling it to go on expanding throughout the Victorian era and to benefit from the patronage of the queen's eldest daughter. In 1913 it acquired an annexe but the First World War and subsequent depression heralded a decline which ultimately led to its closure. It was converted into a museum in 1953. The Harrogate motto 'Arx Celebris Fontibus', inscribed over one of its doors, means 'a citadel famous for its springs'.

Harrogate: *St John's Well, as it is today.*

Situated on the Stray beside the approach road from Wetherby, this small octagonal well-house was built in 1842 as a replacement for the earlier domed building of 1786. It was designed for the Harrogate Improvement Commissioners by Isaac Shutt, the local architect whose Royal Pump Room had just appeared in Low Harrogate on the west side of the developing town. It is still an interesting landmark and reminder of the days when this side of Harrogate, once known as Haregate-head, was a small village whose two chalybeate springs attracted fashionable people from many distant parts of the country.

of the well's pump was moved and a circular domed shelter built over it. This still survives today as a café, leaving the original structure to serve as a gardeners' tool shed.)

Probably the biggest boost to town and spa alike came in 1884 when Harrogate was incorporated as a municipal borough and acquired a new council. The council adopted the motto *Arx Celebris Fontibus*—'a citadel famous for its springs'—and two years later, in 1886, bought Bog's Field which it duly re-opened a year later as the Valley Gardens.

The next venture was in 1888 when the Montpellier estate was purchased and, with the exception of the small octagonal entrance kiosk which now survives as a knitwear shop, Joseph Thackwray's original Montpellier Baths were demolished to make way for the Royal Baths and Winter Gardens. A huge and undistinguished but lavishly equipped late Victorian building, the Royal Baths cost £118,000 and was finally opened in 1897, a year after the council acquired the last remaining private spa, the Cheltenham Spa Rooms.

By this time Harrogate, like so many other surviving spas, was deeply involved in the hydropathic 'cure' and in 1889 the Royal Bath Hospital appeared on the skyline above the Valley Gardens on the site of a hospital founded in 1824 'for the relief of poor persons whose cases require the use of various mineral waters and baths of Harrogate'. The new hospital had virtually everything it could wish for, including the advantages of two huge hydropathic hotels near by. The Harrogate Hydro (a reincarnation of the Old Swan which was to revert to its original name in 1952) was already in operation and the Cairn Hydro was to be opened in 1890.

Among the hydros which were subsequently to appear in and around Low Harrogate was one at Harlow Car (now famous for its gardens run by the Northern Horticultural Society) about two miles to the south-west. Harlow Car was a small separate village, but its chalybeate and alkaline sulphur waters had been known since the 18th century and it seemed an ideal spot for such an establishment. In 1893 extensions were built on to an existing house called Harlow Manor which a Leeds architect, John Milling, had built for himself nearly twenty years earlier. It was suitably fitted out with all the latest hydropathic devices and was soon in business, providing treatment and hotel facilities under one roof.

Unlike its Harrogate contemporaries, however, the Harlow Carr Hydro had the disadvantage of being too far out of town to remain viable as a hotel once the public had lost interest in hydrotherapy and eventually the exten-

Harrogate: *The Montpellier Sulphur Well and Baths, from an engraving.*
Erected in 1835, the baths were fed by a spring originally known as the Crown Sulphur Well which stood in the garden of the original Crown Hotel. (The hotel had been built in 1740 close to the Old Sulphur Well and was the first of any importance in Low Harrogate.) Having discovered the new spring in 1822, the proprietor laid out the pleasure gardens for the benefit of those who came to drink and bathe. However, by 1871, the Improvement Commissioners had rebuilt the nearby Victoria Baths (on the site of the present Municipal Offices) and had embarked on a programme of expansion which was eventually to bring the whole of the spa area under municipal ownership. About 1890, the Montpellier establishment was demolished and the extensive and lavishly equipped Royal Baths (opened 1897) built on the site. Only the tiny kiosk (left of picture), now used as a shop and known as the White Cottage, survives today at the corner of Montpellier Road and Montpellier Gardens.

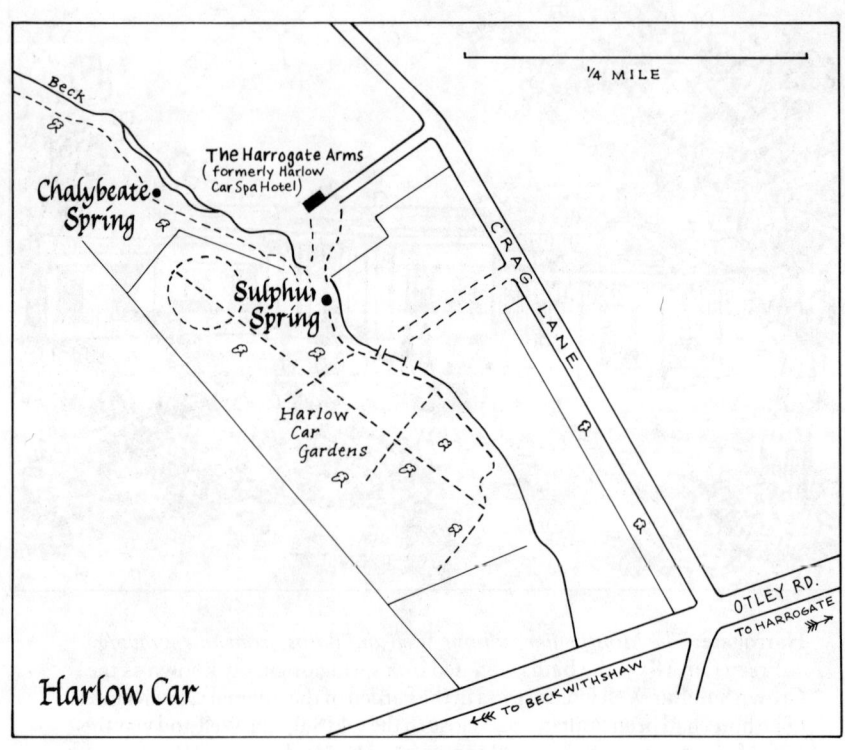

sions were pulled down, leaving only the original house and the name Harlow Carr Hydro still decipherable on the parapet.

Today the sulphur springs of Harlow Car lie hidden beneath metal covers in the Horticultural Gardens and the chalybeate spring on the bank beside the stream can only be located with difficulty. Nevertheless, the place is not without its spa relic for, in a distant woodland setting facing the main entrance to the Gardens, there now stands, like some ancient citadel, a group of classical-style pillars. They are part of the façade of Harrogate's Cheltenham Spa Rooms re-erected here after the building was demolished in 1939.

At the beginning of the 20th century, Harrogate made its final, and as it turned out, misguided gesture of confidence in its spa future. It built the Kursaal (re-named the Royal Hall after war broke out in 1914) and two more enormous hotels—the Majestic in 1900 and the Grand in 1903. In fact, so buoyant was the mood and the demand for Harrogate water that, even as late as 1913, the Royal Pump Room was provided with an extension.

All these buildings have survived, though the days have long since passed when they catered for spa visitors. The Grand Hotel has been renamed Windsor House and is now the Valuations Office of the Inland Revenue, the Majestic is patronised chiefly by conference visitors, while the Royal Hall, situated next to the giant new Conference Centre, now provides light entertainment for everybody.

Many of these changes can be attributed to the 1930s when the changes in medical fashon and social customs finally forced the Royal Pump Room to close its doors. During the sad period that followed, the building was used first as a store and then as a restaurant, before re-surfacing in 1953 as a local history museum complete with a new flatter roof covered with copper tiles in place of the old lead ones (made necessary by collapsing roof timbers).

Today the old sulphur spring, with its basin of clear cold odorous water, can once again be seen and sampled. It stands in the basement of the building at the original ground level, with an effigy beside it of a celebrated Victorian well-woman called Betty Lupton who used to work at the pump outside. Even the old hand-operated pump installed to draw water from one of the other sulphur springs on the site has survived and stands against the wall. Nowadays a modern electrically operated pump supplies an outside tap—though not, from all accounts, with the same degree of reliability as the old hand pumps of Betty Lupton's day.

Some say that Harrogate's spa era ended with the closure of the Pump Room, others that it ended earlier at the time of the First World War when the old order died. Whenever it was, this famous northern spa, which had never once been visited by a reigning monarch, survived the Edwardian era in style and, true to form, was among the last to surrender.

Pharmaceutical Notes

THESE BRIEF pharmaceutical notes are appended for the interest of readers who are curious to know how the active ingredients of the various types of mineral water 'worked', or were presumed to work. They are based partly on information given in the Pharmaceutical Codex of 1907—a time when some spa waters were still being drunk.

The Saline Waters

The purgative action of salts such as magnesium sulphate (Epsom Salt) contained in the natural saline waters is due to the fact that they remain unabsorbed by the blood stream, while withdrawing fluid by osmosis from the surrounding tissues. By this means they are able to increase the quantity of fluid in the intestines. Since removal of fluid from the body causes a reduction in blood pressure, they were considered beneficial in cases of a whole variety of inflammatory and congestive conditions, including dropsy, and were likewise prescribed for gout and liver complaints.

The Chalybeate Waters

By supplying an extra quantity of iron, salts such as ferrous sulphate present in the chalybeate waters were considered good for anaemia and allied complaints caused by deficiencies in the absorption of iron from the alimentary canal. These waters were drunk for their 'tonic' effect and were prescribed for people suffering from virtually any condition associated with 'poverty of the blood', including even those with debilitating diseases such as tuberculosis.

The Sulphur Waters

Although sulphur itself is an inert substance, some of the sulphides and other sulphur compounds present in the natural sulphur waters are antiseptics capable of killing the parasites responsible for certain skin diseases. They also have a stimulating effect upon the skin, particularly noticeable when the water is heated. Because of this tonic effect, hot sulphur baths became popular with people suffering from complaints such as chronic rheumatic arthritis.

N.B. Even today, sulphur compounds are used in conditions such as acne.

Bibliography

Local History Collections
The Spas of Britain (Official Handbook of the British Spas Federation)
The Spas of England by Dr A. B. Granville, 1841 (reprinted Adams & Dart 1971)
English Spas by William Addison (Batsford) 1951
Discovering Spas by R. L. P. and Dorothy M. Jowitt (Shire Publications) 1971
The Spas of England by Peter J. Neville Havins (Hale) 1976
Spas that Heal by William A. R. Thompson (A & C Black) 1978
Bath Portrait by Bryan Little (The Burleigh Press) 1968
Bath—An Architectural Guide by Charles Robertson (Faber) 1973
Pelton's Illustrated Guide to Tunbridge Wells by J. Radford Thomson, 1881 (reprinted by S.R. Publishers 1972)
Tunbridge Wells by Terence Davis (Phillimore) 1976
Royal Tunbridge Wells by Alan Savidge (Midas Books) 1977
The Story of the Pantiles by Martyn Hepworth (The Pantiles Association) 1956
Epsom by Gordon Home (reprinted by S.R. Publishers)
St Ann's Well, Buxton (High Peak publication)
The Crescent at Buxton (High Peak publication)
The Peak District by F. R. Banks (Hale) 1975
Bristol in the 18th Century Ed. Patrick McGrath (David & Charles) 1972
Bristol as it Was by Bruce Winstone, 1971
Portrait of Bristol by Keith Brace (Hale) 1971
A History of Bristol and Gloucestershire by Brian Smith and Elizabeth Ralph (Darwen, Finlayson & Beaconsfield) 1972
The Survey of London by John Stow, 1958 (reprinted by J. M. Dent 1970)
The London Pleasure Gardens of the 18th Century by W. and A. E. Wroth (Macmillan) 1896
Greater London by Edward Walford (Cassell) 1898
Springs, Streams and Spas of London by Alfred Stanley Foord (T. Fisher Unwin) 1910
Greater London by Christopher Trent (Phoenix House) 1965
The Royal Parks of London by Richard Church (HMSO) 1965

The History of Streatham by Frederick Arnold (Elliot Stock) 1886
Read about Sydenham Wells by Joan Read, 1977
The Story of Norwood by J. B. Wilson (London Borough of Lambeth) 1973
Cheltenham by Simona Pakenham (Macmillan) 1971
Southampton through the Ages by Elsie M. Sandell
Brighton by Edward M. Gilbert (Flare Books) 1954
Life in Brighton by Clifford Musgrave (Faber) 1970
Yorkshire, North Riding by Malcolm Barker (Batsford) 1977
Dorton House by Lewis G. Creed, 1957
History and Directory of the Counties of Leicester and Rutland by William White
Portrait of Gloucestershire by T. A. Ryder (Hale)
Leamington, Week by Week (magazine)
A History of Malvern by Brian S. Smith (Leicester University Press) 1964
Malvern Country by Vincent Waite (Dent) 1968
The Sixpenny Ilkley Guide Book
Matlock by B. Bryan, 1903
The Peak District by Roy Christian (David & Charles) 1976
The Matlocks and their Past (Derbyshire County Library) 1977
Strathpeffer Spa by Fortescue Fox (H. K. Lewis) 1889
Yorkshire through the Years by Ian Dewhurst (Batsford) 1975
Boston Spa by Beatrice M. Scott
Askern by Gordon Smith (Spotbrough) 1968
The Companion Guide to North Wales by Elizabeth Beazley and Peter Howell (Collins) 1975
An Account of the Knaresborough Spaw by M. Calvert, 1841
An Atlas of Harrogate by J. A. Patmore (Corporation of Harrogate) 1963
A History of the Wells and Springs of Harrogate by Bernard Jennings (Corporation of Harrogate) 1974
A History of Harrogate and Knaresborough by the W.E.A. History Group (The Advertiser Press, Huddersfield) 1970

Index

Acton Wells, 79, 90, 93
Adam, Robert, 43, 230
Adelaide, Queen, 133, 135, 136, 179
Admaston spa, 153
Aesculapius (god of healing), 81, 82, 115, 119
Akemanceaster (Bath), 3
Aldfield spa, 208, 209, 210
Allen, Ralph, 6
Anne of Denmark, 4, 5
Anne, Queen, 19, 20, 33
Aquae Arnemetiae (Buxton), 37
Aquae Sulis (Bath), 3
Ashby de la Zouch: 150–152, 153; Ivanhoe Baths, 150, 151, 152
Askern spa, 220–223
Astrop (and King's Sutton) spa, 26–30, 37
Aubrey, John, 31, 79
Aylesford, fourth Earl of, 161, 164

Baldwin, Thomas, 11, 12, 13
Bagnigge Wells, 67–69
Bakewell spa, 233
Barium salts, 245
Barnet Well, 77, 95, 96–100, 139
Bath: xv, xvi, xviii, 2–15, 17, 20, 21, 37, 40, 47, 50, 73, 108, 140, 149, 176, 259; Assembly Rooms, 8, 9, 10, 11; Cross Bath, 4, 6, 11, 12, 14, 15; Hemming Bath, 11; Hot Bath, 4, 11, 12, 14, 15; King's Bath, 3–8, 11, 14, 15; Mineral Water Hospital, 9, 15, Pump Room (early), 7, 9; Pump Room (Great), 6, 8, 9, 12, 13, 14, 15; Queen's Bath, 4, 5, 7, 14; Roman Baths, 14
Ben Rydding, *see Ilkley*
Bergavenney (later Abergavenney), Barons, 17, 20

Bermondsey spa, 85
Beulah Spa, 86–88, 89
Billing's Well, 90
Bladud, Prince, 3, 14
Bolton, James, 52
Boston Spa, 216–219
Boswell, James, 201
Bright, Dr Timothy, 261
Brighton: 22, 130, 132–137, 139, 176; German Spa, 132–137; St Ann's Well, 132, 133, 134, 136
Bristol: xiii, 37, 47–52; Colonnade, 47, 48, 49, 50, 52; Hotwell House (First), 47, 49, 50, 105; Hotwell House (Second), 51, 52
British Spas Federation, 169, 209, 281
Bromley spa, 85
Brydon, J. M., 13
Builth Wells, 246–248, 249
Burney, Fanny, 108
Burns, Robert, 201
Burton, Decimus, 87
Busby, Eric, 186, 187
Buxton: xv, xx, 37–46, 47, 192, 233; Buxton Hall, 37, 39; Devonshire Royal Hospital, 40, 42, 43; Grand Assembly Room, 45; Natural Mineral Water Baths, 37, 45; St Ann's Well, 37, 39, 40, 41, 44, 45
Byng, Hon. John, 108

Camberwell spa, 85
Cane, John, 251, 253
Canterbury spa, 232
Carlyle, Thomas, 180
Carr, John, 37, 40, 41, 42, 43
Catherine of Braganza, 6, 18, 47, 50
Causey, Bell, 19
Chaplin, Robert, 151, 152

Charles I, 4, 18, 19, 20
Charles II, 6, 18, 20, 31, 33, 34, 35, 47, 50, 92
Chaytor, Sir William, 203, 206
Cheltenham: xvii, xx, 36, 40, 103, 104–119, 155, 156, 157, 266, 270; Assembly Rooms, 107, 112, 116; Cambray Spa, 104, 112; King's Well, 109, 111; Montpellier Wells, 110, 111, 115, 116; Original or Old Well/Spa, 104, 105, 106, 108, 109, 111; Pittville Pump Room, 104, 112, 115, 116; Rotunda, 104, 110, 111, 113; Sherborne (Dr Jameson's) Well, 111; Sherborne Pump Room (later Imperial Spa), 104, 112, 114, 116
Chippindale, Thomas, 263, 266, 268, 269
Civic Trust, 177, 180
Civil War, 18
Clerk's Well, 56, 64
Cobham spring, 100
Continental spas, xv, xix, 17, 20, 135, 136, 173, 186, 199, 261, 263
Corbett, John, 233, 236, 237
Cotton, Charles, 39
Croft-on-Tees: 303–307; New Well/Spa, 204, 205, 206, 207; Old Well, 203, 206
Cromartie, Earl of, 201
Crowder's Well, 64
Cuffe, Dr., 227
Currey, Henry, 42, 43, 44

Darwin, Charles, 180
Defoe, Daniel, 32, 139
Delves, Sir Thomas, 37, 39, 40, 41
Devonshire, Dukes of, 40, 45
Dickens, Charles, 87, 180
Dodgson, Dr., 213, 215
Dorton spa, 143–147, 149

Droitwich: xxi, 233–237, 239; Royal Brine Baths, 233, 234, 235; Old Saline Baths, 233, 235; St Andrew's Baths, 233, 236, 237
Duke, R. R., 45
Dulwich Wells, 79, 83, 84

East Sheen—Palewell, 89
Edlingham spa, 202
Edward VIII, 255
Elizabeth I, 4, 37, 39, 175
Elliston, Robert, 163
Enclosure Act, 43, 261
Epsom: xvii, 31–36, 37, 61, 73, 79, 139; New Wells, 32, 33, 35, 36; Old Well, 31–36
Epsom Salt, xvi, 31–36, 71, 87, 279
Evans, Rev. Theophilus, 243, 244
Evelyn, John, xvii, 4, 57, 83, 85

Faraday, Michael, 87
Farrow, Mrs Elizabeth, 139, 142
Fauconberg, Lord, 108, 109, 111
Field, Mrs., 105, 107
Fiennes, Celia, xvii, 6, 28, 31, 33, 34, 39, 47, 97, 100, 139, 232, 265
Finsbury Spa, *see London Spa*
Fitzherbert, Mrs., 87
Fitzwilliam, Earl, 211
Fleet, River, 55, 67, 68
Forty, Hannah, 106
Fountain, The, 64
Fountains Abbey, 209
French, Dr John, 262, 265
Fuller, Thomas, 97

Gainsborough spa, 223
George II, 57, 127
George III, 83, 103, 108, 109, 111, 115, 119, 121, 122, 123, 124, 125
George IV, 133, 135, 136
George V, 229
George, Prince of Denmark, 33, 34, 35
Gibbons, Dr., 92

Index 285

Gilsland spa, 202
Gladstone, W. E., 156, 180
Glauber's Salt, 71
Gloucester spa, 154–160
Godstone spring, 100
Goldsmith, Oliver, 69, 92
Graefenburg, 179, 186, 188
Granville, Dr A. B., xix, 22, 23, 52, 136, 209, 211, 219, 225, 227, 239, 281
Grosvenor, William, 249, 251, 253
Gully, Dr James, 173, 179, 180, 181, 182
Gwynne, Nell, 33, 35, 67

Hampstead spa, 77, 92, 94, 95
Harrogate: xx, xxi, 123, 165, 206, 210, 259–267; Cheltenham Pump Room/Spa Rooms, 266, 270, 274, 277; Harlow Car, 259, 270, 274, 276, 277; Montpellier Baths, 271, 274, 275; Old Sulphur Well, 262, 263, 265, 268, 269, 272, 277; Royal Baths, 274, 275; Royal Pump Room, 268, 269, 271, 273, 277; St John's Well (Sweet Spaw), 261, 262, 263, 265, 266, 267, 268, 273; Tewit Well, 259, 261, 263, 265, 266, 267, 268, 269, 272; Victoria Baths, 271, 275
Harvey, John, 6, 8, 11
Hastings, Marquess of, 151, 152
Hawkins, Sir John, 58
Henrietta, Maria, Queen, 2, 18, 20
Henry I, 3, 5
Henry VIII, 37, 61
Hockley spa, 230
Horneyold, T. C., 175
Hotchkin, Stafford, 228
Hotchkin, Thomas, 225, 228
Houghton-le-Spring, 202
Hovingham spa, 211, 212
Hughes, Thomas, 107, 112
Hygeia (goddess of health), 111, 114, 115, 118, 119

Ilkley: 184–189, 191; White Wells, 184, 185, 186, 187; Ben Ryhdding Hydro, 186, 188, 189, 191, 192, 196
Iodine salts, 157, 160, 225, 227, 228, 230, 231, 239
Islington Spa, 56–60, 69

James I, 4, 5, 17, 31, 100, 211
James II, 6, 12
Jameson, Dr., 111
Jelf, Sir James, 156, 159
Jenkins, Mrs., 249, 251
Jephson, Dr., 167
Johnson, Dr Samuel, 107

Kent, Duchess of, 22, 23, 179
Kilburn Wells, 90, 92
King's Sutton, *see Astrop*
Knaresborough spa, 139, 259, 260, 261, 262, 264

Ladywell (Lewisham), 85
Lambeth Wells, 85
Leamington: xx, xxi, 143, 145, 161–169, 173, 233; Abbot's/Smith's Saline Baths, 161; Assembly Rooms, 162, 163, 166; Aylesford Well, 161, 162, 164; Royal Pump Room, 162, 163, 167, 168, 169; Smart's Marble Baths/Imperial Fount, 162, 163; Wise's/Curtis's Baths, 161
Levingstone, apothecary, 33, 35
Llandrindod Wells: xx, xxi, 247, 248, 249–256; Old Pump House and Hotel, 250, 251, 252, 253; Rock Park, 251, 252, 254, 255, 256
Llangammarch Wells, 242, 245
Llanwrtyd Wells, 242, 243, 244, 245
London Spa, 56, 64, 65
Lower, Dr Richard, 27
Lupton, Betty, 277
Lysons, Daniel, 73

Macaulay, Lord, 180
Malton spa, 211

Malvern: xvii, 173, 174–183, 185, 186; Ditchford's/Mary's/Nancy's Well, 175, Hay Well, 174, 175; Holy Well, 174, 175, 176, 177; Priessnitz House, 180, 182, 183; St Ann's Well, 174, 175, 176, 178, 179, 182; Spa Cottage and Villa, 176, 180, 181; Well House and Rock House, 176, 177
Marlborough, Sarah, Duchess of, 47, 50
Marlborough, Dukes of, 19, 133
Mary of Modena, 6, 12, 14
Mary, Queen of Scots, xvii, 37
Mason, William, 105, 109
Matlock: xx, 190–196, 233; Grand Pavilion, 190, 191, 194, 195; Matlock Bath, 190, 191, 192, 193, 194, 195; Old Bath, 191, 193; Old Pavilion, 193, 195; Smedley's Hydro, 191, 194, 195
Melksham spa, 148–149
Middleton, Squire, 185, 187
Miller, William, 107, 108
Milner, Edward, 45
Mistley spa, 230
Moffat spa, 201
Moreau, Simon, 107, 108
Muswell spring, 92, 95

Nash, Richard (Beau), xvii, xviii, 6, 8, 9, 11, 20, 21, 143
National Health Service, xxi, 14, 169, 207, 229, 231, 237
New River, 57, 60, 61
New Tunbridge Wells, *see Islington Spa*
Nightingale, Florence, 180
North, Lord Dudley, 17, 20
Northaw Spring, or King's Well, 100
Norton, Martha, 40
Nottington Spa, *see Weymouth*

Oliver, Dr William, 9
Orange, Prince of, 8

Palmer, John, 11, 13
Pancras Spa, 71, 72, 73

Papworth, John Buonarotti, 112, 113
Parkhurst, John, 33
Parkinson, John, 225, 228
Paxton, John, 43, 140, 141, 142, 192
Pepys, Samuel, xvii, 4, 19, 33, 35, 47, 97
Pilot, Mr., 252, 254
Pitt, Joseph, 112, 115, 118
Powis Well, 56, 64, 66
Priessnitz, Vincent, 173, 180
Prince Hoare, 9
Prince Regent, 22, 129, 130, 133, *see also George IV*

Radcliffe, Dr., 28, 29
Radipole Spa, *see Weymouth*
Richmond spa, 77, 89
Ripon spa, 208–210
Romans, The, 3, 7, 15, 37, 40, 185, 191, 233, 243, 249, 253
Rosoman, Thomas, 63, 65
Rowlandson, Thomas, 11, 14
Rowzee, Dr., 18
Russell, Dr Richard, 133, 134, 139

Sadler, Thomas, 61, 62
Sadler's Wells, 56, 61–63, 64
St Ann, 37
St Chad's Well, 70, 71
St George's Spa, 85
St Govor's Well, 90, 91
St John's Priory, 61, 64
St Mungo/Magnus, 259
St Rumbold, 26, 27, 29, 30
Satchwell, Benjamin, 161, 164
Saxons, The, 15, 37, 143
Scarborough: 133, 138–142, 211; New Spa, 141, 142; Old Spaw House, 140
Shap spa, 202
Shires, John, 217, 218
Shooter's Hill wells, 85
Shore, Thomas, 122, 123
Short, Dr., 262
Shrewsbury, Earl of, 37, 39
Shutt, Isaac, 268, 272, 273

Skillicorne, Henry, 105, 106, 107, 109, 110, 112, 115
Skillicorne, William, 107, 108, 109
Skipton spa, 213–215, 217
Slingsby, William, 259, 263
Smedley, John, 188, 189, 191, 192, 194, 195
Smollett, Tobias, 140, 265
Southampton: 126–130; Bath-on-the-Platform, 126, 128; Dolphin Assembly Rooms, 128; Martin's Long Rooms and Baths, 126, 127, 128, 129
Spa, xv, 17, 20, 135, 136, 261, 263
Spas mentioned by name only, 85, 90, 100, 202, 203, 209, 223, 247
Stanhope, Dr Michael, 261, 267
Stansfield, Hamer, 186, 188
Stow, John, 55
Strathpeffer spa, 200, 201
Struve, Dr., 135, 136
Streatham spas, 77, 78–82, 83
Sul-Minerva (Saxon-Roman goddess), 3, 15
Sydenham Wells, 83, 84

Tenbury Wells, 238–241
Tennyson, Alfred Lord, 180
Tewkesbury—Walton spa, 157, 158, 160
Thackwray, Joseph, 268, 271, 274
Thetford spa, 230
Thompson, Henry, 110, 111, 112, 113
Thompson, Pearson, 112, 113
Tottenham springs, 95
Totteridge springs, 95
Trifriw wells, 243
Tunbridge Wells: xvii, xix, 16–25, 27, 28, 31, 37, 57, 61, 73, 77, 100, 108, 127, 139, 232, 259; Assembly Rooms, 18, 21; Bath House, 22, 23, 25; Colonnade, 19, 20; Walks (later the Parade, Pantiles), 18–25

Underwood, G. A., 111, 112

Verity, Thomas, 142
Victoria, Queen, 22, 23, 145, 167, 178, 179, 196, 272
Villiers, Barbara, 31

Wall, Dr John, xvii, 175, 176, 180
Walpole, Horace, 127, 230
Wanstead spa, 100
Weighall, Sir Archibald and Lady, 227, 229
Wellington, Duke of, 112, 115, 116, 119
Welwyn springs, 95
Wesley, John, 49
West Tilbury spa, 232
Weymouth: 120–125, 127; Nottington Spa, 120, 121, 122, 123, 125; Radipole Spa, 120, 121, 124, 125
White Conduit House, 69
Wicker, Henry, 31
William IV, 133, 135, 136
Williams, John, 266, 268, 270, 271
Williamson, Robert, 210
Willis, Dr., 27
Wilson, Dr James, 173, 179, 180, 181, 182, 186
Wittie, Dr Robert, 139
Wood, John, 6, 9, 10, 11, 12, 40
Woodford and Chigwell spas, 100
Woodhall Spa: xx, xxi, 223, 225–232; Bath-house and Pump Room, 227, 228; Victoria Hotel, 225, 227
World Wars, xiv, xx, 14, 116, 118, 188, 189, 193, 207, 227, 228, 229, 239, 240, 244, 254, 255, 272, 278
Wragg, George, 191